LISTENING, THINKING, BEING

LISTENING, THINKING, BEING

TOWARD AN ETHICS OF ATTUNEMENT

LISBETH LIPARI

The Pennsylvania State University Press
University Park, Pennsylvania

Library of Congress Cataloging-in-Publication Data

Lipari, Lisbeth, 1960– , author.
Listening, thinking, being : toward an ethics of
attunement / Lisbeth Lipari.
p.   cm
Summary: "Explores listening as a fundamental
human endowment connected with language and
thought, and its potential for social, personal, and
political action. Incorporates historical, literary,
intercultural, scientific, musical, and philosophical
perspectives"—Provided by publisher.
Includes bibliographical references and index.
ISBN 978-0-271-06332-4 (cloth : alk. paper)
1. Listening (Philosophy).
2. Thought and thinking.
3. Psycholinguistics.
I. Title.

B105.L54L57   2014
128'.3—dc23
2014004638

The Pennsylvania State University Press is a member of the
Association of American University Presses.

It is the policy of The Pennsylvania State University Press
to use acid-free paper. Publications on uncoated stock
satisfy the minimum requirements of American National
Standard for Information Sciences—Permanence of Paper
for Printed Library Material, ANSI Z39.48–1992.

This book is printed on paper that
contains 30% post-consumer waste.

To the memory of my Father, SALVATORE LIPARI

CONTENTS

ACKNOWLEDGMENTS

It may sound cliché, but it's by no means a stretch to say that birthing a book, not unlike raising a child, takes the proverbial village. Many, *many* people— teachers and students, friends and family, colleagues and neighbors—helped shape the listening, thinking, and being that led to this book. Its ideas spring from a lifetime of learning in and out of the classroom, and perhaps, most especially, in encounters with the works of myriad artists, conversationalists, musicians, mystics, novelists, and poets whose love of truth and beauty have graced the world. It also goes without saying that scholarship in every field is a perpetually unfolding conversation, constantly being amended, revised, redrawn, and expanded. No scholar stands separate and independently on her own, and each owes a debt of gratitude to all who went before her, even those with whom she most vehemently disagrees. So in that spirit I wish to thank communication scholars of the past and present, both named and unnamed, without whose work this book would simply not be.

I am extremely grateful for the Robert C. Good Fellowship granted by Denison University, which provided the time and solitude needed to breathe life into these pages. I also thank the Young India Fellowship for granting me an opportunity to carry some of the ideas in this book back to Bhārata Māta, from whom so much precious wisdom derives.

As for the people whose lives have directly touched my own, I would like to thank the following. First, members of the Levinas study group of the National Communication Association, which I joined in November 2000. I offer my tremendous gratitude to the founding members of that group— Chris Poulos, Jeff Murray, Ken Chase, Michael Hyde, Ron Arnett, Roy Wood, Pat Gehrke, and Spoma Jovanovich—who for over a decade have graciously and generously listened me to speech. I am also indebted to many friends and colleagues past and present, whose influence directly and indirectly shapes these pages. Among those I especially wish to thank are Alina Halliluc, Alison Regan, Amanda Gunn, Annette Holba, Barbara Engh, Bill Kirkpatrick, Bill and Julia Brodie, Chuck Morris, Clark and Perdita Strand, Dana Cloud,

David Gilbert, David Oh, Eric Saranovitz, Hollis Griffin, Jeff Kurtz, Jeff Temnick, John Arthos, Kathleen Battles, Kathy Ritchie, Lama Kathy Wesley, Laura Russell, Marie-Cécile Bertau, Pam Magelaner, Ping Yang, Priya Kapoor, Rhunette Diggs, Sally Scheiderer, Sangeet Kumar, Shirley and Larry Cox, Star Andrews, Stuart Tannock, Suzanne Condray, Terri Karis, Tim Anderson, Toni King, and Yoshi Miike. I am also extremely grateful to both Kendra Boileau and Robert Turchick not merely for their expertise and assistance, but for their faith in and hopes for this project. Many thanks also to John Morris for meticulous (and at times exhausting) copyediting. His expertise has made this a better book.

Students, far too many to name, have taught me surprising lessons of their own—special thanks to Arpitha Upendra Kodiveri, Austin Bailey, Camillo McConnell, Chiteisri Devi, Danielle Gadomski, David Brade, Lindsay Gund, Maddie Katz, Shashank Rai, Tomar Brown, and Vanessa Miller for passion and curiosity that continue to inspire. Many teachers have also helped water the tree that has become this book, and for the wisdom, inspiration, and encouragement offered many years ago I want to especially thank Professors Elizabeth C. Traugott, John Mowitt, John Thayer, Rod Hart, Steve Chaffee, and Susan McClary.

Closer to home, I am grateful beyond words for the love and support of my family—Emma Ryan, Ilene Lipari, Neshama Rose Lipari, Nicklaus Ryan, Samuel Lipari, Steven Lipari, and our many furry friends, whose generous love and laughter make the world a better place. My deepest gratitude goes to the wonder who is K. Lee Ryan, my beloved better half.

Lastly, beyond my appreciation for all who helped shepherd the life that birthed this book, I retain the right to claim any and all errors as exclusively my own.

Note

A brief portion at the end of chapter 4 contains redacted excerpts from the following essays by the author: "Listening for the Other: Ethical Implications of the Buber-Levinas Encounter," *Communication* 14, no. 2 (2004): 122–41; and "Listening, Thinking, Being," *Communication Theory* 20 (2010): 348–62.

Chapter 7 contains redacted elements from the following essays by the author: "Listening Otherwise: The Voice of Ethics," *International Journal of*

Listening 23, no. 1 (2009): 44–59; "Rhetoric's Other," *Philosophy and Rhetoric* 45, no. 3 (2012): 227–45; "The Vocation of Listening: The Other Side of Dialogue," in *"After You!": Dialogal Ethics and the Pastoral Counselling Process*, ed. Axel Liégeois, Roger Burggraeve, Marina Riemslagh, and Jozef Corveleyn (Leuven: Peeters, 2013), 15–36.

INTRODUCTION

It is the disease of not listening, the malady of not
marking, that I am troubled withal.
SHAKESPEARE, *King Henry IV, Part II*

Midway through *Bowling for Columbine,* a 2002 documentary about gun violence in the United States, filmmaker Michael Moore explores the influence
that heavy metal music might exert on teenagers. Does it make them violent?
The film shows an intense musical performance by shock rocker Marilyn
Manson, who screams into the mike wearing black-and-white face paint,
black lipstick, and an overall ghoulish look. Clearly, if any music ever had the
power to turn kids to violence, this would be it. Backstage after the performance, Moore interviews Manson, who sits serenely, legs crossed. Moore asks
Manson his thoughts about the Colorado teens who shot dozens and killed
fifteen people, including themselves, in 1999. "If you were to talk directly to
the kids at Columbine or the people in that community, what would you say
to them?" Moore asks the vampire-toothed Manson, who reflects for a
moment or two and then responds in a quiet voice: "I wouldn't say a single
word to them, I would listen to what they have to say. And that's what no
one did."[1]

This insight, powerful and obvious as it may be, rarely makes an appearance in most of our daily public and private conversations. In fact, there are
few places today where listening enjoys the same emphasis and value as speaking. Certainly, we understand that listening, as the inevitable counterpart to
speaking, is central to human experience. But the matter seems to end
there—most of us think of listening as a relatively straightforward process in
which we either accurately or inaccurately receive and decode information
sent to us from a speaker. The few domains with a more nuanced approach to

listening—such as spiritual traditions and psychological practices—are so small and specialized that the majority of us encounter none of these insights in our everyday experience. Rather, the dominant emphasis in U.S. culture—in education, politics, law, or religion—is on speech and speaking rather than on listening. High schools have debate teams, colleges teach courses in "Public Speaking," "Persuasion," and "Argumentation." In legislatures, on talk radio and television shows, verbal wrestling matches masquerade as dialogue, and listening occurs only, if at all, as a means of preparing one's next move in the spectacle. And even when listening is addressed in classrooms, courtrooms, or television studios, it is done primarily with the aim of conquest and control. We either listen to our adversary's arguments so we may defeat them, or we listen in order to "master" some material, facts, or theories.

At the same time, ironically, *some* kind of listening is happening everywhere, all the time. A stroll through a nearby shopping mall or down a city street today features many people engaged in private listening, plugged into pods, pads, tablets, or cell phones while walking, running, or driving through crowds. In many homes the sound of the TV or radio is ever present. And in many public spaces like airports, doctor's offices, and shopping malls, you can't avoid the blare of a TV or canned Muzak. But in another, deeper sense, truly engaged listening hardly happens anywhere.

Our aversion to silence masks our failure to listen in the same way it disables our ability to listen. For the silence of listening is, like its visual counterpart of the shadow, an invisible presence. Listening is the absence of speech, a gap, a lacuna, a fissure. It is the red light I wait at until I may speak again. It is "killing time," "doing nothing," or contrarily, it is rigorously goal oriented: when is he going to get to the point already? Or, Hey, I'm not following you. So why don't we listen? What's at stake in our failure to listen?

This book embarks on a journey meant to turn everything you knew, or thought you knew, about language and communication, listening and speaking, inside out. It's not about how to be a good listener or the ten barriers to good listening. It's about how listening brings humans into being. In this book we challenge the readily taken-for-granted suppositions about listening, language, and communication in order to develop a new way of thinking about listening that we will call *akroatic thinking*.[2] As we will discuss in the chapters ahead, *thinking listening as a way of being* creates the possibility of an ethics driven neither by rules and obligations nor by outcomes and consequences, but rather, one that is drawn toward an ethics of attunement—an awareness of and attention to the harmonic interconnectivity of all beings and objects. By changing our thinking about listening, we may be freed to dismantle the linguistic prison houses that confine us to misconceptions of our own making about who we are, what we do, and how we might live peacefully together with others on this planet.

The purpose of the book is threefold: first, to bring readers' awareness to the value and importance of listening as a fundamental human endowment that has been consistently overlooked in Western culture; second, to bring readers' attention to the complexity of listening from personal, cultural, and philosophical perspectives; and third, to teach readers to understand listening as an essential form of constitutive communicative action and see its potential for social, personal, and political transformation. The work synthesizes a range of multidisciplinary perspectives on listening to engage a variety of questions, from the practical to the philosophical, and to develop new conceptual frameworks with which to theorize, study, and practice listening. The next eight chapters of the book create a spiral of sorts that begins with embodiment and harmonic vibration, winds through language, moves on to communication, curls from there into social interaction, and then leans into ethics, finally returning, at the end, back to embodied attunement again. This spiraling movement of inquiry journeys through several intellectual fields and historical pathways to craft a holistic and integrated study of communication in which listening and the ethical relation are central. We begin with the body, the materiality of sound, and the phenomenology perception, and then move through language and the various ways scholars have theorized its relation to thought and speech for over two millennia. We next explore the dialogic dimensions of communication and then turn to an investigation of social interaction and the nondual nature of speaking and listening vis-à-vis the concept of interlistening and its relation to time. In the penultimate and final chapters of the book we expand upon these insights to explore listening as both an ethical relation and a way of being in the world.

The How, What, and Why of It

Throughout the following chapters we will be developing a densely layered montage that interleaves interdisciplinary ideas from affect studies, communication, linguistics, philosophy, psychology, sound studies, and theology. Both implicitly and explicitly, we will listen to the listening of these various disciplinary "gazes." Even when not explicitly stated, listening will always already be understood as the warp and woof of human interaction—whether it be listening *with, in,* and *out* of our bodies; *with, in,* and *out* of language; or *with, in,* and *out* of others. Throughout, we will be developing a holistic model of human communication that integrates ideas from a wide swath of scholarship to sketch the outlines of a philosophy of listening and an ethics of attunement.

Briefly, in chapter 1, "Akroatic Thinking," I introduce several underlying themes and frameworks for *thinking listening* in new ways. Beginning with a brief examination of the importance and nature of misunderstanding, I then introduce the concept *interlistening,* which aims to account for the multiplicitous and nondual relationship between speaking and listening. Next, I introduce the distinction between thinking about communication as an instrument for channeling messages and conceiving it as a maker of worlds. Lastly, I turn to *akroasis,* which German musicologist Hans Kayser calls "a very specific mode of thinking,"[3] in order to develop an account of listening and communication that proceeds from holistic rather than atomistic perspectives as a basis for understanding our shared sonic worlds.

In chapter 2, "Vibrating Worlds and Listening Bodies," I explore the embodied materiality of vibration, sound, and listening. When we listen, our bodies move. We vibrate with sound waves pulsing toward and then through us. We are, as the deaf percussionist Evelyn Glennie explains, participators who touch the sound. This chapter explores how, as embodied beings, we are participants in a vibrating material world. Beginning with an examination of the physics of sound and music, we proceed to investigate the relationship between sensation and perception and the role attention plays in all our experiences. We then conclude with a discussion of embodied listening and how we can bring more awareness to our listening selves.

The third and fourth chapters, "Premodern Perspectives on Language and Thought" and "Contemporary Perspectives on Language and Thought," begin with a historical exploration of how, even after twenty-six hundred years of research and debate, linguists, psychologists, and philosophers continue to argue about the relationship between language and thought. What is language? What is thought? Are they the same or different? How? In chapter 3 we examine the relationship between language and thought through its long and storied history, beginning with the ancient Indian grammarians and ancient Greeks, through the European Enlightenment. In chapter 4 we continue this discussion in regard to contemporary approaches in linguistics and cognitive science, examining these schools of thought from atomist and holist perspectives. We wind up chapter 4 by examining what this history offers to an understanding of listening and how akroatic thinking can reshape the ways we think about language and thought—especially in respect to how we habituate to already existing linguistic categories, concepts, and structures and then mistake these conceptual formations for the truth of the way things are and have to be.

In chapter 5, "Communication and a Nice Knock-Down Argument," we explore how even the most lonely monologue, even one uttered on an isolated windy beach, is fundamentally dialogic because of the ways in which words from the past as well as the future continually reverberate with sounds, phrasings, voices, and meanings far distant from their utterance at any given moment in time. Through an investigation of what is often theorized as "inner speech," we return to the ancient Indian grammarians to explore how selves and society are continually reconstituted in an ongoing intersubjective dance of word, rhythm, and meaning that begins when infants listen in the womb. Here we build on insights from the previous chapters to craft a dialogic understanding of human being—one always in dialogue with selves, others, and worlds.

In Chapter 6, "Interlistening and the *Tout Ensemble*," we examine the ways in which listening, speaking, and thinking are not three distinctly separate processes, but are in fact three facets of a single integrated communicative whole. Building upon the previous chapters, I here introduce *interlistening* as a new model of dialogic interaction that can reckon with aspects of the embodied polymodal, polyphonic, and polychronic processes of human communication. Among other things, this chapter recasts intersubjectivity from a spatialized *between* generated by individual subjects, to interlistening as a dense movement of interactional and con-fused temporality wherein listening, speaking, and thinking co-occur in living synchronous, diachronous, and simultaneous polyphony. As we will have explored in previous chapters, to study dialogue as interlistening is to see how every now always echoes with past and future nows; how every speaking is at the same time a listening (and vice-versa); and how even "innermost" thoughts require words from "outside."

In chapter 7, "Listening Others to Speech," I elaborate on the ethical implications of thinking with listening. For too long scholars have taken speech and speaking as stand-ins for the *logos*. But a *logos* that speaks without listening is no *logos* at all. In this chapter we examine "listening" as a transitive verb in order to convey the ways in which listening enacts ethics that are constitutive of and always prior to speech. Here we will theorize listening as an invocation, a calling forth of speech, that generates possibilities for the ethical response. Just as intersubjectivity opens conceptual spaces for scholarly inquiry outside the self-other binary, so listening others to speech opens new pathways for ethics and understanding.

The final chapter, "Toward an Ethics of Attunement," brings us back via "a commodius vicus of recirculation" to the beginning, where we can, perhaps, "arrive where we started and know the place for the first time."[4] In this chapter I return to the discussions of harmonics, sound, and vibration from chapter 1 to take up the temporal dimensions of listening vis-à-vis the embodied, nonlinear, and rhythmic aspects of being together with others. Here I develop an understanding of *ethical attunement* as an interplay between *akroatic thinking* and the ancient rhetorical concepts of *kairos*. I conclude the book by pointing to several recurring themes that may shape an ethics of attunement: interconnection and generosity, impermanence and humility, iteration and patience, and invention and courage.

A Concluding Word on Words

Throughout the book, I will use words, metaphors, and examples intended to help open up your thinking about listening. You may find some terms more useful than others—don't worry. The idea is to bring a fresh awareness and conscious intentionality to the way you listen to yourself, others, and the world. Whether it's *akroatic thinking, interlistening, sphoṭa, listening otherwise, listening others to speech, a listening eye, an ethics of attunement,* and so forth, feel free to hold the meanings of these ideas loosely in your mind as you attend to the overall tenor of the argument, *thinking akroatically* as you go along. Let these ideas stretch and challenge your everyday understandings, listen to the sounds of the words and of your own understanding, and most of all, be willing to misunderstand.

I

AKROATIC THINKING

Nobody means by a word precisely and exactly what
his neighbour does, and the difference, be it ever so
small, vibrates, like a ripple in water, throughout the
entire language. Thus all understanding is always at
the same time not-understanding, all concurrence in
thought and feeling at the same time a divergence.
—HUMBOLDT, *On Language*

Misunderstanding

When we think about listening in the ordinary way, we usually (but not
always) make a distinction between hearing as the physiological process of
perceiving sounds, and understanding as our interpretation of those sounds.
Most of us recognize both physical and psychological impediments to hearing—deafness, distraction, self-absorption, denial, and so forth. And most of
us think misunderstanding is an impediment to effective communication
that interferes with the aim of being a good listener. The perspective offered
in this book challenges these perspectives on listening. It challenges the ideas
that (a) misunderstanding can be avoided, (b) speaking is at the center of
communication, and (c) communication is, at heart, the accurate or inaccurate exchange of messages. The book not only rejects the above suppositions,
but it goes further in grounding the human experience of *being* as an ethical
relation with others that is enacted by means of listening.

The view that misunderstanding, while perhaps inevitable, is bad and
something to be avoided enjoys a long tradition in the European philosophy
of hermeneutics, the theory of interpretation. In the nineteenth century,

Schleiermacher, widely considered the father of modern general hermeneutics, was the first scholar to theorize "the art of understanding" in all of its varied manifestations, from dense theological texts to everyday conversation. But while he acknowledged the impossibility of eliminating all misinterpretation, Schleiermacher's whole approach was shaped by an aspiration to perfect "the art of avoiding misunderstandings."[1]

From the perspective of this book, however, misunderstanding is not only an inescapable aspect of communication, it is, moreover, both valuable and indispensable. Why? Because misunderstanding reminds us, again and again, that our conversational partners are truly "other" than us; that each of us lives at the center of our own world; that we each arrive independently "on the scene" of communication with different histories, traditions, experiences, and perspectives; that the self is not the world; that perfection is impossible; and that, although human language is infinitely generative, there are important aspects of human existence that are, simply, ineffable. In short, misunderstanding opens the doorway to the ethical relation by inspiring (or frustrating) us to listen more closely to others, to inquire more deeply into their differences, and to question our own already well-formed understandings of the world. Rather than turn away or shut the conversation down, misunderstanding can invite us to move with more humility, patience, and generosity than we might have otherwise. It asks us to give up easy certainties, to endure what may seem like endless repetition, and to cultivate a courage that could "sustain blows of any kind and still remain alert."[2] As the Italian philosopher Gemma Corradi Fiumara, one of the twentieth century's deepest thinkers about listening, argues, "listening involves the renunciation of a predominately moulding and ordering activity; a giving up sustained by the expectation of a new and different quality of relationship."[3] These ideas about misunderstanding will form the background of much of the coming chapters and be addressed in greater detail in chapter 6. For now, however, it is sufficient to highlight the importance of including misunderstanding as both an ethical practice and an inextricable partner in the process of communication.

Interlistening

The second supposition that underlies most ordinary conceptions of listening is that it basically involves a two-step process of hearing and understanding. From the perspective of this book, this two-step model fails to address some of the complexities of listening, such as, Why do we have two words, "listening" and "hearing"? Are they synonyms? What is listening, anyway? When I'm thinking silently to myself, am I speaking or listening? If I'm speaking (or listening), then who's listening (or speaking)? And along those lines, do I listen not only to words with my mind, but also to the music of the voice in my ears, the posture and gesture of the body with my eyes, the vibrational rhythm of the others' pulsations, movements, and intonations in my body? And what does it mean to say that I "understand" something? When I'm listening to you, are your words, sounds, and movements a code that I simply decode? Does understanding mean that I translate your words into mine, and thereby project my meanings onto your words?

Even in our most sophisticated thinking about communication, listening is all too often regarded as a second thought, dragged along as speaking's necessary but slightly embarrassing, dull partner. As a result, listening has been relegated to a shadowy penumbra or black box—something both there and not there, obligatory but irrelevant. Our ordinary conceptions of communication typically presume speaking to be the active construction of meaning and listening its passive reception. But in this book we will consider the possibility that there is no speaking without a simultaneous listening, nor a listening without a simultaneous speaking. We will explore instead how speaking and listening are inseparable processes, inextricable counterpoints rather than opposites; to cleave them apart would be like touching without being touched in kind. In order to describe this somewhat hidden aspect of communication, I use the term "interlistening" to inhibit the speech-centricity of our perspectives and bring the many connotations of "inter-" (i.e., interbeing, interaction, interdependence, intersubjectivity, etc.) into the foreground. The idea of interlistening thus aims to describe how listening is itself a form of speaking that resonates with echoes of everything we have ever heard, thought, seen, touched, said, and read throughout our lives.

One of the few things that scholars of communication and listening will readily agree upon is that we know too little about the process of listening. We have theories about empathic listening, interpretive listening, effective listening, and so forth, but we have yet to advance our understandings to a point where we theorize listening and speaking as fully inseparable, interdependent aspects of communication processes—where listening receives the acknowledgment, attention, and regard that centuries of scholarly study have afforded speaking and speech. Cognitive psychologists have begun to address part of this question from the intrapersonal perspective; they explore what happens when your words mingle with my neurons; how the brain responds to various language stimuli; how concepts are categorized, where they are stored, and so on. Other scholars have begun to focus on the relational and intersubjective spaces of listening—how listeners and speakers collaborate in moment-to-moment communication processes, how synchronous movements and rhythmic entrainment invisibly coordinate speakers in dialogue.

Other questions, however, remain without answer: Are thoughts themselves a form of communication; are they the same as or different from speech? And if so, are they enactments of speaking or listening, or perhaps both? And if thoughts are a form of communication, then who is speaking and who listening when one is thinking? Moreover, are the thoughts that one listens to and/or speaks truly one's own? Or are they in some ways quasi-public and social? Do I speak language, or does language speak me?[4]

Words to Worlds

How and what we think about communication very much influences how we communicate and what we "do" with communication. For most of the twentieth century at least, communication has been understood with what James Carey calls the "transmission model." This model depicts communication as a means by which message-objects are transmitted over space and time from senders to receivers. Communication is thus understood as a mode of information transportation where we move ideas, like corn in a freight train, from one brain to another. We can hear this idea when we define the Internet as an "information superhighway" or a conversation as an "exchange," or when we describe how advertisements "deliver" messages to audiences and audiences to advertisers. We also participate in the transmission model of communication when we think of education as a process by which teachers "send" ideas out to students, who "receive" them, write them down, "retain" them, and are said to have (more or less successfully) learned something. When viewed as a kind of information transfer, communication becomes a merely mechanical routine wherein things like the accuracy of the message, the efficiency of delivery, and the precision of reception are in the foreground while other much more interesting and important aspects of communication are missed.

Another somewhat limited model of communication is what communication scholar John Stewart calls the "semiotic perspective," a view which conceives of communication as a symbolic process in which words are signs that symbolize, depict, and generally re-present the world.[5] According to Stewart, the semiotic view distinguishes between two worlds, one linguistic and one nonlinguistic, with language serving as a means to accomplish tasks in the nonlinguistic world. From this perspective, language creates mental impressions "inside" our minds to represent things "outside" our minds, like how a highway exit might represent a town near the highway. While it is not wrong to see the road sign as a symbolic tool, it would be quite limiting to understand it in *only* this way. Imagine, for a moment, that you're in the United States driving east on Interstate 80 and you pass signs for places like Sparta, Dover, Netcong, Buttzville, Lake Hopatcong, or the New York state line. Each of these "word signs" names not just a place, but a time as well, and the names resonate with history, language, and culture. Moreover, these words create individual and collective identities that may for some people bestow a sense of ancestral affinity or even home, while for others they may convey a sense of racism, injustice, and even genocide. At the same time, many sports fans from these towns might identify as New Jersey Nets supporters, but if they're from Hopatcong, they'll more likely root for their high school team rather than Parsipanny's. According to this perspective, which Stewart calls the "constitutive view," communication not only signifies or represents, but also constitutes "world" between persons, creating correspondences not between language and a nonlinguistic world, but between speakers and listeners mutually co-constituted in the linguistic world. In his influential study of how the telegraph shaped news-gathering, writing, and reading practices in the mid-nineteenth century, James Carey draws upon cognates of the word "communication" such as *communi*on and *communi*ty to describe what he calls a ritual view of *communi*cation. In contradistinction to a transmission view, Carey's ritual view describes the act of "reading a newspaper less as sending or gaining information and more as attending a mass, a situation in which nothing new is learned but in which a particular view of the world is portrayed and confirmed. News reading, and writing, is a ritual act and moreover a dramatic one. What is arrayed before the reader is not pure information—but a portrayal of the contending forces in the world."[6] Similarly, the scholar John Shotter gives the example of the world-making power of the phrase "I love you."[7] Think for a moment back to your teens or early twenties when, for the first time, you or a beloved uttered those words in a romantic sense. Was information merely transferred? Or did something much richer happen, such as creating a whole new world—of delight, discomfort, or perhaps even unrequited despair—between and you and your beloved?

In this way, communicating is how we coconstruct worlds with ourselves and others, from groups as small as two people to organizations as large as an international congress and everything in between. Thirty-nine influential and wealthy men sign a piece of paper, and a new country is "constituted." The Catholic Church refuses to annul Henry VIII's marriage to Catherine of Aragon, and a whole new state religion is born. Moreover, we cannot date someone who is not dating us, and if we decide to get married, we won't be able to do it alone; society has to take part. Two people each can say "I do" to each other, but without a duly empowered representative of society—court clerk, justice of the peace, pastor, rabbi, or imam—to "pronounce" them married, they are not married. Thus, our communicative acts give birth to worlds—declaring war brings a world of war into being, declaring an enemy creates an enemy, verbally harassing someone brings a hostile environment into being, and so forth. We use language to create relationships, organizations, governments, and laws. Consider, for example, the fact that the legal concepts of sexual harassment, date rape, and domestic violence didn't exist thirty-plus years ago, or that gay rights, let alone gay marriage, didn't exist as a publicly recognizable concept until the last several decades. In other words, acts of communication do more than represent—they bring worlds into being. Your wife or husband takes their wedding ring off, and your whole world changes.

Here's the important thing, though: none of these views of communication—the transmission, semiotic, ritual, and constitutive views—are wrong; they are each partial and incomplete. Certainly we use communication to transmit messages in space, to encode and decode signs, and to construct, celebrate, and repair community. Each of these views lets us see different things and leads us to ask different questions. And while no single view captures the whole, each captures something important. Unfortunately, however, the cultural dominance of the transmission and semiotic views of communication keeps us from understanding communication in this other vitally important way—as the way in which we make worlds. As the German philosopher of language Hans Georg Gadamer puts it, "Language is not just one of man's possessions in the world; rather, on it depends the fact that man has a world at all."[8]

But one more thing: notice how easy it was in the previous paragraph to take "speech" and "speaking" as synonyms for "communication." That's because in most scholarly, public, and personal arenas, *listening* is marked off as *other* in ways not dissimilar from how certain professions, attributes, or activities mark women and people of color as *other*. Markedness refers to category memberships that are by default unmarked for some members but require marking for others—the implication being that the unmarked version is natural, inevitable, or the norm. For example, the phrase "Asian actress" contains two levels of markedness—one for race and one for gender. In contrast, the unmarked "actor" would be assumed to be white and male. Along these lines, in April 2013 it was discovered that hundreds of novelists were deleted from the category "American novelists" on the ostensibly egalitarian Wikipedia website ("the biggest multilingual free-content encyclopedia on the Internet") and added to the category "American women novelists."[9] In this way, the Wikipedia editor erased women from the unmarked category of American novelist and in so doing marked them as *other*. Similarly, words and phrases pertaining to speech (i.e., "free speech," "public speaking," "saying I do," etc.) are unmarked because they need no explanation—they are self-evident categories of communication. In contrast, such oddities as "free listening" or "public listening" would require further explanation. Taking this problem of speech-centricity as an inevitable but often invisible background, it will be important to sketch why and how we come to the theoretical paradigm taken in the book—a holist perspective on listening, language, and communication.

Holism and Atomism

From medicine to engineering and from physics to analytic philosophy, most fields of study consider what we call the scientific method to be a pretty good procedure for separating the true from the false (or the fact from fiction, the myth from the reality, etc.), not to mention building pretty good stuff like computers, bridges, and fast-flying airplanes. But this book takes a slightly different path, employing not the analytical atomism of science, which tends to break things into parts in order to understand how they work, but a holistic process-oriented synthesis that integrates insights from multiple disciplines in order to better understand the relationships between practice, performance, and experience in our taken-for-granted everyday social interactions.

A great deal of (though by no means all) research in the disciplines of communication, perception, and linguistics is undertaken from the perspective of the scientific method, which is defined in the *Oxford English Dictionary* as "a method of procedure that has characterized natural science since the 17th century, consisting in systematic observation, measurement, and experiment, and the formulation, testing, and modification of hypotheses." In many fields, such as classical physics, the scientific method has been grounded in a mechanical view of a "clocklike universe" that is governed by "the assumption that everything in the whole universe can be reduced completely and perfectly to nothing more than the effects of a set of mechanical parameters undergoing purely quantitative changes."[10]

Although the scientific method remains useful in many ways today, some of the underlying assumptions of the mechanistic view have led to unforeseen problems, and, further, have been contradicted by twentieth-century insights about the role of probability and chance in quantum physics. As a result, some scientists and scholars are revamping their models and theories based on these changes, while others continue to adhere to the well-established boundaries of the classic model. But, as in all things, change is slow and often difficult. As Thomas Kuhn has observed, challenges to widely accepted paradigms that govern normal scientific practice are often vehemently resisted. But they also, more often than not, herald a scientific revolution. For example, Kuhn argues that Galileo's "discovery" of the regular motion of pendulums arose because of a shift from the Aristotelian paradigm of bodies in motion as a change of state to the medieval scholastic theory of bodies in motion as a process. "Until that scholastic paradigm was invented, there were not pendulums, but only swinging stones, for the scientists to see. Pendulums were brought into existence by something very like a paradigm induced gestalt switch."[11] Kuhn describes similar paradigm shifts that initially encountered fierce criticism and yet enabled other scientific "discoveries" (which in turn generated new paradigms) such as Copernican astronomy, Dalton's atomic theory, Lavoisier's oxygen, and Roentgen's X-rays. According to Kuhn, X-rays "were greeted not only with surprise but with shock. Lord Kelvin at first pronounced them an elaborate hoax."[12] Wide swaths of scholarship in some fields (including communication, psychology, and linguistics) remain largely within the classical paradigm. Thus, one goal of this book is to bring a more holistic and integrated perspective to the study of communication in general, and to listening in particular. So in an effort to keep things clear but also simple, I want to describe three important changes the quantum perspective has presented to the classical or mechanistic model of science. The first pertains to the relationship between actuality and probability, the second relates to the question of substance and materiality, and the third relates to causality and locality.

In the classical model, "systematic observation'" means that the scientist (the subject) doing the observing is completely independent of the phenomena being observed (the object). Scientists test theories in controlled experiments that rule out anything thought to be unrelated to what is being examined. The basic goal is to find objective and accurate explanations for why things are the way they are and, as a result, be able to manipulate, and predict, outcomes—this is a primary goal in medicine, physics, engineering, geology, and so on. But due to several remarkable insights by physicists in the early part of the twentieth century, some of the underlying assumptions of the mechanistic view of the universe and the role of "systematic observation" came into question. Einstein's famous theory of relativity was one of the first key insights in this regard. In very, *very* simple terms, the idea is that speed and direction are not immutable properties that are everywhere the same, but instead are relative phenomena that depend upon the speed, direction, and location of the observer. For example, have you ever been a passenger lying down in a car stopped in traffic when suddenly other cars begin to move past your car? If your only frame of reference is the other cars and the sky, it might appear and even physically feel to you that your car is moving backwards.

Another wrinkle in the mechanistic view of the universe pertains to the so-called particle-wave duality, wherein at the infinitesimally small quantum (i.e., smaller than atoms) level "all manifestations of matter and energy seemed to have two possible aspects, that of a wave and that of a particle."[13] This means that the kinds of certainties about the physical world that we take for granted every day (such as nothing can be in two places at once, that what goes up must come down, and that New York exists whether I see it before my eyes or not) are not at all certain in the world of quantum particles. According to the physicist Werner Heisenberg, "what one deduces from an observation is a probability function, a mathematical expression that combines statements about possibilities or tendencies with statements about our knowledge of facts."[14] Therefore, unlike the Newtonian mechanical laws of classical science, which were thought to unwaveringly govern all phenomena in the universe, regardless of size or scale, quantum physics discovered uncertainties in the form of probabilities at the atomic level. According to Bohm, "the notion of an atomic path has only a limited domain of applicability. In a more detailed description the atom is, in many ways, seen to behave as much like a wave as a particle. It can perhaps best be regarded as a poorly defined cloud, dependent for its particular form on the whole environment, including the observing instrument."[15] Thus, not only did quantum physics discover uncertainty with regard to the essence, location, and direction of subatomic phenomena, but it demonstrated that the observer's measuring instruments themselves played a role in the experimental findings. "The equation of motion for the probability function does now contain the influence of the interaction with the measuring device. This influence introduces a new element of uncertainty."[16]

While some physicists, such as Heisenberg and Bohm, were convinced that quantum insights required a radical reinterpretation of classical physics, others, like Einstein, were convinced that other underlying laws or theories would be found to explain and bring certainty to the uncertainty of this quantum world. This conviction is reflected in Einstein's famous quip "God does not play dice with the universe." According to Heisenberg, these physicists wanted to "change the philosophy without changing the physics . . . [and] come back to the idea of an objective real world whose smallest parts exist objectively in the same sense as stones or trees exist, independently of whether or not we observe them. This, however, is impossible or at least not entirely possible because of the nature of the atomic phenomena."[17] Thus, quantum physics revealed that the underlying mechanistic notions of "systematic observation" needed to be augmented with a more complex understanding of the interrelationship of observer to observed, wherein, at the quantum level at least, the observer and the observed were "a single indivisible entity." As we will examine later, this insight gives us ground for questioning such atomistic separations as those between, for example, speaking and listening or listener and speaker.

A second change in the mechanical paradigm pertains to assumptions about what any single solitary thing actually is, whether it be an atom, a person, a planet, or a universe. When I was in graduate school, one of my professors who held pretty closely to the classical view of science said that the most important first thing a researcher had to do was decide what "one" is—what is "one" unit of attention, cooperation, or intention? How will it be measured? But ironically, the more closely scientists look into any one thing, the more they see that it is composed of many things—from the tiny bits of matter called "atoms" surmised by ancient Greek and Indian philosophers to the atoms in the atomic theory discovered by John Dalton in the nineteenth century; and from the subatomic bosons, leptons, and charm- and strange-"flavored" quarks of twentieth-century quantum physics to the even tinier filaments of twenty-first-century superstring theory. And what's amazing is that the more closely scientists look (i.e., magnify things), the more they realize that what they thought was "one thing" is really made up of many interrelated things. Moreover, they discover how most entities are made up of mostly "empty" space. As Bohm describes it, "the illusion that the self and the world are broken into fragments originates in the kind of thought that goes beyond its proper measure and confuses its own product with the same independent reality. . . . [F]ragmentation originates in essence in the fixing of the insights forming our overall self-world view, which follows on our generally mechanical, routinized and habitual modes of thought about these matters."[18]

Twentieth-century improvements in technology that greatly enhanced the power of measurement and observation, whether up into the sky or down into the subatomic sphere, demonstrate that as much as we inhabit infinite space, we are also inhabited by it. George Leonard poetically describes the way human flesh appears through a microscope with increasing magnification: muscle fibers appear crystalline, with long spiraling molecules "swaying like wheat in the wind." Magnifying the molecules reveals atoms that appear as "shadowy balls dancing," whose interiors are "lightly veiled by a cloud of electrons." Upon increased magnification, the shell of the atom

> dissolves and we go on inside to find . . . *nothing.*
>
> Somewhere within that emptiness, we know, is a nucleus. We scan the space, and there it is, a tiny dot. At last, we have discovered something hard and solid, a reference point. But no—as we move closer to the nucleus, it too begins to dissolve. It too is nothing more than an oscillating field, waves of rhythm. Inside the nucleus are other organized fields: protons, neutrons, even smaller "particles." Each of these, upon our approach, also dissolves into pure rhythm.[19]

Another example of how space infuses all things at both subatomic and cosmic scales can be seen in a film by the innovative inventor/designers Charles and Ray Eames (inventors of, among other things, the eponymous classic Eames chair) that demonstrates the recurring patterns of density and emptiness found at all scales of the universe.[20] Beginning with two people lounging on a picnic blanket in a park as seen from a distance of ten meters, the camera's range finder moves farther and farther away by factors of ten every ten seconds. The image ascends from the picnic to the park to the city of Chicago, then to Lake Michigan, then to North America, then to the earth from a distance of 1 million meters, and on to the solar system, the Milky Way galaxy, and on and on until you what you see is mostly space, and finally at ten million light years, the Virgo Cluster of galaxies. Then the range finder moves back to the picnic blanket and reverses the process, this time magnifying the image more and more by factors of ten every ten seconds. First you see an image of one person's hand, then you see magnification into the layers of the skin, then the blood vessels , then a white blood cell, then into the cell's nucleus and into the DNA, and on down to the molecule, the hydrogen atoms, the electrons, then the proton at a distance of one nanometer, on to an image of what might be leptons and quarks and so on, until what you see is mostly vast inner space.

Thus, these two big ideas behind the classical scientific method—that what we perceive as separations between things are, in fact, actual separations in the world, and that things can be understood relatively separately from other things—have proven to be mere assumptions based upon our ways of looking, not on "reality" as it exists "out there." To each of us, our bodies feel solid, as if they are "one" thing, but from the perspective of an atom, our bodies are an entire universe. "I sing the body electric; / The armies of those I love engirth me, and I engirth them,"[21] wrote Walt Whitman. Thus, the classical scientific view of the universe as a well-oiled machine composed of separate but interacting parts is increasingly being replaced by the view of the universe as a deeply complex, interrelated whole, which brings us to the third change in the underlying assumptions of the scientific method: the relationships between causality, nonlocality, and nonlinearity. As we will examine in greater detail in coming chapters, each of these changes in perspective has fascinating implications for the study of communication, from macroscopic global perspectives to microscopic neural perspectives, and everything beyond and in between.

In the mid-twentieth century, thinking in physics and brain science started to interact, and a key insight was made by Harvard neuroscientist Karl Pribram. He and his colleagues were trying to understand why individuals with serious brain damage were able to recall specific memories in spite of the destruction of the associated brain areas.[22] It seemed to Pribram that memories were not stored locally, in specific areas of the brain, but were instead distributed widely throughout the brain. But why? Drawing on insights from Bohm, Lashley, and Gabor, Pribram theorized that the brain stored memories the way holograms store images, each part containing an image of the whole. If you tear an ordinary photographic plate in half, for example, only half of the image will remain. But if you tear a holographic plate in half, or even quarters, or hundredths, the whole image will remain and be reconstructed from any part.

The reason for this is that unlike regular photographic plates, which record the stream of light waves that bounce off an object, a hologram records two streams of laser light, one bouncing off the object and the other directly from the laser, that create an interference pattern on the holographic plate. The resulting pattern of wave interference records a three-dimensional image of the whole. For example, if you were to drop three pebbles into a shallow pool of water, each pebble would send out a pattern of waves that would intersect. This intersection of wave formations is called an "interference pattern." Remarkably, it is possible to trace back the location of each of the three pebbles from any point in the pattern—which is what makes it a hologram.[23] Figure 1 illustrates a two-point interference pattern produced in a ripple tank. It is possible to trace back the origin of the two pebbles from any smaller subdivision of the image. As Bohm describes it, "The different parts of the hologram are not in correspondence with different parts of the object. But rather each one is somehow impressing something of the whole."[24] The physics of holography has to do with quantum theory and wave frequency dynamics and is far more complicated and detailed than we need to discuss, but suffice it to say that holograms have been theorized as the fundamental organizing principle of everything from cognition to cosmology.

For example, in 1982, Dr. Alain Aspect conducted experiments that discovered "that subatomic particles, like electrons, can communicate instantaneously, regardless of distance," a finding that lends support to Bohm's theory of the universe as a hologram. Although the particles appear to be separate and therefore somehow in communication, Bohm believes that "on a deeper level of reality they are actually just different aspects of a deeper cosmic unity. . . . The picture of reality Bohm was developing was not one in which subatomic particles were separate from one another and moving through the void of space, but one in which all things were part of an unbroken web."[25]

Another apparent confirmation of a holistic view of the universe comes from the discovery of unexpectedly recursive fractal patterns found to exist in the natural as well as the social world. In the 1960s, the mathematician Benoit Mandelbrot began to devise formulae to describe seemingly chaotic, unpre-

FIG. I   Wave interference pattern. A two-point pattern produced in a ripple tank. Image from Wikimedia Commons (photo: Armedblowfish).

dictable data. Using cotton prices as his data set, he saw a pattern that astonished him. "The numbers that produced aberrations from the point of view of normal distribution produced symmetry from the point of view of scaling. Each particular price change was random and unpredictable. But the sequence of changes was independent of scale: curves for daily price changes and monthly price changes matched perfectly."[26] In the 1970s, Mandelbrot designed computer algorithms that used pixels on a screen as colored data points to create

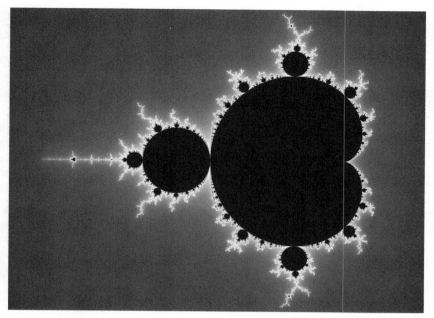

FIG. 2 *Initial image* at the start of a Mandelbrot set of fractals. Not unlike Bohm's holograms, each subdivision (part) of the Mandelbrot fractal set contains the whole. Series created by Wolfgang Beyer with the program Ultra Fractal 3. Images from Wikimedia Commons.

Zoom 1: Head and shoulders. This image depicts a zoom magnification of a small section located near the middle of the first image, at the intersection of the main heart-shaped body (the head) and the smaller circular body to its left (the shoulder).

Zoom 2: Seahorse valley. This image depicts a zoom magnification of a small section of the head and shoulders image, taken from the mid-lower-right quadrant where the two shapes form a valley.

Zoom 3: Seahorse. This image depicts a zoom magnification of a small section of the seahorse valley image, taken from its middle-right quadrant and containing the second from the top in the row of four similar, vaguely seahorse-shaped, forms located on the right side of the image.

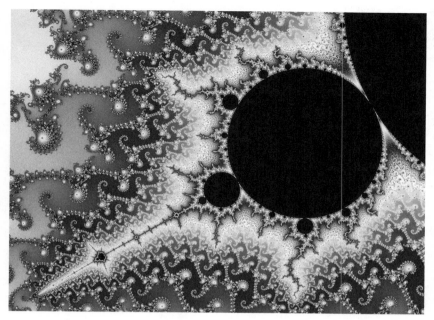

Zoom 8: Satellite antenna. This image is the eighth iteration in the set, five generations (or steps) of detail from Zoom 3, the seahorse valley image.

visual representations of the fractal patterns. Figure 2 illustrates several iterations of what is known as the Mandelbrot set. The resulting beautiful iridescent series of paisley swirls of the fractal patterns is, in James Gleick's words, "a way of seeing infinity."[27] Figure 3 is a close-up image of a Romanesco broccoli that demonstrates the recursive self-similarity found in nature and fractal algorithms as well as in the part-as-whole relationships found in holograms.

Just as the Eames film *Powers of Ten* demonstrates recursive self-similarity at different scales of the cosmos, so do the branching patterns of trees and riverbeds, the spiraling patterns of galaxies and shells, and the geometric symmetry of crystals and ice, to name but a few fractal patterns found in nature. The two key principles of chaos theory, self-similarity and repetition, are seen in the alternating patterns of density and emptiness that recur again and again as the Eameses' view moves from the microscales of the atomic world to the macroscales of the human world and up through the megascales of the cosmos. It is suggestive to imagine that these patterns of cosmic density and emptiness are analogous to the patterns of compression and decompression of sound waves as they move longitudinally through matter and space, as

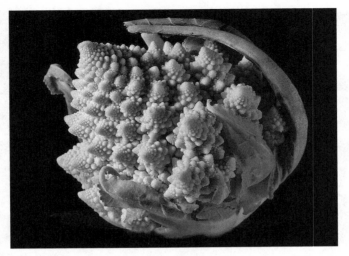

FIG. 3   A Romanesco broccoli that illustrates fractal patterns of
self-similarity at different scales as they appear in nature. Image from
Wikimedia Commons (photo: Jon Sullivan).

perhaps suggested by the ancient cosmologies of India, Egypt, and Greece.
But for that discussion, we must wait for the next chapter.

And Your Point Is . . . ?

So how does this all tie in with listening? Because the world is such a huge and
complex amalgamation of things, both holist and atomist perspectives are
needed. Given that academic scholars tend to specialize in one particular area
of study, separating it from everything else in the world. Combine this special-
ization with a classically atomistic and mechanical view of wholes composed of
parts, and you get what Bohm sees as a distorted view of the world. So while the
mechanism of the classical scientific model can be valuable for approaching
phenomena at the human scale—it gets in-depth and focused on one thing and
produces some wonderful things like hearing aids, penicillin, bicycles, air conditioning, and solar energy—it fails to account for the complex interrelationships that may not be visible to a specialist's view. So it is important to stress
that just as we need *both* the transmission and the constitutive models of
communication, so we also need *both* the atomistic and holistic models of
research. Thus, although I will not be engaging much research in communication

studies that approaches listening from more atomist perspectives, there is much important and valuable work done and yet to be done from that paradigm.[28]

The holism of complex fields of interaction such as the human body, social organization, the weather, and the cosmos can be seen in recent discoveries of fractal geometry and chaos theory. Rather than describing orderly, linear, sequential organization as the prototype standard of all life processes, chaos theory illuminates how both order and chaos interact in a dynamic and non-linear process where an infinite number of phenomena influence the whole, alternating between predictable and nonpredictable patterns. That is to say, causes are not linear, moving from a to b to c, but are instead recursive, feeding into the system and thereby building and changing it from there. In chaos theory, as in quantum physics, linear causality is replaced by complex relationships of probability, wherein everything effects everything, directly and indirectly. "[A]ll causal laws known up to the present have been found to lead eventually to contingencies that are outside the scope of what can be treated by the causal law in question. . . . [E]very mechanical law applies only to an isolated system, because its behavior depends on boundary conditions that are determined in essentially independent systems external to the one under consideration."[29]

In terms of our shared social world, the atomism of the mechanistic perspective has led us to some highly shortsighted ideas and actions. As will be discussed in the next chapter, the 1940 collapse of the brand-new Tacoma Narrows Bridge in Washington State is a good example of the damage that can be wrought by an atomism that ignores complex interactions and contingencies. In the case of Tacoma, a combination of unexpected factors and wind turbulence created increasing forces that magnified over time, generating enough force to destroy the bridge. Similarly, even a patch of ice on an airplane wing can lead to unbelievable damage. According to Briggs, "The unpredictability of turbulence exists because dynamical systems made of liquid or gas are hypersensitive. A fluid system is easily folded back on itself, and its folds can grow quickly. . . . A few grains of ice on the wing of a jet liner, for example, can cause a wrinkle in the air current that feeds back upon itself, multiplies, and spirals to create turbulence that may be great enough to cause a plane crash."[30]

And while we are aware of and celebrate the contributions made by coal- and gas-burning energy, which fueled the industrial and technological revolutions, we tend to neglect the many complex interactions that lead to economic, environmental, geopolitical, and human health problems caused by coal mines, oil wells, fracking for natural gas, and carbon exhaust, to name but a few. When we operate from a mechanistic model that sees the world in terms of single separated objects related only through linear causality, we fail to take into account all the nonlinear and interdependent relationships between all phenomena in the world.

For example, for decades some economists have criticized the way governments measure economic and social well-being using a formula known as Gross Domestic Product (GDP). The basic model for calculating GDP is based on a formula that includes the ratio of exports to imports, government and consumer spending, and industrial investment. But "[e]conomists have warned since its introduction that GDP is a *specialized* tool, and treating it as an indicator of general well-being is inaccurate and dangerous. However, over the last 70 years economic growth—measured by GDP—has become the *sine qua non* for economic progress."[31] Other economists note that in addition, the current formula for GDP fails to account for other economic contributions such as nonprofit work, housework, and charity or, conversely, costs such as pollution, dislocation, and divorce. "Of particular concern is that GDP measurement encourages the depletion of natural resources faster than they can renew themselves. . . . GDP encourages depletion because clear-cutting a forest for lumber is valued more in GDP terms than the ecosystem services that forest provides if left uncut. These services—including biodiversity habitat, reducing flooding from severe storms, filtration to improve water quality in rivers and lakes, and the sequestration of carbon dioxide and manufacture of oxygen—are not part of the market economy and as a result are not counted in GDP."[32]

In the area of acoustic ecology, another example of the damage wrought by fragmentation is demonstrated by the work of Bernie Krause, who studies the bioacoustics of natural sonic habitats. According to Krause, in undisturbed natural environments, all the biological life forms contribute to the creation of a biophony, in which "a delicate acoustic fabric is almost as well-defined as the notes on a page of music."[33] Each different being in the environment occupies its own unique acoustic niche, with its own unique pitch, rhythm, sequence. When combined together, the chorus of these sounds

> creates a protective audio screen thwarting predators from locating where the sound is coming from. The synchronized frog voices originate from so many places at once that it appears to be coming from everywhere. However, when the coherent patterns are upset

by the sound of a jet plane as it flies within range of the pond, the special frog biophony is broken. In an attempt to reestablish the unified rhythm and chorus, individual frogs momentarily stand out giving predators like coyotes or owls perfect opportunities to snag a meal. While recording the rare spade foot frogs above the north shore of Mono Lake in the Eastern Sierras one spring, a similar event actually occurred. After the jet disappeared, forty-five minutes passed before the frogs were able to reestablish their protective chorus. In the dusk light we saw two coyotes and a great horned owl feeding by the side [of] the small pond.[34]

Krause's observations about biophony warn us of the terrible consequences that can arise from not attending to the complex interrelationships of our shared world. As we will discuss in the next chapter, many negative outcomes—from the destruction of habitats, ecosystems, and bridges to the potentially fatal injustices of economic calculus and eyewitness testimony—arise from our failures to think akroatically. Which brings us to the question of what a holistic perspective on listening might sound like. So before we go on with our investigation of sound, vibration, perception, and embodied listening in the next chapter, it may be helpful to briefly consider the fact that a holistic perspective on listening is not really new. As we will discuss in chapter 2, thousands of years ago the ancient Greek philosopher Pythagoras had a holistic theory of music and the relationship between sound and number, which he may or may not have inherited from the Egyptians. Similarly, as we will discuss in chapter 3, even further back in time, ancient Indian cosmology and philosophy had a holistic theory of sound and language. It turns out that there may in fact be an ancient holistic theory of listening that has been buried in the sands of time.

In 1946 the German musicologist Hans Kayser revived the ancient Greek term *akroasis* (from the Greek for "hearing," ακρόασις) for the title of his beautiful treatise, *Akroasis: The Theory of World Harmonics*. To Kayser, listening is a form of thinking rooted in Pythagorean harmonics, which he describes as a gestalt-series of correspondences that, like quantum physics, calls into question mechanical models of certainty and linear causality. According to Kayser, "anyone accustomed to thinking and feeling akroatically knows that there is no 'objectivity' in the sense of a world of facts detached from human beings."[35] Over a decade later the German scholar Günther Wille wrote a 1958 *Habilitation* on the phenomenology of acoustics that examined the ways in which "the sense of hearing is a key feature of being, disclosing the inner and outer realms."[36] Like Kayser, Wille traces *akroasis* through numerous ancient sources to describe a holistic perspective on acoustics that combines physics, mathematics, and music. We will further investigate the theory of harmony and akroasis in chapters 2 and 8, but in the meantime it may suffice to say that akroatic thinking will be a primary thread running throughout the book.

2

VIBRATING WORLDS AND LISTENING BODIES

> Many people travel to Syria and Iraq and meet only
> hypocrites. Others go all the way to India and see
> just merchants buying and selling. Others go to
> Turkestan and China and find those countries filled
> with sneak-thieves and cheats. We always see the
> qualities that are living in us. A cow may walk from
> one side of the amazing city of Baghdad to the other
> and notice only a watermelon rind and a tuft of hay
> that fell off a wagon.
>
> —RUMI, *The Illuminated Rumi*

I never really realized how much America lived inside me until I traveled to India for the first time and discovered there the truth of the old proverb: "Wherever you go, there you are." Driving into Delhi from the airport in a swirling chaos of traffic far worse than anything found on New York's Cross Bronx Expressway, I was astonished by the randomness of beings, objects, and their movements in the road. Cars, pigs, bicycles, children, trucks, cows, and dogs, and at one point, a family of four on a very small motorcycle. Forget about traffic lanes, they're just, well, "guidelines." And though there was pavement for cars, rickshaws, and motorbikes, there were no sidewalks or special lanes for the nonmotorized traveler. Everyone seemed to have agreed that the freedom to move was more important than the rules of the road. But the *sound* of that traffic is what fascinated me most; it was almost symphonic, with layers of horns at different pitches, timbres, and volumes, speaking in different voices, and singing for different lengths of time. In the United States we seem to have only one or two kinds of horn honking—it's either the more or less polite horn tap from behind that reminds you to get going, or it's the rudely impatient blare from any direction that shouts, "Get the h@$^ out of my way!" But in the Delhi traffic, there seemed to be all sorts of horn honks, from light taps that gently nudge, "I'm here," to staccato trills that chant, "Like it or not here I am," to triplets of impatience that nag, "Get going already." But strangest of all was a kind of long sigh that seemed to say something like, "Come on, people, we're moving, moving, moving."

There's also an entirely different tonality to the traffic in Delhi. Perhaps because all the vehicles are mostly small from an American perspective and the motorcycles and auto-rickshaws seem to outnumber cars, there was a softer underlying hum rising from the chorus of motors. Moreover, most of the vehicles are unassuming—I never did hear a Harley roar, nor did I hear the pulsing throb of sub-bass woofers, the roar of a kicked-up muscle car, or the unwelcome din of ear-splitting rock and roll. And when, a few days later, I braved the crazy river of traffic in an open auto-rickshaw (which is basically a three-wheeled motorcycle with a canvas tent on top and a tin shell to sit in), all my muscles were clamped tight in anticipation. But it was far less frightening than I expected. In fact, being closer to the ground and riding alongside all the other moving things felt like being more a part of the flow, as if the rickshaw were a big fish swimming with a shoal of metal fishes, or dancing with the freewheeling bees. It took quite a while for me to lose my American ears and let these new sounds become the unconscious background of my daily life. But whoever knew that *traffic* was a cultural form?

The point is simply this: culture is more than values, ritual, custom, belief. It is more than art and architecture, clothing or music. More even than food or kinship, child rearing or language. Culture is a living being, and its habitat is the body. Embedded in the five senses, the cultured body lives and breathes in moving corporeality, enacting and reenacting itself moment by millimeter, with every gaze and passing sigh, moving with the rhythmic pattering of gestures, posture, and everyday talk. We humans are embodied beings—we live in and with and from our bodies. But as many artists, thinkers, and scholars note, many of us tend to live from the neck up, "between the ears," as it were. But do we? The Euro-American philosophical tradition has tended to separate mind and body, thought and emotion, but as recent advances in neuroscience and biology are demonstrating, such separation is an illusion—mind and body are deeply interconnected, if they are even two things at all. So, following this idea, what if our ears aren't really in our heads, but are our whole body? What if our entire body is one giant listening organ, one great resonating chamber? What if we are, in some sense, all ears?

It's not as big a stretch as you might think. Sound waves can travel in many different materials—through air, water, steel, and stone—with enough power to bend, break, and move matter. Sound waves can melt a kidney stone or dismantle a bridge, and they can render human beings immobilized. They can also, irresistibly, urge us to tap our feet or even dance. When we hear sound, acoustic waves travel through the air and then pass through the boundaries of our bodies: first through the skin of the tympanic membrane (our ear "drum") and then along the bones of our inner ear and into the mysterious cochlea, a fluid-filled membrane lined with hair cells that are each tuned to a different frequency, which in turn trigger auditory neurons that fire up the auditory nerve and travel into the brain.[1] So when we listen, our bodies vibrate with the sound waves pulsing toward and then through us. When you are listening to music, the music is not just playing in you, it is, rather, playing you, your body becoming a musical instrument, a resonating chamber. The music echoes through your mind, reverberating your bones and synapses such that you become the music. Listening may or may not compel you to wiggle your hips or bounce your head, but the waves of sound are nevertheless moving you.

The award-winning Scottish percussionist Dame Evelyn Glennie—who happens to be profoundly deaf—explains how, as listeners, we are in fact *participators of sound* because we actually *touch* the sound. After she became deaf at age twelve, Glennie switched from piano to percussion. Of course, at the time many people thought her efforts to play music were pathetically futile, but, with the support of her parents and teachers, she persisted. A major breakthrough came when her percussion teacher placed Glennie's hand on the wall next to a big kettledrum and asked her to feel the vibrations on her palm as he struck the drum. As Glennie became increasingly sensitive to the vibrations, her teacher moved her into the hall entirely outside of the music room, where he was pounding a kettledrum. By placing her hand on the wall outside the room, Glennie learned to differentiate between two pitches of the drum. Over time, she came to notice that she felt higher pitches in the fingers and lower pitches toward the heel of her hand and down her wrist. Eventually, she developed the ability to distinguish the pitch and volume and rhythm of different instruments, including all sorts of drums, marimbas, and bells. Today Glennie is an internationally acclaimed percussionist who has mastered the ability to listen by *touch*. She writes, "I can also tell the quality of a note by what I feel, I can sense musical sound through my feet and lower body, and also through my hands; and can identify the different notes as I press the pedal according to which part of my foot feels the vibrations and for how long, and by how I experience the vibrations in my body."[2]

So one crucial thing about listening is that it takes place in the body. And one of its key elements is rhythm, which, as George Leonard points out, is the pulse of life: "in the vibrant molecular realm, everything is rhythm and electricity."[3] Research in a variety of fields has revealed how pulsations and rhythm underscore everything from the dance of subatomic particles to the mysterious spiraling of super galaxies and everything in between—including the gestures and movements of the human body as we move about in our everyday social interactions. Basically, as Bergson noted over a hundred years ago, "Matter thus resolves itself into numberless vibrations, all linked together in uninterrupted continuity, all bound up with each other, and travelling in every direction like shivers through an immense body."[4]

Consider, for example, the rhythmic pulse of a heartbeat and the uncannily proportional relationship between heartbeat and life span, where, across animal species, the faster the heartbeat, the shorter the life. "While a mouse's heart and lungs beat rapidly compared to an elephant's, both mouse and elephant count the same number of beats and breaths per life. It is as if mammals are assigned 1.5 billion heartbeats and told to use them as they like. Tiny mice speed ahead in a fast-forward version of an elephant's life."[5] Or consider the steady pulsations or "heartbeat" of a computer or a machine. Later today, perhaps, you'll sit before the sleek computer screen aglow with possibilities, your fingers caressing the keys. They know this terrain; it is the mother tongue your digits speak to the CPU, their listener. The laptop shell is cool beneath your wrists, and you can feel the machine hum before you can even feel your own pulse, but the two commingle. Are they in sync? Is there some unheard duet, a rhythmic concerto between your pulse and that of the machine? A computer today pulses somewhere around 2.26 gigahertz (or 2.26 thousand million cycles per second). In contrast, your heart beats at about a dawdling 70 cycles per minute. But does your pulse change when your wrists, naked and vulnerable, rest on the laptop? What rhythms or counterrhythms resound when the pulse of the human body commingles with that of the machine? And rhythmic pulsation isn't the only embodied waveform arising between the interaction of you and your computer.

In the sounds of the keyboard tapping there's a pattern to the alternating clicks and clacks—a stutter here as you revise a word, then a flurry of clicks as a whole sentence roars out. This rhythmic movement of plastic on plastic, the dots and dashes of keyboard English, may be audible to many, but is understood by few. Clever thieves can obtain passwords and account numbers by the beeps and pings of a cell phone keypad. Could a blind person be trained in such listening? Might this Helen Keller of keyboard English be able to listen as your fingers speak? With each key stroke and mouse click, your body, the embodied materiality of communication, reverberates with the combined sound of human and machine, the rhythm of heartbeat and gigahertz. And lest you think this is a mere flight of whimsy, consider this: a professor of computer science at the University of Iowa is developing a biometric identification program that will use the patterns of your own unique and individual way of typing on a keyboard instead of a password![6] With all the dazzle and glare of our communication technologies, it's easy to forget that we *are* our bodies.

We can trace the embodied materiality of communication to a scene in fifteenth-century Germany, where the printer Johannes Gutenberg is fingering the letters as he readies to print his Bible, his hands blackened with ink, the machine groaning with the weight of iron on wood. Or even further, to the Sumerian scribe in 3000 B.C.E., sitting cross-legged on the ground, the dry earth warm beneath his buttocks, his fingers coiled around the stylus as he cuts wedges into clay, the clay moist and yielding to his reed pen, the pen barely noticeable nestled between thumb and forefinger. Focused on his work, the scribe bends forward, his neck and shoulders tired from the curving down. Or we can remember the rugged materiality of the medieval messenger, transporting secret scrolls over land day and night, the horse's hooves pressing into the warm earth of desert or forest, or clattering over stones. This is another kind of typing, each footprint a letter in the translation from fingers to eye. And what embodied materiality marks your communication right now, dear reader? Are you poised over your keyboard or hunched from the hours slouched in your chair? As you read these words, do your fingers curl around a coffee cup coated with the prints of your hand? What sound waves are vibrating the bones, membranes, and synapses of your body as you read?

Sound and Vibration

So what is sound? Well, as with most things, it turns out that how we define it depends on our point of view. From an anthropocentric perspective, you can't get much more human-oriented than the good old *Oxford English Dictionary,* which defines sound as "the sensation produced in the organs of hearing when the surrounding air is set in vibration in such a way as to affect these." But sound can also be defined apart from our ability to hear it with our "organs of hearing." The answer to the old philosophical chestnut "If a tree falls in the forest but no there's no one there to hear it, does it make a sound?" depends both on how you define sound and how you define "one." If only hearing *humans* count as "one," then perhaps the tree falls without a sound. But if we define sound as a physical process that involves the transfer of energy in the form of pressure waves, then yes, indeed, the falling tree makes noise—which raises an entirely new question about the difference between sound and noise. But we will get to this later.

Meanwhile, sound waves are created when objects collide with enough force to compress the atomic particles together. When the particles move from their pre- to their postcollision state, they transfer the energy of the original movement to nearby particles, which in turn transfer the energy to the next and so on, creating a wave pattern that spreads out from the source of the initial collision, not unlike the patterned undulations of a Slinky toy. When you strike the head of a drum with a stick, the pressure from that collision creates vibrations that travel as waves through the drum down to the floor and beyond, as well as through the stick into your hand and up your arm, and through the air to the walls, windows, and doors, traveling through any material (such as bone, wood, glass, water, or air) in its path. We call it a wave because in the process of traveling, the particles moving in one direction leave a gully-like gap behind them, as was illustrated in figure 1. As the wave moves, each gap in the pattern is filled with the particles moving forward from behind, producing a repeating pattern of compression and release, not unlike the density/emptiness patterns of space. Sound waves move longitudinally in the same direction they travel, like an earthworm scrunching up and then stretching out. But unlike the belly muscles of an earthworm, sound waves can travel through any medium.

But sound waves are only one kind of wave phenomenon—light, water, gravity, and electromagnetic radiation also travel in waves. Basically, any repetitive movement creates some form of wave, whether it's a bee's wings vibrating back and forth or an electron racing in vast orbits around a nucleus. So long as the movement repeats in a cycle (either back and forth or around and around), a wave pattern is created. A clock pendulum swinging back and forth creates waves, as does a planet spinning on its axis, or the heart muscle beating in your chest. When a hummingbird that weighs about the same as a penny hovers over a trumpet flower to sip some nectar, its wings flap about seventy times a second to produce the humming sound after which it is named. Scientists find that pretty much everything in the universe vibrates, from the infinitesimally tiny subatomic filaments of string theory to massive supergiant stars like Betelgeuse—and therefore produces waves.

When the contractions and expansions of the human heart produce pressure waves that pump blood through the body, each completion of the contraction and expansion cycle is a beat, and heart rate is calculated by the number of beats per minute. Other vibrating phenomena, like the neurons in the human brain, are measured in seconds. When we're in a deep sleep, the brain pulses in cycles of about 4 times a second, emitting what are called delta waves. When we're alert and thinking hard, the brain pulses about 14 times a second, emitting what are called beta waves. Really, really fast repeated cycles, like those in computer processors, are measured in millions of beats per second. Still other kinds of wave phenomena are measured in rotations, as in the cycle of the earth rotating (or revolving) around the sun once a year or the CD in your computer rotating around 300 times a minute. When a ten-thousand-pound Coast Guard helicopter hovers over the ocean on a sea rescue mission, its blades rotate about 125 times per minute. When the dentist is fixing your cavity, the ultrasonic drill rotates about 800,000 times a minute. And all of these cyclical repetitions produce wave forms. You might have noticed another pattern here: the faster the rotation, the higher the pitch. In what follows, I will provide an extensive explanation for why this is so by delving into considerable detail about the physics of sound and the nature of perception. If the material is new or unfamiliar to you, try not to get bogged down in the details—just keep reading with an open and akroatic mind, listening for holistic patterns, shapes, and relationships. For just as one can sometimes see things more clearly out of the corner of one's eye rather than looking dead on, sometimes simply joining in and listening *with* the text can be more fruitful than striving for mastery. The point of this mass of detail is to provide you with a rich vocabulary for thinking generatively about sound, voice, and listening in new and unexpected ways.

Waves are typically measured in three dimensions, amplitude, wavelength, and frequency; or, in layman's terms, height, width, and speed. Amplitude measures the height of the wave, wavelength measures its width, and frequency measures its speed. In sound waves, amplitude is related to volume—the bigger the amplitude, the louder the sound. Frequency is related to pitch—the more wave cycles per second, the higher the pitch.[7] Wave frequency (number of wave cycles per second) is measured in hertz (Hz), named after the German physicist Heinrich Hertz. A heart thumping at a rate of 60 beats per minute will have a frequency of 1 Hz, that is, one pulse per second. The average adult can hear sounds between 20 and 16,000 Hz, the average infant up to 20,000 Hz, and the average dog up to 45,000 Hz (which is why dog whistles can't be heard by humans). The amplitude (volume or energy) of a sound wave is measured in decibels, a somewhat arbitrary measure based on the amount of volume change that an ordinary person can perceive. So, for example, a whispered conversation has an amplitude of about 20 dB, whereas an average lawnmower runs at about 100 dB. Anything over 130 dB will damage your ears, which is why many former rock musicians now need hearing aids.

As mentioned above, pitch relates to wave frequency, and Western musicians use frequency to tune their instruments together to what is called "concert pitch." Whether you have two violinists or fifty musicians playing together, you want them to be in tune so that the notes that are *supposed* to sound the same actually *do* sound the same, and so the notes that are supposed to harmonize beautifully, or not, actually do so. Since the mid-twentieth century or so, Western orchestras have tuned their instruments together with an internationally agreed upon standard measure (a kind of musical yardstick), where the middle A of their instruments (whether it be on a violin, flute, or double bass), vibrates with a frequency of 440 Hz, or 440 cycles per second.[8]

While there have long been many different systems of measuring pitch over the history of the world, as a basic frame of reference, today the lowest note a bass opera singer might be able to produce is about 87 Hz and the highest note a soprano might reach is about 1200 Hz; at that pitch, depending on the volume of the note, one might be able to shatter a wine glass. Thus, as mentioned above, the frequency of sound wave motion is directly related to pitch, wherein slower frequency equates, to our ears, to "lower" pitch. Importantly, however, not all cultures map pitch with height metaphors as we do in the West. In some cultures, such as in Bali and Java, musicians use the metaphor of size (small and large) instead of high and low, whereas in the Amazon, some cultures use metaphors of young and old.[9]

But regardless of what metaphors we use, what is remarkable about all this is the fact that the ear can distinguish incredibly precise differences in pitch as well as rhythm. According to the physicist Hermann von Helmholtz, "It is well known that when two pendulums are ticking near one another, the ear can distinguish whether the ticks are or are not coincident, within one hundredth of a second. The eye would certainly fail to determine whether two flashes of light coincided within 1/24 second; and probably within a much larger fraction of a second."[10] This sensitivity to pitch is what enables us to perceive when things are out of tune, even by the slightest fraction. When you have two violinists playing the same notes together, but one player is a bit off key—say he's a bit sharp, playing a 449 Hz note rather than 440 Hz—the resulting sound will be unpleasant and perhaps even painful to most Euro-American listeners. In some cultures, however, this kind of combination of sounds not only perfectly correct but quite pleasing, as in the Balkan singing style, which features very close intervals of sound. Why? Because as described in the last chapter, what we call one "note" is not really "one" thing, but a vibrating confluence of notes that make up the harmonic series. We will return to this issue when we address issues of resonance shortly, but it is worth noting that pitch also plays an important role in tonal languages, such as Athabaskan, Bantu, and Chinese. In these languages meaning is based not simply on pitch itself, but also on the melodic patterns and direction of pitch movement (rising, falling, or dipping). Not surprisingly, scholars have found that far greater numbers of tonal language speakers (such as Vietnamese and Chinese) possess absolute pitch, "the ability to name or produce a note of particular pitch in the absence of a reference note," than nontonal language speakers (such as English), who consider absolute pitch a remarkably "mysterious and exceptional musical endowment."[11]

And just as systems of pitch measurement have varied throughout history and culture, so have what we call musical scales. One of the first musicians to theorize the relation of sound and measure was the ancient Greek philosopher Pythagoras (about whom we will learn even more in chapters 3 and 8). Pythagoras (or his Egyptian teacher's teacher's teacher) discovered that there is a precise mathematical correspondence between the proportions of the string length and the sounds produced. When you divide a string, whether in half, in thirds, in fourths, and so on, you get proportionately related sounds. So when you divide a string in half and pluck it, you get a sound that is both identical to and different from the sound of the full string—the note sounds the same, but it is higher in pitch. That is, when you divide the string exactly in half you double the frequency—so the smaller string sounds higher. But, because the frequency of the divided string is proportional to the open string, with a ratio of 2:1, we hear the two notes as equivalent. We call this sonic same/difference relationship the octave, and the notes between the octaves form a scale. So no matter how long your string is, if you divide it in half you'll get an octave. But that's not all. Pythagoras also noted other consistent

Table 1   Relationship of string length to frequency, harmonics, and music

String length ratio	Frequency (Hz)	Harmonic (partial)	Musical note	Relation to tonic	Multiple of tonic
1	256 Hz	1st	C	Tonic	× 1 (same)
1/2	512 Hz	2nd	C	Octave	× 2 (double)
1/3	768 Hz	3rd	G	5th (dominant)	× 3 (triple)
1/4	1024 Hz	4th	C	Octave	× 4 (quadruple)
1/5	1280 Hz	5th	E	3rd	× 5 (quintuple)

*For numerical simplicity, middle C is here given as 256 rather than the standard 261.6 Hz.

corresponding relationships between string length (number) and sound (tone), which we call the harmonic series. Divided in thirds, the string sounds with a tone exactly three times the frequency of the original open string, which we hear as what is called the fifth. Table 1 illustrates the relationships between string length, frequency, harmonic proportion, note, and scale position.

If you sing *do, re, mi, fa, sol,* the relationship between *do* and *sol* is a fifth (or if you hum the song "Twinkle, Twinkle, Little Star" the first twinkle is *do* and the second twinkle is *sol*). Similarly, if you divide the string in fifths, the tone will be exactly five times the frequency of the original open note, and will sound as what we call the third (or *mi*). According to Kayser: "Apart from the practical musical activity, the third, the octave and the fifth are seen as the fundamentals of every theory of music since the earliest times. These intervals must have been *heard* by ancient theorists, as proved by Chinese and Indian traditions, as well as by the Pythagoreans."[12]

In Western music, the notes between the octaves are divided into twelve equally spaced intervals (called semitones), seven of which form the diatonic scale *do, re, mi, fa, sol, la, ti, (do)*. In traditional Indian music, the octave is divided into twenty microtones (the distinctions between which are hard for Westerners to hear), and in Japanese music, the octave is often divided into five tones (the pentatonic scale), which can be heard by playing only the black keys on the piano. There are many different kinds of scales, though most Western music is built around the twenty semitones of the octave. Today, these semitones are tuned at standardized equal intervals (known as equal temperament), whereas before Bach's time they were not. These pitch relationships can be seen on a contemporary piano, which has twelve keys in each octave and a range of eight octaves, where the lowest note, called A0, vibrates at 27.5 Hz, and the highest note, C8, vibrates at 4300 Hz. Notice the pattern—27.5 (A0) doubled is 55 Hz (A1), which when doubled is 110 Hz (A2), doubled again is 220 (A3), doubled again is 440 (A4), and so on. To the human ear, all these A notes, whether they are very low or very high in pitch, sound similar because they share something in common—their fundamental rates of vibration are proportionately related.

We call these proportional vibrations harmony, and they are one of the qualities that make music pleasing to the ear. When the Beach Boys sing their classic song "Good Vibrations," for example, it's not just the words but also their close harmonies that create the vibrations that, to many listeners, feel good. We thus experience vibrations with our bodies—from the jackhammer's jolt in the soles of your feet as you pass the construction site to "bad vibes" you sense from a new acquaintance, and from the pulsing ball of energy felt by the tai chi practitioner in the park to the throbbing bass of a passing car. In short, everything vibrates, and the quality of those vibrations as well as our ability to perceive them are due to the periodicity of the cycles, which in turn resonate with other vibrating bodies, which produce yet another series of vibrations, in a virtually infinite rippling effect.

So, for example, when a cellist draws her bow across the fattest string of the cello (C2), that open string will vibrate with a specific frequency (65.4 Hz), called its fundamental frequency, or natural resonance. Whether she plucks the open string with her teeth, fingers, or toes, or whether she strokes it with her bow, a pencil, or a glass, it will vibrate at its fundamental frequency. But that's not all: the C2 string will also vibrate with what are called overtones, or harmonic partials, which are derived from multiples of the fundamental frequency. The first overtones of C2 are the octaves at C1, C3, C4, and so on, which is the fundamental frequency doubled (130 Hz) or halved (32.5 Hz). The second overtone is the frequency tripled (195 Hz, which is the note G1) or divided in thirds. The fourth is the frequency quadrupled or divided in four, and so on.

What's important to note here is not the numbers themselves, but the proportional relationship between the vibrations, which recur at every scale, regardless of size, shape, or velocity of the sound waves produced by the strings. Perhaps most amazingly, these harmonic patterns have also been found to recur in nature, be it in the arrangements of leaves on a plant, the recurring geometric patterns produced by crystals, the proportions of the human body, or, as we will explore in chapter 8, sound itself.[13] Therefore, when the cellist plucks the C2 string, it will vibrate not only at the fundamental frequency but also with its overtones of Cs, Gs, and Es as well. If she plucks the next string, G2, it will vibrate its overtones as well as the resonant overtones on the C string. The quality and quantity of these vibrations are what create the color, or timbre, of the sound, and can vary according to the kinds material used to make the cello as well as the body and style of the musician. For example, a recording of Pablo Casals playing the Bach cello suites sounds quite different from Yo Yo Ma's version, even though both cellists are virtuosos playing the exact same notes and both their cellos are tuned to A440. Neville Marriner, the conductor of the Minnesota Orchestra, once told my music class in a guest lecture that given a choice between hiring a virtuoso oboist or a highly competent journeyman, he would choose the latter. Why? Because virtuosos, having more color and slightly altered timing compared to run-of-the-mill excellent players, will tend to stand out rather than blend in with the rest of the section. And with orchestral music, you want your section players to sound with "one" voice.

Resonance

When sound waves travel through earth, air, and water, some of their energy vibrates (or is absorbed by) the material they move through. When the A4 note on the piano is struck, for example, it makes other piano strings vibrate in what is called "sympathetic resonance." The "sympathy" is actually a numerical relationship of frequency rates—playing A4 makes all other strings on the piano with multiples of 440 vibrate at their fundamentals and partials. But it doesn't end there. The A4 sound waves will make other things in the room (both those we can hear, such as other instruments or a window, and those we can't hear, like our bones or the dog's teeth) vibrate. The resonant frequency of these other vibrating objects is determined by a number of factors, including the size, weight, density, and tension of the material that is vibrating. As composer Pauline Oliveros notes, humans sense the sonic envelope of the earth, which she calls the "sonosphere," "according to the bandwidth and resonant frequencies and mechanics of the ear, skin, bones, meridians, fluids and other organs and tissues of the body as coupled to the earth and its layers from the core to the magnetic fields as transmitted and perceived by the audio cortex and nervous system (all with great variation, of course). All cells of the earth and body vibrate."[14] The kinds of mechanical differences in the sonosphere also create differences in the sounds of the human voice—such as the size and thickness of the vocal folds, the size and shape of the palate, the tongue, and the lungs—as well as the sounds of musical instruments. For example, while the six strings of a steel-string guitar are of equal length, they differ in thickness, density, and tension. The thicker the string, the more slowly it will vibrate and therefore the lower the pitch. In contrast, the same note sounded on a plastic or gut classical guitar string will have a different timbre (warmer, rounder, softer, etc.) than the same note sounded on a steel-string guitar (cooler, biting, fresh, etc.).

But when sound waves vibrate other materials besides musical instruments, things can get very bad, very fast. Perhaps you have seen someone make a crystal wineglass sing by rubbing a finger in circles along the lip of the glass—the finger movement creates vibrations in the glass that will resonate with the harmonics of the fundamental frequency of the crystal that makes up the glass. Speeding up or slowing down the movement will change the volume but not the pitch, just as hitting a piano key hard or soft, fast or slow, changes its volume and color but not its pitch. Now bring an opera singer into the room and ask her to sing loud and high. If she gets a note that matches the vibrational frequency of the crystal, the glass will shatter, as the famous 1970s Ella Fitzgerald Memorex commercial will attest. But the destructive power of sound resonance is not limited to advertising or parlor tricks.

As touched upon in the last chapter, a famous example happened in 1940 when the Tacoma Narrows Bridge in Washington State collapsed because of resonance only a few months after completion. Even though the wind was blowing only about forty miles per hour, a complex series of vibrational interactions set the bridge shuddering with enough building force to rock the bridge laterally back and forth. This rocking in turn created a twisting or torsional wave that generated enough force to destroy the bridge. What caused the destruction of the bridge was not the force of the wind or energy of the waves, but the fact of sympathetic vibration. The wind was "singing" at just the right frequency to set the bridge a-rocking and with enough force to cause its collapse. Another example of the power of wave energy is shared by physics professor Benjamin Crowell, who tells a tale of the genius inventor Nikola Tesla, which is also reported in several Tesla biographies.[15] According to Crowell, Tesla told a "credulous" newspaper reporter that he attached a pocket-sized electric oscillator to a steel beam of a building under construction in New York City. Tesla said that after he had presumably tuned the vibrator to the resonant frequency of the beam, "In a few minutes, I could feel the beam trembling. Gradually the trembling increased in intensity and extended throughout the whole great mass of steel. Finally, the structure began to creak and weave, and the steelworkers came to the ground panic-stricken, believing that there had been an earthquake. . . . [If] I had kept on ten minutes more, I could have laid that building flat in the street."[16] And lest we forget, the destructive power of sound has even been weaponized not just by the army of the Third Reich but also by police forces in the United States and around the world. For example, in 2004, 2010, 2011, and 2012, in cities including New York, Chicago, Oakland, and Pittsburgh, civilian protestors (in the Occupy and other movements) were threatened with the "nonlethal" force of Long Range Acoustic Devices (LRADs), which blast painfully debilitating super-high-frequency sonic waves in short bursts. The devices were also deployed in London for the summer 2012 Olympics and have been used against protesters in the United States in 2009 and 2011 and in Azerbaijan in 2013.[17]

What makes wave phenomena especially powerful is their ability to move the material they travel through without the material itself traveling along with it. Thus, the wave forms of earthquakes and tsunamis travel through earth and water without actually pushing the material forward. That's why a duck lounging in the pond moves up and down, rather than being shoved toward the shore, when a wave passes beneath it. When a passing boat creates waves that travel towards the duck, the water molecules don't move with the wave, but in little circles below it. So a wave is a pattern of energy moving through a medium where the greater the energy, the higher the peaks and valleys of the waves.

In sound waves, these heights and valleys are related to volume. As discussed above, greater sound energy equals greater volume, but greater energy doesn't necessarily translate to greater speed. The velocity of a sound wave is determined by both the type and force of the original collision, as well as the density (or viscosity), depth, and shape of the material it travels through. Sound waves moving through water or flesh travel much more quickly than they do through air, which is what makes them especially valuable for navigation and medical procedures. When ships use sonar (sound navigation and ranging), they send out a steady stream of sound waves that bounce off objects in the distance and return to the ship. The speed, shape, and pattern of the returning sound waves provides information about the size, shape, location, and distance of any objects around the ship, allowing it to safely navigate the waters (or search for treasure buried beneath the sea). Sonar, also called echolocation, is also how dolphins and whales navigate the oceans.

But because sound waves are reflected and absorbed at different rates depending on the type of material they travel through, they do not travel at the same speed through all fluids, which is why they are useful for medical procedures. If you go to the doctor for an ultrasound exam, the machine emits sound waves that travel through your flesh at such a high frequency that you cannot hear them. When the sound waves encounter a change in density or viscosity, such as a boundary between a liver and a spleen, or between a kidney and a kidney stone, the sound waves bounce back to the machine at different speeds and directions, which can be translated into a visual image projected on a screen. Later, if for example a kidney stone is found, sound waves can be used to break up the stone by sending out a shock wave that shatters the stone like an opera singer shattering a champagne glass.[18]

Thus, the physics of sound, music, and sonar (electron, guitar string, dolphin or whale) tell us something important about listening: not only are our ears incredibly sensitive to vibration, but so are our bodies and the bodies of all beings and forms of matter on the planet. We will return to the relationship between sound, vibration, music, and listening in the last chapter, but these ideas form the background of the holistic and embodied perspective offered in various forms throughout the book. In short, everything vibrates and everything resonates, and whether it is audible or not, our bodies always are in touch with sound. Consider this: Daniel Kish, president of the World Access for the Blind foundation, was born blind and has trained himself to "see" through the use of sound and audition. Mr. Kish's foundation teaches blind and low-vision people from all over the world how to navigate through space using echolocation, or what he prefers to call "FlashSonar." The process involves producing tongue clicks that bounce off objects in the surrounding environment, yielding information about the size, shape, location, distance, and solidity of things in the near to middle distance.

Kish and his colleagues teach students three different kinds of tongue clicks—"cluck click," "giddy up click," and the very soft "tsk tsk click," which, while barely noticeable by sighted people, yields an extraordinary amount of information about everything from walls, open windows, and doorways to curbs, steps, and fire hydrants, and from pedestrians, trees, and parked or moving vehicles to chain-link fences, soccer balls, and mud puddles. According to Mr. Kish, "the greatest advantage to FlashSonar is that an active signal can be produced very consistently so the brain can tune to this specific signal very intently. This allows for relatively easy recognition of echoes even in complex or noisy environments. It's like recognizing a familiar face or voice in a crowd. The more familiar is the voice, the easier it is to recognize."[19] So far, Mr. Kish has trained other "perceptual mobility specialists" who teach blind, low-vision, and even sighted people to navigate through unfamiliar environments on foot, skates, and bicycles in the wild or on the streets. In other words, perceptual mobility means using multiple senses to move through space. And this raises a question: what is perception, and how is it different from sensation?

Perception

We encounter, in each nanosecond of our lives, billions of sensations, some of which we are aware and many, many more of which we are not. The vast majority of these sensations are ignored by our conscious mind, while those that we recognize and name become perceptions—categorized sensations of which we are consciously aware. Consider a conversation between two people in a crowded café. The air is filled with a cacophony of sound that includes the murmuring of voices, the clanking of spoons, the hiss of the various coffee-making machines, the faint strains of Muzak, and the ring of the cash register. Similarly, the air is also thick with the sharp aroma of coffee as well as of cologne and baked goods, and is also perhaps peppered with a sharp waft of perspiration or the faint odors of sour milk and ammonia. At the same time, thousands of colors, shapes, and patterns surround the pair in the short and middle distance—even when each looks steadily at the other's face, their peripheral vision observes movement, color, size, shape.

Though neither person may be aware of it, the skin and bones of both their bodies receive thousands of simultaneous touches—the smooth warmth of the coffee mug beneath the fingers, the hard wood of the chair on the sit bones, the soft rubber of the mat under their feet, and the cool metal of the table under their wrists. They might even feel a mordant burn in the solar plexus when a tricked-out muscle car passes by outside, subwoofers roaring. And at the same time, there may be a sharp tang of Sumatra dark roast on one's tongue, balanced by a sweet burst of cranberry and orange from a morning muffin. All of which is not to even mention the thunderstorm of thoughts in both their heads—everything from worries and plans to memories and dreams tumbling around like clothes in a big round laundromat dryer. And all of this is happening together, at the same time, while one friend tells the other about the disturbing dream he had last night.

So in order to listen, one must zero in and pay attention to the speaker and his or her words, and thereby ignore the zillions of other sensations competing for awareness. The better one can do this, consciously, the better one's focus, concentration, and presence. The American epidemic of ADD (attention deficit disorder) is a disturbance of conscious focus that makes concentration tremendously difficult for some people. And while most of us can choose (to greater or lesser degrees) where we place our attention, our brains are in fact doing this unconsciously all day long. According to neuroscientists, the brain receives vastly more sensory information per second than it can process, so it has to filter things out and organize the remaining sensations into patterns and categories. This filtering and classifying process is what we call perception, and it illustrates the difference between sensation and perception. Since the eighteenth century or so, some Western philosophers, such as Immanuel Kant, Henri Bergson, and William James, have surmised that objects presumably "out there" in the "real world" are not entirely "out there," and that, in fact, the human mind is partly responsible for constructing our perceptions. Kant's legendary dictum that without concepts ("thoughts") our perceptions ("content") are empty and without perceptions ("intentions") our thoughts are blind basically means that sensations need to be processed by the mind before they can be considered perceptions.[20] Similarly, William James observed how "[t]he baby, assailed by eyes, ears, nose, skin, and entrails at once, feels it all as one great blooming, buzzing confusion."[21]

During the second half of the twentieth century, neuroscientists and cognitive scientists began to identify the actual physical processes that transform sensations into perceptions. According to this new scientific paradigm, everything we perceive, including "external reality," "is a construction of the brain. Our senses are confronted by a chaotic, constantly changing world that has no labels, and the brain must make sense of that chaos. It is the brain's correlations of sensory information that create the knowledge we have about our surroundings, such as the sounds of words and music, the images we see in paintings and photographs, the colors we perceive."[22] Thus, perception is a process of distilling sensations into culturally distinct patterns—what transforms that blooming buzz into more or less organized perceptions is largely a linguistic and cultural process that describes, names, and gives meaning to those zillions of sensations. The neuroscientist Israel Rosenfield describes how "there are no colors in nature, only electromagnetic radiation of varying wavelengths (the visible spectrum is between 390 and 750 nanometers). If we were aware of our 'real' visual worlds we would see constantly changing images of dirty gray, making it difficult for us to recognize forms . . . colors themselves are not in our surroundings."[23]

While color recognition may be a universal human perception, the kinds and numbers of categories named for color in a given language can differ greatly from culture to culture.[24] A few cultures have no semantic category for color, and of those that do, the number of basic colors can range from eleven (as in English), to a two-color system (containing black and white or warm and cool) and combinations in between.[25] Consider: I just this moment glance out the window and am caught by a bloom of red and dying leaves, the wind animating the branches of the giant maple in my neighbor's yard. Then a flash of yellow as a neighbor's child pedals by on her bike on the sidewalk in the rain. This brief experience is not a transcription of visual sensory input, but is instead a kind of linguistic tableau filled with culturally imbued words, meanings, and categories—it is as much a description of me (my nationality, age, race, gender, social class, etc.) and my language and culture as it is of the scene itself.

Thus, perception is not always conscious and intentional; in fact, it is far more often also unconscious and habitual, and this often creates problems. It's one thing when we jump back and recoil at the sight of a big snake, only to realize it's an old, tattered piece of rope. It's quite another when we unconsciously (or consciously) make presumptions about a person's ability on the basis of the color of their skin, the tones of their accent or dialect, or the style and quality of their clothing. All too often, we habitually and automatically respond to sensory information in ways that we may not be consciously aware of. For example, the sounds of human footsteps carry a vast amount of social information that people pick up on and respond to, often unconsciously.[26] Even while unaware, people can infer the mood, gender, social status, and even personality traits of the walking person by only listening to their footsteps. As it turns out, even our footfalls, like traffic, music, and color, are culturally shaped.

So *what* perceptions get named, as well as *how* they get named, is ultimately a social and political matter. In the United States, unless the speakers are artists or designers, the use of certain color words such as "mauve" and "chartreuse" tends to be associated with female gender and gay male sexuality. Similarly, the choice of words used to describe skin color carries significant political weight with meanings that differ depending upon who the speaker is. For example, while African American speakers describing someone's skin color as "mocha," "dusky," or "yellow" may be quite acceptable ordinary practice, these descriptions are likely to signify differently when uttered by a white speaker. But the political and social dimensions of skin color play even more powerfully in large-scale social formations, such as the U.S. Census. For example, the first U.S. Census of 1790 sorted people according to white males sixteen and up, free white males under sixteen, free white females, other free persons, and slaves. But the gender only of free white persons was noted—the gender of "other" people, whether free or enslaved, was not categorized, named, or counted. One hundred years later, the 1890 census separated gender from skin color and asked each person in the household to identify their "Race" as "White," "Black," "Mulatto," "Quadroon," "Octoroon," "Chinese," "Japanese," or "Indian."[27] Here we have people sorted and labeled by color, proportion of ancestor color, ethnicity, and nationality. Notice, however, that neither European ethnicities nor nationalities are named or counted.

Forty years later, in 1930, the question had changed to "Color or Race" and the categories included white, black, Mexican, American Indian, Chinese, Japanese, Filipino, Hindu, and Korean. Here we find categories of color that are not sorted by ancestry, along with the continued categorization of only non-European ethnicities, nationalities, and, now, religion.[28] By the year 2000, the census asked people to self-identify their "Race" in an open-ended question, and to indicate whether they were Spanish, Hispanic, or Latino—a combination of national, ethnic, and linguistic categories. As we can see from this brief historical account, for over 220 years the U.S. Census has categorized, named and counted people by various and continually changing "racial" and "color" labels. The bare *fact* of this naming, in addition to the fact that these words and categories have changed over time, indicates just how much racial categories are social and political signifiers that attach meaning to skin color and ethnicity in ways that correspond to politics, power, and the social order.

But the social and political dimensions of language are of course not limited to what we name, because what we name also has a bearing on what we observe. Consider the question of eyewitness testimony, which often plays a key role in police investigation and court testimony. Eyewitnesses are considered, by and large, to be a highly credible form of evidence, especially when confirmed by seemingly objective tests like a police lineup. People observe something firsthand, and what they honestly report seeing is presumed to be what "is." But researchers have demonstrated that a variety of factors—such as police procedural errors, faulty memories, and racial bias—make eyewitness testimony far less certain than television police dramas would have you believe. For example, even tiny details in the way police construct and administer a lineup have been shown to influence how witnesses respond to suspect identification. Witnesses often want to help police catch criminals and are therefore highly susceptible to conscious and unconscious cues from police.

"Lineup administrator behavior that biases a witness towards a positive identification decision obviously can have devastating consequences if the outcome is the misidentification of an innocent suspect."[29] Moreover, witness recall is likely to be inaccurate to begin with. Numerous studies demonstrate that witnesses have a tendency to identify innocent bystanders rather than assailants as the criminal. Perhaps even more disturbing, the research shows that witnesses are far less accurate in identifying people of a different race from their own.[30] The numerous exonerations of convicted felons made possible by the recent introduction of DNA evidence that contradicts eyewitness testimony is a case in point.

The issue of what is called "change blindness" is another example of how our perceptions are freighted with social judgment combined with our environment. In the 1970s, psychologists began to study the relationship between attention and perception. In one famous study, they asked people to watch a videotaped basketball game and press a button every time they saw the ball passed.[31] About thirty seconds into the tape, a woman in the video walks through the middle of the basketball court carrying an open umbrella. When the observers were questioned about the tape about a minute later, only six of the twenty-eight observers noticed the woman with the umbrella. Subsequent studies over the next several decades have confirmed these findings, most recently with a person wearing a gorilla suit who rambles through the middle of a game. Apparently some of the observers not only didn't notice the gorilla, but further, had to be shown the videotape again to convince them that it was actually there. These studies "show that attention plays a critical role in perception and in representation. Without attention, we often do not see unanticipated events, and even with attention, we cannot encode and retain all the details of what we see."[32]

Thus, selective looking, like selective hearing, is not just dime store psychobabble, but an inevitable part of our perceptual processes. Most challenging, however, is the way that witnesses will reinforce their own faulty memories over time, and the more they report their observations, the more convinced they are of the accuracy of their reports. "Once witnesses state facts in a particular way or identify a particular person as the perpetrator, they are unwilling or even unable—due to the reconstruction of their memory—to reconsider their initial understanding."[33] Similarly, witnesses can be cued to "remember" events that did not occur. In the 1970s, psychologist Elizabeth Loftus (who later came to develop the controversial "false memory syndrome") created a laboratory experiment to study eyewitness testimony of automobile accidents.[34] Participants viewed a film of a car accident and then were asked to fill out a form first describing the accident in their own words and then answering several specific questions. Half of the subjects filled out a form containing a question that described the accident with the word "smash," and the other half filled out a form different only in having the word "hit" rather than "smash."

Loftus and her colleague discovered that participants who answered the questionnaire with the word "smash" tended to give a higher estimate of the cars' speed than did those who answered the questionnaire with the word "hit." When, one week later, the participants were asked to recall features of the accident, those who had previously answered the questionnaire with the word "smash" were more likely to report seeing broken glass, when in fact there was no image or sound of broken glass in the film. What this means is that the word "smash" not only influenced the estimates of speed, but actually influenced people's memory of the original event. And this leads to the question of what memory is—is it like a film recording, or is it, like perception itself, a complex gestalt influenced by linguistic and cultural formations? What and where *is* memory, anyway? As it turns out, it lives much more in our bodies than we might imagine.

Embodied Listening

Unlike Evelyn Glennie or Daniel Kish, for mortals who employ sound as well as sight, the auditory process typically unfolds as a sequence that occurs so incredibly quickly it is experienced simultaneously. In a nanosecond, physical sensations are transformed into thoughts, memories, and feelings. When slowed to a standstill by explanation or illustration in a book, the process looks like a linear succession of events where one step follows another. But for listeners, the auditory experience is as a whole instantaneous. It begins when sound waves enter the outer ear and travel toward the tympanic membrane (or ear drum) and into the middle ear. The tympanic membrane, like the surface of one of Evelyn Glennie's kettledrums, pulses in response to the sound waves that hum through the air, then transfers these vibrations to a series of three small bones in the inner ear—first the malleus (mallet), which strikes the incus (anvil), which in turn moves the stapes (stirrup), which acts like a lever to bounce against a tiny "window" that separates the middle ear from the fluid-filled inner ear (or cochlea). Then comes the really crazy part.

The cochlea is filled with auditory neurons that connect to the brain. The hair cells in different regions of the cochlea are tuned to different frequencies, so when sound waves pass through the cochlea they trigger neurons that then travel up the auditory nerve toward the giant tree-like network of the brain. In fact, one of the theories about Evelyn Glennie's deafness is that the hair cells in her cochlea have been so damaged that they cannot pick up and transfer most sound energy to her brain. However, while her brain does not respond to any speech sound, it does respond somewhat to musical sound. That fact, in combination with her highly sensitive body and her ability to "hear" the music she reads from scores, has enabled her to perform as a featured soloist with major orchestras around the world, win two Grammy awards, and play everything from solo Bach fugues on the marimba to xylophone in a Balinese gamelan and even garbage-can lids with Oscar on the children's television show *Sesame Street*.

But if Dame Evelyn Glennie can "listen" without her ears, what does that say about listening? How do we even define it? As it turns out, in the English language we have two words for the auditory process: "hearing" and "listening." The verb "to hear" derives from the Middle English *heren* and is related to Old High German *hōren* and Latin *cavēre*. *Webster's* defines "to hear" as "1: to perceive or apprehend by the ear" and "2: to gain knowledge of by hearing." Similarly, the *Oxford English Dictionary* (OED) defines "to hear" as "To perceive, or have the sensation of, sound; to possess or exercise the faculty of audition, of which the specific organ is the ear." The verb "to listen," in contrast, is derived from the Middle English *listnen* and is defined by the idea of attention to sound. Harper traces the word "listen" to the Sanskrit *srosati* "hears, obeys," and derives the word "obey" from the Latin *obedire*, to "give ear, literally 'listen to,' from *ob* 'to' + *audire* 'listen, hear.'"[35] This etymology illustrates that "listen" and "hear" are not simply synonyms, but are inflected with different meanings that suggest different ways of being in the world. Etymologically, "listening" comes from a root that emphasizes attention and giving to others, while "hearing" comes from a root that emphasizes perception and receiving from others. Indeed, the ideas of "gaining" and "possessing" evoked by the word "hearing" tend to foreground the self's experience, while the ideas of attention and obedience resonating in the word "listening" tend to focus on the other.

For this book, we will examine listening as a holistic embodied process and expand our definition of listening to include nonauditory phenomena, and we will also do some damage to atomist separations between phenomena such as language and thought, speaking and listening, inner and outer, and past, present, and future time. In this way, the examples of extraordinary humans like Dame Glennie and Mr. Kish, who have taught themselves to perceive the world despite the loss of one or more senses, tell us something interesting about listening—they reveal how listening, for humans, is not solely an auditory process, but a multimodal process that involves (or can involve) all five of our senses, in a process I call *polymodality*, which will be discussed in more detail in chapter 6. For example, nonverbal communication scholars understand communication as an embodied process and study communication in multiple modes—auditory, visual, tactile, kinesthetic, and, sometimes, smell and taste. Thus, a polymodal study of humans communicating would include not only words but also embodied, physical features such as gesture, posture, facial expression, and eye gaze; sound features such as intonation, prosody, pitch, rhythm, and inflection; relational features such as proximity, touch, and eye contact; and discourse features such as interruptions, turn taking, and so on.

So listening is not only done with our ears, but also with other parts of our bodies such as nose, eyes, bones, and hands. But it all depends on what we pay attention to. Sherlock Holmes was not just a brilliant logician with a capacious memory, he was also an astute observer who used all of his senses to "listen." One day, after returning from a long separation, the fictional Holmes shocks his faithful friend Watson by applauding the good doctor for resuming his medical practice after a long absence. Watson is astonished and, after noting that Holmes "would certainly have been burned, had you lived a few centuries ago," asks how he knew. "It is simplicity itself," responded Holmes. "[I]f a gentleman walks into my rooms smelling of iodoform, with a black mark of nitrate of silver upon his right forefinger, and a bulge on the right side of his top-hat to show where he has secreted his stethoscope, I must be dull, indeed, if I do not pronounce him to be an active member of the medical profession."[36]

While few people can compete with Holmes's extraordinary abilities, most of us do have the capacity to listen with more of our senses than we typically do. Moreover, we can recognize the degree to which we (mostly unconsciously) elect to observe and/or ignore the innumerable sensations that surround us at each moment. As described above, most of our conscious and unconscious selections about what to notice and what to ignore come from culture. Etiquette, for example, contains a set of "rules" that govern what we notice or ignore. In some cultures, noticing the smell of someone's breath is standard greeting practice, whereas in other cultures it is considered rude. Of course in addition to culture, our choices may also be shaped by our gender, ethnicity, family, social standpoint, profession, and personality, to name but a few. The French sociologist Pierre Bourdieu developed the concept of "habitus" to describe the constellation of deeply embedded and experientially shaped patterns of thoughts, attitudes, practices, tastes, preferences, and so forth that each person acquires as a result of socialization. The resonance of "habitus" with the word "habit" echoes the largely unreflective and/or unconscious ways we take on and enact these patterns, whereas the word "habitat" echoes the way we actually live within these patterns (habits) that are shaped by our surroundings and their history (our habitats). In an innovative recent study of the relationship of musical "taste" to the social conditions of impoverished young men living in a housing project in Newcastle, England, the cultural studies scholar Mark Rimmer deploys the term "musical habitus" to examine music's role in creating and sustaining group membership as well as providing "strategies of negotiating some of the shared problems of poverty, boredom and stigma."[37] Just as many teens around the globe develop a musical habitus reflective of their social identities and locations, so do all of us.

But let's take this concept a step further and explore how beyond a musical or other symbolic habitus, we each develop ways of listening (or not) that are partly shaped by culture and our social location within it, and partly by our personalities and particular life experiences. This is what we might call our listening habitus, which is based on a combination of cultural, social, and personal experiences. Each of us habitually inhabits and perform ways of listening that are shaped by the social worlds we inhabit and that inhabit us. But whereas Rimmer's musical habitus tends to emphasize symbolic and social meanings, our conception of a listening habitus pertains not just to meaning, but also to perception itself, including how we listen, what we listen to, what we ignore, and so forth. When I am teaching, I ask students to reflect on how the identity or social position of a speaker affects their listening. At first, they usually argue that it makes little difference. But as the course progresses, students begin to notice how their listening, like their speaking, varies from situation to situation. They start to understand how, inadvertently, their listening habitus deafens them to others. One student described a story told by her grandmother that reflects an understanding of how social location relates to listening. According to the student, Arpitha Kodiveri, her grandmother encountered the real burden of embodying the group identity of both a Hindu and an Indian. She was living with her older sister in Belgaum and spent most of the day tending to household chores. There was one household chore that she was not made to do, which was of cleaning the latrine box. It was left to the local untouchable in the community to come and clean the filth. She never used to look him in the eye, but it so happened that one day she fainted having worked long hours in the hot sun, and no one came to her side but Malappa the community untouchable. In his attempt to wake her up he splashed water from above and on waking up my grandmother was shocked and in a fervent tone told him, "I would have ideally said that I have been polluted but I have now realized that it was I who was seeing you in the wrong light." She thanked him profusely for his efforts. Till today this has remained with her and the reason being that she was able to lay down the burden of her group identity.

There is thus a politics of listening, and it relates to who speaks and who doesn't, what is and is not said, how what is said is said, as well as, of course, to whom it is said and what is and is not heard, and *how* what is heard is heard. And of course there is also a politics, as well as a poetry, of silence, even in the most unsuspected domains of life. A politics of listening prevails, for example, in the world of Western music, where structures of sound, such as the diatonic scale, based on the octave and the fifth (called, ironically, the dominant), are both shaped by and shape cultural and political formations. For example, feminist musicologist Susan McClary traces the way Western classical music asserts a patriarchal ideology through harmonic patterns of dominance and even tonality itself.[38] Similarly, in his "Reflections of a Progressive Composer on a Damaged Society," the American composer John Cage describes the limitations of European music both in terms of the sounds it excludes as well as in the structures of organization, which impose ideas and order rather than inspiring and including them. "When I think of a good future it certainly has music in it, but it doesn't have one kind of music. It has all kinds. And it goes beyond anything that I can imagine or describe."[39] We will return to a discussion of the politics of listening when we take up questions of ethics in chapters 7 and 8.

Because we have all, over the course of our lifetimes, developed habitual perceptual routines that we barely notice, one way to bring awareness to our listening habitus is to exercise what sound designer and music educator Murray Schafer calls "ear cleaning," "a systematic program for training the ears to listen more discriminatingly to sounds, particularly those of the environment."[40] Schafer begins by teaching his students to "respect silence" by refraining from speaking for one day, an exercise that I have adopted in my classes. Students respond to this exercise with everything from delight to trepidation, and some even give up before long. Perhaps not surprisingly, the most challenging aspect of this exercise arises in student's interactions with other people. Many students report feeling socially isolated during this exercise, and some experience outright rejection by their peers. According to one student, "I felt rude and awkward the whole time I was silent. Since I couldn't speak I realized people didn't want to be around me." Students also report experiencing some alarm when their internal thoughts became more audible to them because of their silence. Another student described how "when I listened to myself it scared me because I felt I was listening to an individual who was hollow." We will return to an examination of the ethical dimensions of listening later, but for now it is worth noting how difficult it is to listen to people and things in themselves, instead of the myriad meanings, interpretations, and significance we associate with them.

Another exercise from Schafer that we employ in class is a listening walk, where together as a class we walk across campus in and out of different buildings, quadrangles, parks, and parking lots. Students are astonished to notice the sounds of wildlife (insects, birds, trees whispering) as well as the percussive sounds of our footsteps in the stairwells and across the floor. They are surprised at how loud a car sounds driving through an underground garage, and then they notice the Doppler effect, where the sound of a moving object (in this case a vehicle) lowers in pitch as it passes by. During this exercise, we try to experience what philosopher Don Ihde calls "listening phenomenologically": "more than an intense and concentrated attention to sound and listening, it is also to be aware in the process of the pervasiveness of certain 'beliefs' which intrude into my attempt to listen 'to the things themselves.' Thus, the first listenings inevitably are not yet fully existentialized but occur in the midst of preliminary approximations. Listening begins with the ordinary, by proximately working its way into what is as yet unheard."[41] In these exercises, we are attempting to listen beyond words and meanings to the sounds and sensations of the world around us. We try to observe which sounds we notice and which we ignore, and we strive to pay careful attention to the sounds we might otherwise avoid or disregard. In the early part of the semester, I will play different sounds from the BBC sound effects library in class and ask students to pay attention to how they physically, not mentally or emotionally, respond to these sounds. Students report clenching their teeth, tightening their stomachs, relaxing their shoulders, feeling a tingling in their hair, in response to sounds that range from the comforting lapping of waves on a beach to the agonizing wails of a child crying in full tantrum mode.

We also, following Ihde and Schafer's prompting, try to listen to sound as sound, rather than meaning. At first students try to describe sound by its shape, its feel, whether it has a foreground or background, whether it has color, or weight, density, and so on. We explore what might be the horizon of sound— where it begins and where it ends. We listen for the loudest, the shortest, the closest, the lowest sounds around us. Then we examine the shape of sound— does it have shape? Does it have extension, depth, or texture? How do sounds surrounding us fit together, do they clash, harmonize, pierce, or chafe? Here's how one student, Shashank Rai, described listening phenomenologically during a jog at a nearby university:

> The cold wind that blew across my face, rushing past the leaves of the trees, made me turn around more than a few times. It was my social conditioning that stopped me from going wild, but as I jogged the meaning of "losing yourself" became clear to me. I could hear the trees sing. . . . As I breathed heavier, my breath became part of the experience, part of the music. The wind was the flute, my feet were the drums, and my breath formed the guitar piece. Everything was beautiful. The kids on their bike and the sound of the pedals, the couples talking on their evening walks, the old man dragging his feet, the car speeding past me, the guard on his round shouting at someone, the motorcycle punk honking his horn, my shoe laces bouncing off my shoes . . . everything became part of the orchestra.

This musical dimension of sound and the world is well understood by art music composers Cage, Oliveros, and Pierre Schaeffer, who employ phenomenological listening for compositions that expand traditional Western musical vocabularies and break down the culturally constructed barriers between sound, noise, and music. They also work to expand the audience listening habitus by challenging listeners to notice their habitual and embodied responses to sound, and then, perhaps, open up to them. Pauline Oliveros describes this as a process she calls "deep listening," which involves "learning to expand the perception of sounds to include the whole space/time continuum of sound—encountering the vastness and complexities as much as possible."[42] Oliveros describes how when she goes on stage, her performances are based on moment-by-moment improvisation that does not follow preconceived ideas but instead responds to a listening that includes everything in the auditory environment. Similarly, French composer Pierre Schaeffer has crafted an elaborate inventory of sonic and musical "planes of reference" to theorize what he calls "concrete music," an assemblage of recorded sounds "from the ski tow to the noise piano" that are combined, repeated, and manipulated into musical compositions.[43] His intention in these compositions is to twist free of the constraints imposed by tonality as well as the "language of signs" and meanings inevitably sewn into sound. For example, while Schaeffer admires the attempts of twelve-tone serialist composers (also known as dodecaphonists) like Arnold Schoenberg to escape the constraints of tonality, he decries their use of the twelve-semitone division of the octave because it submits to the governing relationship between the tonic and the dominant fifth that rules Western music. According to Schaeffer, what underlies our appreciation of Western music is "not about pleasure, or beauty, or ugliness; rather, it is about a perfect conformity between man, who is sensitive to the dominant, and a music that exploits the phenomenon of the dominant."[44] Further, Schaeffer argues that listeners cannot escape the relationship of meaning and sound as conveyed by familiar musical instruments. "When Wagner uses the brass," says Schaeffer, he uses them "much more for the brass sound than for the melody he gives them."[45] Like Ihde's concept of phenomenological listening, Schaeffer's music endeavors to break free of the predictable sound-meaning relationships of Western music, which are organized around the dominant. To Schaeffer, because composers like Schoenberg remained within the parameters of tonic and dominant, they could not claim to be atonal, even though they employed a twelve- rather than an eight-tone division of the octave. "The only true atonality, ultimately, is in concrete music if the elements of a series do not trigger any ideas based on tonality."[46]

Thus, one of the greatest challenges to listening holistically is to interrupt the habitus, the habitual attributions of meaning that language and culture impose on our everyday experiences. To examine what this kind of listening "sounds like," another exercise we do in class is to listen to the Wallace Stevens poem "The Snow Man," which offers a beautiful example of embodied listening. Stevens's poem asks us "not to think / Of any misery in the sound of the wind, / In the sound of a few leaves"; that is, the poem asks us to listen behind the meanings we might attribute or the interpretations we might impose—to listen to the sounds themselves. Stevens's "mind of winter" is a mind at once attuned to and at one with the snowy world around it, and his listener is a hologram—a part of the whole containing the whole. Stevens closes the poem by reminding us not to forget the vast nothingness that is both within and outside us.[47]

When we inquire into the phenomenon of nothingness, we are led naturally to the question of silence. What is it? Does it exist? The *Oxford English Dictionary* defines silence as both the absence of speech and as the utter absence of all sound. Whereas Henry David Thoreau tends toward the first of these definitions with his famous "It takes a man to make a room silent,"[48] the composer John Cage asks us to inquire into the second when he asks, What happens when we listen to silence? What does silence sound like? In his famous composition *4'33"*, Cage invites the audience to listen carefully, daring us to describe the experience as an absence of sound. The title describes the music: the conductor raises her baton, the orchestra members sit at attention with their instruments at the ready, and for four and a half minutes the orchestra members remain in place without playing a single note. Sitting in the music hall, the audience becomes aware of the sounds all around them, of people breathing or rustling around, of the shuffle of feet or the echo of a lonely cough, of the whisper of fabric against fabric or the distant howling of a police siren. Cage's musical composition thus calls into question our easy distinctions between sound and music and noise, and suggests that music is all around us all the time.

As with all our perceptions, our listening habitus is shaped by our social conditioning and our places and relations in the social world. Whether we ignore or notice a sound, whether we find it pleasing or jarring, or whether we welcome silence or find it uncomfortable is not an inevitable response, but depends on a whole interrelated set of social and cultural phenomena that we will explore in the following chapters. We will further expand our understanding of embodied listening in chapter 6 when we take up the multimodal dimensions of interlistening, and in chapter 8 when we return to the relationship between vibration, harmonics, and listening in order to develop our thinking about the ethics of attunement. But in the meantime, it is time to turn to the listening word, or what Nancy calls "hearing say," rather than "hearing sound."[49] In the next chapter we will journey on a historical world survey of the differences between holist and atomist perspectives on language, thought, and listening.

3

PREMODERN PERSPECTIVES ON
LANGUAGE AND THOUGHT

> Not only the entire capacity to think rests on lan-
> guage . . . but language is also the center of the
> misunderstanding of reason with itself.
> —HAMANN, *quoted in O'Flaherty, Unity and Language*

I'm driving to work, down a long highway that curves between pastures, meadows, and hillocks of corn and soy. Cows to the left of me, orchards to the right. Here I am. It's early morning and I'm steering two thousand pounds of steel while thinking about thinking. Specifically, I'm pondering the relationship between language and thought. Is thinking the same as speaking? Or is it more like listening? Come to think of it, are thoughts even language? And what is language anyway? Is it a divine spirit that possesses the power to create and destroy? Or just a useful tool for conveying thoughts and exchanging information? Or, perhaps, in the gloomy outlook of a Flaubert character, "human speech is like a cracked cauldron on which we knock out tunes for dancing-bears, when we wish to conjure pity from the stars."[1] Miles go by before I realize that I'm in the car, on the exit ramp, and heading into town. I don't remember the ten miles between the orchard and the exit, but I was driving, right? How did I get here? And who was driving while I was so busy thinking/speaking/listening?

As is most often the case, the answer to these questions depends on who and how you ask. After all, scholars have been arguing about them for over three millennia. In terms of written history, we know that the relationship between language and thought has a long and storied past that dates back at least to Indian, Chinese, and Greek philosophies in the fifth century B.C.E. But even after some twenty-six hundred years of research that prods and probes the human mind and the mysteries of language, today's linguists, psychologists, and philosophers *still* argue about language and thought. In this chapter we will explore a bit about the history of these arguments with an ear out for the role that listening has—and has not—played for lo, these three millennia. We begin with the grammarians of ancient India.

Ancient Perspectives East and West

Who causes my tongue to speak?
—*Kena Upanishad*

The earliest-known studies of the relationship between language and thought date back at least to fifth- or sixth-century B.C.E. India, where the Sanskrit grammarians, Pāṇini, Yaska, and later Patañjali, created an extensive and systematic analysis of the categories and rules of language and meaning.[2] The impetus for these scholars was the study of the Vedas, the epic Hindu scriptures, which are thought to date back to at least 1500 B.C.E. and are said to "bring to us an idea or a glimpse of what we may call the mind beyond mind or the mind of our mind."[3] Two elements of the Vedas make them an especially important place for us to begin our discussion of language and thought. First, Hinduism is, as Guy Beck notes, at heart a "sonic theology" wherein sound and word are joined in an interdependent sacred relation.[4] One reads in the Vedas a reverence for speech and sound as gifts from the divine if not divinity itself. Each of the four Vedas is a compilation of ancient hymns and commentaries, and the *Rig Veda* (thought to be the oldest of the Vedas) contains several hymns in praise of speech, which is depicted as the divine origin of the cosmos itself. In one hymn, for example, the goddess of speech praises speech as the source of all: "I am the one who blows like the wind, embracing all creatures. Beyond the sky, beyond this earth, so much have I become in my greatness."[5] In another hymn, speech is praised as "the final abode where all the gods have taken their seat. . . . The whole universe exists through the undying syllable."[6] In yet another hymn, the mysteries of speech are said to elude many: "There are those who though perceiving cannot see speech; others again though listening cannot hear it. There are again others to whom she reveals herself as a well-dressed wife desiring her husband would."[7]

The second reason for us to begin with the Vedas pertains to ideas presented in the Upanishads, which are thought to have been composed around

600 B.C.E. and are called Vedanta, the last of the Vedas. Said by some scholars to be "the foundations upon which the later philosophies and religions of India rest,"[8] the Upanishads are more like a genre of texts than a homogenous text. Although they are often studied as a group, some scholars argue that they derive from different schools of thought in different periods of time. Further, because the texts are thought to have been transmitted orally for centuries before being written down, dating them is quite difficult and scholars disagree about definitive origin.[9] Among other things, the Upanishads emphasize the paradoxical nature of thought and mind and present a nondualist perspective on consciousness. "Who makes my mind think?" asks the student of the *Kena Upanishad.* "Who causes my tongue to speak?" The answer given by the student's teacher is the deathless Self, "the ear of the ear, the eye of the eye, the mind of the mind, the word of the words, the life of the life," which exists "beyond the duality of the knower and the known."[10] The Upanishads, which some scholars claim are a response to the growing dominance of caste hierarchy among the Brahmin priests,[11] seem to be an invitation to spiritual insight that can "enable [one] to hear the unheard, think the unthought, and know the unknown."[12] This undifferentiated oneness of all things known and unknown is beautifully captured in the preface to the *Isha Upanishad:*

> All this is full. All that is full.
> From fullness, fullness comes.
> When fullness is taken from fullness,
> Fullness still remains.[13]

To the singers of the Vedic hymns, because "word, speech, hearing, knowledge, and creation" are an interrelated whole, correct pronunciation, grammar, and rhythm were essential skills for preserving their sacred integrity.[14] But it was the study of grammar that "was regarded as the gateway to other disciplines" of Veda study, which also included disciplines such as phonetics, etymology, metrics, and ritual.[15] For over a thousand years the Vedas were transmitted orally from generation to generation. And because of the importance placed on divine speech, the ancient priests greatly emphasized correct speech, from matters of pronunciation to the proper use of grammar. Accordingly, the early Vedic philosophers and priests studied the language of the Vedas in order to develop means of teaching students correct speech. The great Sanskrit philosopher of language Pāṇini created the world's first systematic analysis of the categories and rules of language and meaning. At approximately four thousand rules, Pāṇini's grammar includes both phonetic and syntactic rules with a level of detail and theoretical complexity that led the American linguist Leonard Bloomfield to declare in the 1930s that it was "one of the greatest monuments of human intelligence. It describes, with the minutest detail, every inflection, derivation, and composition, and every syntactic usage of its author's speech. No other language, to this day, has been so perfectly described."[16] Similarly, the Finnish linguist Itkonen writes that "[t]o me it is beyond question that at least until the year 1970 a comparable grammar was produced nowhere in the world, that is, a grammar that would have to the same extent combined extensive coverage of data with theoretical sophistication."[17]

For at least several centuries, Pāṇini's grammar was transmitted orally—as the Vedas themselves had been for perhaps a millennium—and thus required exacting and extensive memorization by priests, scholars, and students. Itkonen quotes a Chinese Buddhist traveler to India in the sixth century c.e. who gives a description of what the learning of grammatical science involved:

> The teaching begins when the pupils are six year[s] old. At the age of eight they memorize Pāṇini's grammar, which takes about eight months. Then during several years they are taught to understand [it] at an elementary level. At the age of fifteen they start to learn a more advanced commentary on Pāṇini, [which] takes about five years. After learning additionally logic and metaphysics, they spend a couple of years in places that we might call universities. . . . [T]he true scholars continue with the study of grammar. . . . [T]his takes some additional five years. It is only now that they may call themselves "well-informed."[18]

In other words, the rigorous study of speech in ancient India seems to have rivaled that of advanced postgraduate study today, with the addition, of course, of copious amounts of memorization. The work of two other Indian grammarians made a long-lived impact on the study of grammar and the philosophy of language prior to the common era: Yaska (fifth century b.c.e.), who developed word classifications and etymology, and later Patañjali (second century b.c.e.), who published extensive commentaries on Pāṇini's grammar and focused centrally on semantics (the relationship between word and meaning).[19] According to the contemporary Indian philosopher Bimal

Krishna Matilal, Patañjali's central question is "What is a word?" Patañjali's answer begins with an understanding of the relationship between words and their meanings as fixed and unchanging, due to their divine origin.

Through centuries of studies of the Vedas, Indian scholars developed multiple and competing perspectives on thought and perception. The grammarians who studied the Vedas rapidly began to develop their own philosophies of language and meaning, which eventually developed into different schools of thought—some radically and some subtly different from one another. One driving question debated by the different schools concerned the question of truth, which was important because the Vedas, considered the absolute truth, could not contain any errors or contradictions. Therefore, anything that appeared wrong or contradictory had to be explained, which gave rise to debate. For the most part, these arguments can be characterized as coming from two perspectives—idealist and realist. For the idealists, "[t]he so-called external world is only a creation of the mind; the 'stuff' of the world is made of consciousness only."[20] The realist wing, in contrast, held that the external world existed outside the mind and that perceptions were accurate representations of phenomena. According to Matilal, the realists "wanted to combat skepticism, idealism, and solipsism—all in one blow—by denying completely the possibility of error of illusion or even hallucination."[21]

Aside from the grammarians, other ancient Indian schools of thought involving the philosophy of language included the Jain, Buddhist, Nyāya-Vaiśeṣika, and Mīmāsā schools. Without getting into all of the many complexities and nuances differentiating these schools, a few points are worth noting. Some of the realist schools, such as the Nyāya, developed full-blown systems of logic, argumentation, and debate. The Nyāya school, which arose around 200 B.C.E., held to a theory of logical realism that involved a five-step syllogism[22] (in contrast to the Aristotelian three-step syllogism), which placed a premium value on inference as "the sole reliable means to philosophical knowledge."[23] To the Nyāya, everything, including knowledge, self, and world, is a distinct, independent object that can be known by the mind. "For as mind is an object, any other object . . . is what it is in relation to this object—the mind. The independence of the object of all subjective influence logically implies the individuality and distinctness of each object. Realism in fact invests every object with a self-hood; each object is significant by itself."[24]

In contrast to the grammarians, who held that word meanings were related to cognition rather than external objects in the world, the Nyāya held to a representational view of language wherein words referred to things. The Nyāya considered external objects as the source of meaning and speech as an instrumental way of knowing, comparable to (yet distinct from) "a perceptual episode or an episode of knowledge through inference based on evidence."[25] Thus, causality was not just the principal means by which objects related to one another, but "a form of our thought, a mode of intellect, a tie to bind all experiences."[26] The Nyāya logicians created a logical formula for language governed by a form of predicate calculus. Their linguistic calculation combined the active causal agents of a sentence (which they called *instruments* and we might call a *grammatical subject*), with actions performed by those agents (which they called *operations* and we might call *verbs*). The combination of instruments (I) plus operations (V) resulted in meaning (R). This was written as I + V > R. Matilal uses the example of writing with a pen as an illustration of the causal model. "The pen is an 'instrument' (the most efficient causal factor) for the end-product, writing on the paper. But besides the agent (the writer, who is not considered in this skeletal account), the pen needs to be in physical contact with the paper to produce writing. . . . (I + V) > R where 'I' stands for the 'instrumental cause', 'V' for the intermediate vyāpāra, and 'R' for the end-product."[27]

For the grammarians, in contrast to the Nyāya, meaning was located inside, not outside, the mind. We will return to a detailed discussion of the grammarians' more idealist perspective on language later in the chapter when we examine the relevance of their perspective to a holist theory of listening. For now, however, it suffices to say that the relationship between thought and language, rather than between reality and representation, was at the center of grammarian inquiry. As Deshpande describes it, "Whether or not things are real, we do have concepts. These concepts form the content of a person's cognitions derived from language. Without necessarily denying or affirming the external reality of objects in the world, grammarians claimed that the meaning of a word is only a projection of intellect."[28]

In addition to the debates between and among the grammarian, Nyāya-Vaiśesika, and Mīmāmsā schools, there were at the same time also debates between the Hindu and Buddhist approaches to the relationship between language and thought. In partial response to the elitism of the Hindu Brahmin priests and the caste system generally, two new religious schools of thought arose around 500 B.C.E.—the Jain and the Buddhist. Both schools were nonviolent and rejected the bloody sacrificial rituals of the Vedas. They were also egalitarian for men, and eventually in Buddhism for women as well.

The Buddha was a former prince who renounced his wealth in order to search for enlightenment, and sought to find the cause and end of suffering. After attaining enlightenment, he spent the remaining forty years of his life teaching a "middle path" between ascetic renunciation and hedonistic indulgence. He taught morality, nonviolence, and a form of mindfulness that rejected rational thinking as a means to enlightenment.

To the Buddha, the debates between realists and idealists and the employment of logical argumentation and dialectic were useless forms of speculative hair splitting that led neither to enlightenment nor to the cessation of suffering. The Buddha regarded all questions about whether the world and everything in it is real or unreal, eternal or not eternal, or finite or infinite as "a thicket of views, a wilderness of views, a contortion of views, a vacillation of views, a fetter of views. It is beset by suffering, by vexation, by despair, and by fever."[29] One of the most famed teachings about thought attributed to the Buddha is found in an early (300 B.C.E.) collection of verses called the *Dhammapada*. The verse relates to the power of thought to shape experience, for good or ill, and begins, "All that we are is the result of our thoughts; it is founded on our thoughts and made up of our thoughts. With our thoughts we make the world. If a man speaks or acts with a harmful thought, trouble follows him, as the wheel follows the ox that draws the cart."[30]

The Buddhist perspective on thought thus reaches between and beyond realist/idealist dualism. In Buddhism, thought is a paradox in that it both *is* and *is not;* it grants that while thoughts have enormous power to create, shape, and influence our actions and experience, it also considers that thoughts are, in and of themselves, nothing. The practices of meditation taught by the Buddha instructed monks to pay attention to thoughts without getting lost in following them and to keep one's attention focused on either the body, the feelings, the mind, or mind-objects. According to the *Mahasatipatthana Sutta,* a central sutta from the Pali canon regarding the four foundations of mindfulness, the Buddha taught that awareness and contemplation of mind—whether it be deluded or open, distracted or focused—is foundational to liberation.[31] According to the sutta, "here a monk abides contemplating body as body, . . . feelings as feelings, . . . mind as mind . . . mind-objects as mind-objects, ardent, clearly aware and mindful, having put aside hankering and fretting for the world."[32] In another sutta on consciousness, the Buddha explains that perception precedes knowledge, but that the causes and conditions of perception (whether pleasure or pain) can arise and pass away through mindfulness training. Through consistent practice, a monk gradually proceeds stage by stage to eventually pass beyond bodily sensations and reach the "Spheres of Infinite Space, Infinite Consciousness, No-Thingness." As described in a different sutta, "[W]hen a monk has gained this controlled perception, he proceeds from state to stage till he reaches the limit of perception. When he has reached the limit of perception it occurs to him: 'Mental activity is worse for me, lack of mental activity is better. . . .' And then, in him, . . . other, coarser perceptions do not arise. He attains cessation.'"[33]

During this same period, in fifth-century B.C.E. China, the Taoist sages Lao Tzu and Zhuangzi (sometimes spelled Chuang Tzu) offered similar perspectives on the paradoxical nature of consciousness and thought, albeit in a more whimsical spirit. In response to other dominant philosophies in China at the time, such as the moral absolutism of Confucian hierarchy and the mechanical formulations of the Mohist logicians—the Taoists held that enlightened thought should follow a path beyond the constraints of logic and the rule of noncontradiction.[34] In one of the Inner Chapters, attributed to Chuang Tzu, the sage writes, "What is this is also that, and what is that is also this. That is both right and wrong. This is also right and wrong. So is there really a this and a that? . . . Making a point to show that a point is not a point is not as good as making a nonpoint to show that a point is not a point."[35] Chuang Tzu's parables are characterized by a penchant to "put dents in, if not annihilate altogether, human thought processes. . . . While he is dubious about the efficacy of reason to solve all human problems, he does not assert its utter futility."[36] In one famous parable, Chuang Tzu dreams he is a butterfly flitting happily about. When he wakes up, he doesn't know if he, Chuang Tzu, had dreamed of a butterfly, or if the butterfly was dreaming that he was Chuang Tzu. Later, the ability to question reality and put what appears to be self-evident truth into doubt, became a central feature of the newly emergent school of thought known as Chan, which, influenced by traveling Buddhists from India, combined elements of Buddhism and Taoism and subsequently became known in Japan as Zen.

At the same time that Taoist and Buddhist philosophers were expressing doubts about the ability of logic and pure rationalism to explain consciousness and thought, the sixth- and fifth-century B.C.E. Greek philosophers were coming to systematize logic and put a great deal of emphasis on the mind and thought. Known retrospectively as the pre-Socratics (because they preceded Socrates), early Greek philosophers such as Pythagoras, Heraclitus, and Parmenides were principally interested in the study of nature and the cosmos rather than thought and consciousness, and they placed considerable emphasis on the use of reason and logical inference. According to Waterfield, the thinking of the pre-Socratics was a revolutionary "shift from mythos to logos."[37] That is to say, the pre-Socratics began to move Greek thinking away from myths and legends and toward empirical reasoning as the source for explanations about the ways and means of the world.

Much of what is known of the pre-Socratics comes from a combination of text fragments and discussions of them by later scholars who were influenced by Socrates and Plato and did not always take the thought of the pre-Socratics seriously. Similarly, Mahāyāna Buddhist scholars of the Common Era at times unfairly characterized the thought of their "elders," the Theravādans. As a result, depending on the number and source of the fragments, some depictions of the pre-Socratics are more questionable than others. One of the largest text fragments is a proem by Parmenides, who figures large in Plato's dialogues and is frequently referenced by numerous other philosophers. Although his text is notoriously cryptic, it has provoked and inspired the thinking of generations of philosophers.

What makes the ideas of Parmenides special for our purposes is not just what he said, but how he said it—by using logical deduction. For example, while one of his most famous arguments states that everything is one unified and unmoving whole, it is expressed almost as a syllogism. In a meditation on the question of existence, or *being,* Parmenides argues that the idea that being "came from what is not I shall not allow / you to say or think—for it is not sayable or thinkable / that it is not. And what need would have impelled it, later or earlier, to spring up—if it began from nothing? Thus it must either altogether be or not be."[38] To Parmenides, thought was being, and his idea of "infallible reason" meant that opposites, or contradictions, could not at the same time be true. According to Sextus Empiricus, a second-century C.E. scholar, Parmenides "condemned the sort of reason associated with belief . . . but supposed that the sort of reason associated with knowledge, or infallible reason, was a criterion of truth."[39]

As in India, there were many competing schools of thought in ancient Greece about mind and reasoning, including the Eleatic school, exemplified by Parmenides, and the Pythagorean school, named after Pythagoras, who, as described in chapters 1 and 2, theorized the relationship between sound and the cosmic world as "music of the spheres." There is considerable evidence that in spite of some significant differences, Plato was highly influenced by the Pythagorean school; we will have more to say about their ideas in chapter 8.[40]

The form of reasoning employed by the pre-Socratics, and Parmenides in particular, was immortalized in the dialogues of Plato. In Plato's *Republic,* his epic dialogue on questions of justice and politics, he formulates Parmenides' reasoning as the principle of noncontradiction: "It is obvious that the same thing will never do or suffer opposites in the same respect in relation to the same thing and at the same time."[41] These ideas would be immortalized in Aristotle's syllogism, a discourse "in which, certain things being stated, something other than what is stated follows of necessity from their being so."[42] Aristotle considered it without question that "the most indisputable of all beliefs is that the contradictory statements are not at the same time true."[43]

While the so-called classical Greek schools of Socrates, Plato, and Aristotle came to dominate Western philosophy, later schools also evolved. Epictetus, a Stoic philosopher, claimed that "man is disturbed not by things, but by the views he takes of them"; the Cynics, such as Diogenes, lived, like dogs, in accordance with nature, not society; and the Skeptics, such as Pyrrho, suspended judgment and claimed "nothing is either fine or ignoble or just or unjust." Some of these schools developed after the Alexandrian invasion of India in 326 B.C.E., and there is some evidence of mutual influence between Indian and Greek philosophies.[44] But the atomist forms of logical inference, whether invented or described by Aristotle, eventually came to exemplify what future Western scholars would consider reason itself.

At roughly the same time that the grammarians, Buddhists, and Jains were developing their theories of language, ancient Greek thinking was organizing around the concept of *logos,* which since antiquity "has been interpreted in various ways: as *ratio,* as *verbum,* as cosmic law, as the logical, as necessity in thought, as meaning and as reason."[45] One of the earliest written uses of the word *logos* has been found in the work of the pre-Socratic Heraclitus, whose work, like that of Parmenides, is preserved only in text fragments and quotations by later Greek scholars. One fragment known as B 50, is typically translated along the lines of "Listening not to me but to the *logos,* it is wise to agree that all things are one."[46] Here *logos* seems to mean words or meanings, with the idea that listeners should pay attention not to the speaker, but to the speech of wisdom itself. Another gloss on *logos* is found in the work of Epicharmus, a close contemporary of Heraclitus, who writes that "the *logos* guides men and keeps them always on the straight and narrow. A man has reasoning, but there is also divine *logos.* Human reasoning is born from the divine *logos.*"[47]

Subsequent scholars have used *logos* in a great diversity of ways. Corradi Fiumara, for example, groups the meanings of *logos* into ten different categories, such as computation, relation, law, narrative, word, common talk, divine utterance, assertion, command, and truth.[48] Nevertheless, the legacy left by Plato seems to posit *logos* as logical reasoning and thus the epitome and exemplar of thought. Although some Western scholars have challenged the doctrine of logic and the dualistic principle of noncontradiction, these nevertheless became largely undisputed in Western philosophy and science.[49] Later in the chapter we will return to a discussion of the centrality of *logos* in communication scholarship and its implications for a holistic philosophy of listening.

Although many competing views of language were held by the Greek thinkers of fifth century B.C.E., it was the atomist views of Plato and Aristotle that ultimately prevailed in the West. Plato separated language and thought and claimed that words merely represented thoughts "by means of vocal sound with names and verbs."[50] Plato also distrusted language because, he claimed, it made deception so very easy and because, even at best, language could only offer a secondhand image of truth. The worst abusers of language, according to Plato, were the Sophists, who were itinerant teachers of rhetoric and philosophy and who, unlike Socrates, charged a fee for their teachings. Plato ridiculed the Sophists in many of the Socratic dialogues, and described their teachings as "the art of contradiction-making, descended from an insincere kind of conceited mimicry, of the semblance-making breed, derived from image-making, distinguished as a portion, not divine but human, of production, that presents a shadow-play of words—such are the blood and lineage which can, with perfect truth, be assigned to the authentic Sophist."[51] Plato banished poets from his *Republic* because, he said, they traded in illusions and falsehoods. He argued that like the Sophists, poets were betrayers of the truth, who "impose by means of words that cheat the ear, exhibiting images of all things in a shadow play of discourse, so as to make them believe that they are hearing the truth."[52]

Despite the eventual dominance of Platonic and Aristotelian perspectives on language, some pre-Socratics, like the Indian grammarians, debated the relation of sound and meaning in language. Johnstone, for example, cites a number of contemporary scholars who read in the Sophists a more productive and less referential view of language. For example, according to the Sophist Gorgias (who is much derided by Plato), speech does not convey content or re-present "reality." "Rather, our experienced 'reality' is brought into being through speech."[53] Similarly, Heidegger found in Heraclitus a kind of speaking and listening that differs considerably from the Platonic view of language.

Nevertheless, by Plato's time, such debates were settled by a highly instrumental and representational conception of language. In Plato's dialogue *Cratylus,* for example, Socrates and his student friend discuss whether sound is intrinsically tied to meaning (*physis*) or whether it is merely an arbitrary convention (*nomos*). When Cratylus, another Sophist, argues that sounds have a natural relationship to meaning, Socrates goes to work investigating the question of where names come from. At first, Socrates pokes a bit of fun at a Sophist named Prodicus. "If I had not been poor, I might have heard the fifty-drachma course of the great Prodicus, which is a complete education in grammar and language—these are his own words. . . . But, indeed, I have only heard the single-drachma course, and therefore, I do not know the truth about such matters."[54] After next dispensing with the relativism found in the famous claim of the Sophist Protagoras, that "man is the measure of all things" (and therefore that names are not merely conventional but also purely subjective and individual), Socrates begins to investigate the nature of sounds and how they may or may not be related to meaning.

Here we see the atomistic work of logical reasoning at its finest. Statements are forwarded, corrected, enhanced, and then conclusions are derived from them. The first claim to be tested is the idea that language is a tool wielded by craftsmen, both skilled and unskilled, and that therefore words are "names" that serve as "an instrument of teaching and of distinguishing natures, as the shuttle is of distinguishing the threads of the web."[55] The second claim to be tested by Socrates is the idea that language represents things in the world—that it is an instrument of labeling "real" objects. "You are aware that speech signifies all things, and is always turning them round and round, and has two forms, true and false?"[56] Notice here the implication that language is unreal and that only things in the world are real. Language is thus thought of as a tool that we use to stand for and represent the things of the universe that language names: "the knowledge of things is not to be derived from names. No; they must be studied and investigated in themselves."[57]

With this dialogue, Socrates lays the foundation for what would become the background understanding of language that would dominate Western philosophy: language is by and large separate from and secondary to rational thought, and words are tools that we use to represent "real" things in the world. "[N]either will he so far trust names or the givers of names as to be confident in any knowledge which condemns himself and other existences to an unhealthy state of unreality; he will not believe that all things leak like a pot, or imagine that the world is a man who has a running at the nose. This may be true, Cratylus, but it is also very likely to be untrue."[58] Thus, besides cleaving language and thought, Plato constructed a clear hierarchy between them—thought or "philosophy" was crowned queen and language or "rhetoric" depicted as a lowly court jester. It should go without saying here that of course rhetoricians, scholars of communication, and even some philosophers dispute (and adeptly refute) the Platonist view of language. But as we will continue to explore in the coming chapters, in some fields, such as philosophy and cognitive science, the atomistic view of language and communication tends to overshadow the holist, for Plato's depiction carries no inconsiderable weight. As one notable early twentieth-century philosopher wrote, "The safest general characterization of the European philosophical tradition is that it consists of a series of footnotes to Plato."[59]

Nearly a thousand years later, long after Pāṇini, Heraclitus, and Plato, another great grammarian emerged in India to challenge the atomistic representationalist view of language with a holistic view that theorized an interconnection between sound and word, as well as between speaking and listening. The third great Indian philosopher of language, Bhartṛhari, challenged the dominance of formal representational view of language and meaning found in the Nyāya school. Although "all [philosophers of classical India] believed in the close correspondence between language and reality,"[60] Bhartṛhari's thinking is distinctly holistic, emphasizing the underlying interconnection and indivisibility of language and thought. Bhartṛhari's central text, *The Vākyapadīya* (On words and sentences), begins with an incantation in praise of the word, much like the hymns to Om and speech in the Vedas and Vedanta (as well as the holy letters of the Hebrew alphabet, the originary biblical word of John, or the divine utterances of the Koran): "That beginningless and endless One, the imperishable Brahman of which the essential nature is the Word, which manifests itself into objects and from which is the creation of the Universe."[61] To Bhartṛhari, language does not reflect objects in the world but makes them manifest. With this, Bhartṛhari offers a productive rather than a representative view, wherein language is a means for bringing the world forth. Unlike the Nyāyas, who differentiated perception and speech, Bhartṛhari considered that "each awareness, including sensory perceptual awareness, must be, in order to be of any use to us, also linguistic, i.e., penetrated with words."[62] To Bhartṛhari, thought and language are one and the same thing; "there is no cognition without the operation of the word; shot through and through is cognition by the word."[63] What made this possible was Bhartṛhari s development of Patañjali's earlier concept of *sphoṭa*, or "true" sounds, which are to be distinguished from "uttered" sounds. *Sphoṭa* is "true" because it refers to the initial yet silent awareness of sound, and is thus considered "the real vehicle of meaning . . . a word or a sentence is not just a concatenation made up of different sound units arranged in a particular order, but a single whole."[64]

Building on and expanding Patañjali's theory of *sphoṭa,* Bhartṛhari theorized that the word in the mind causes speech sounds in a way similar to how "the fire stick acts as the cause for further lights."[65] Unlike the Mīmāṃsā and Nyāya schools, which held that phonemes were the fundamental elements of language because speech sounds could be subdivided no further, Bhartṛhari held that "the whole is greater than the sum of its parts."[66] Thus, in contrast to the Nyāya, Bhartṛhari held that the apparently atomistic structures of language—such as the temporal sequentiality of speech or the grammatical units of words, stems, and roots—do not exist in the word in the mind. "For . . . Bhartṛhari, there are no divisions in speech acts and in communicated meanings. . . . Such divisions are useful fictions and have an explanatory value in grammatical theory, but have no reality in communication. . . . The sentence-meaning becomes an object or content of a single instance of a flash of cognition (*pratibhā*)."[67] That is to say, *sphoṭa* illuminates everything all at once, not atomistically as sequential separately ordered parts, but holistically as an undifferentiated, simultaneous whole.

We will return to an investigation of *sphoṭa* and Bhartṛhari's theory of language in the next chapter when we investigate the phenomenon of "inner speech," but for the present it is worth noting the ways in which atomistic conceptions of language have influenced contemporary interpretations of Bhartṛhari and *sphoṭa*. For example, some scholars depict the debates between Bhartṛhari and the Mīmāṃsā and Nyāya schools as a debate about the priority of sentences versus words—the very idea of which implies the very atomism that Bhartṛhari's theory refutes. But when examined in terms of the debates between language and thought, the conflicting perspectives of these ancient schools derive not from category disputes, but from an underlying conflict between the synthetic holism of Bhartṛhari's gestalt understanding of *sphoṭa* and the analytic atomism found in the representational view of language. The unacknowledged and largely unchallenged dominance of the atomistic view of language has obscured how fundamentally Bhartṛhari's holistic gestalt process differs from the atomistic representative process.[68] The invisibility of this difference has even led to a tendency among some scholars to connect Bhartṛhari with Saussure and Plato. In short, there is, as attested by the subsequent renunciation of Bhartṛhari's theory of *sphoṭa* by some Indian philosophers of language, a historical obscuration that bears correction. We will see below how the separation of language and thought (or rhetoric and philosophy) in ancient Greece led Western philosophy of language to develop in a direction closer to the Nyāya logicians than to the grammarians. And after Plato, language was not merely split from thought, but relegated to second-class status, where, in Samuel Johnson's words, "Language is the dress of thought," "and words are but the signs of ideas."[69]

European Enlightenment Perspectives

Cogito ergo sum.

—DESCARTES, *Discourse on Method*

Although many of the ancient insights about mind and reason were lost to the West in the dark ages that followed the collapse of the Roman Empire, they were preserved in the medieval Middle East. Thanks to the roughly four-hundred-year (711–1085) Muslim rule in Spain that introduced Greek rationalism and Indian mathematics into European thought through the remarkably cosmopolitan cities of Islamic Spain, where Christian, Muslim, and Jewish thought were combined with Arabic and Greek mathematics, science, and philosophy.[70] But when the Christian Europeans conquered Spain in the early Middle Ages, the rising Christian monarchies were far less tolerant of religious difference and intellectual innovation, and remained so for several hundred years. For example, when Galileo discovered astronomical evidence in support of Nicolaus Copernicus's then far-fetched claim that the earth revolved around the sun, the Catholic Church was outraged because Galileo's finding challenged the authority of the Holy Bible, which held that the world cannot be moved. Even in the face of mathematical proofs and astronomical evidence that supported the arguments for heliocentrism, the church upheld the Christian Bible as the sole authority on knowledge and reason. As a result, in 1616 the Catholic Inquisition tried Galileo for heresy and forced him to abstain from teaching his theories. It took over fifty years for Isaac Newton's mathematical calculations to bring the debates about the "Copernican revolution" to at least a pause, if not a final denouement, in 1687.

Eventually more European philosophers began to argue for the priority of reason and thought over religious authority, not only in the natural world, but in the theaters of human life involving morality, government, and law. The stage for making mind and reason the star of the whole show was set by the seventeenth-century French rationalist philosopher René Descartes, who, after doubting the existence of everything in the world, determined that the only thing that he could really be sure of was the fact that he was thinking. He came to this conclusion by reasoning that even if everything he perceived was an illusion or hoax perpetrated by some mad evil genius, he could still count on the fact that *he was thinking,* and, therefore that he *was,* that he existed. Descartes's Latin expression for this insight was "Cogito ergo sum" (I think, therefore I am). He wrote, "I could pretend that I had no body and that there was no world or place that I was in, but . . . I could not . . . pretend that I did not exist . . . from the very fact that I thought of doubting the truth of other things, it followed very evidently and very certainly that I existed."[71] In this way, Descartes's atomism separated the mind (or the subject) from the world of "brute facts" (or objects) and claimed that mind was the only thing that could reliably be held to exist. This manner of thought became known as rationalism and was taken to an extreme by the British philosopher Berkeley, whose school of thought came to be called "dogmatic" idealism.

Of course, not all European Enlightenment thinkers were pure idealists, and another rationalist school of thought contested the idea that only the mind exists and everything else is an illusion. As with the debates between the grammarians and the Nyāya of ancient India, so the European school of idealism came to be countered in the seventeenth and eighteenth centuries by the British empiricist philosophers John Locke and David Hume—the latter of whom doubted that we could know anything except what we experience. How do we know the billiard ball will sink into the pocket? asks Hume. Because we have seen it happen dozens of times before. We don't know about the principle of causality until we experience it firsthand—until we have placed our palms on the burner, for example and experienced the causal relationship between fire and pain. Just as the ancient Indians debated realism versus idealism and the ancient Greeks wrestled with the tensions between myth and logic, so European Enlightenment thinkers navigated between idealist and empiricist paradigms of knowledge and thought.

It was in a remote European outpost far to the east that a middle ground between the extremes of idealism and empiricism was found at the end of the eighteenth century. Trained and influenced by the German rationalists and idealists of the early Enlightenment, Immanuel Kant had an intellectual breakthrough after reading Hume. Coming to what he called his own "Copernican revolution," Kant reformulated the idealist/empiricist debate by creating his own system, in which human understanding arose from a synthesis of the sensations we experience in the world—empirical knowledge—and mental categories of understanding that pre-exist experience, which he called a priori knowledge. As we touched upon in the previous chapter, rather than assuming that our minds either reflect (empiricism) or create (idealism) objects in the world, Kant argued that our experiences in the world are conditioned by a set of pre-existing "pure" concepts such as quantity and quality, without which we cannot think or perceive phenomena in the world. Drawing on four of Aristotle's categories of understanding, Kant refashioned them as "pure" concepts that were each subdivided into two opposite terms (antinomies) and a third term that synthesized the two.

For example, Kant subdivided the category of quantity into two opposites, unity and plurality, which were synthesized by a third, totality. Thus, Aristotle's quality was subdivided by Kant into reality, negation, and limitation; relation was subdivided into substance, causality, and community; and modality was subdivided into possibility, existence, and necessity. Kant argued that because none of these concepts could be derived from experience, they must already exist in our minds as a priori pure intuition when we are born. For instance, he claimed that our ability to recognize that there was a relationship between water and ice depended on the a priori category of substance (the atomist's "one" thing that we discussed in chapter 1) and the subcategory of causality—for example, that cold causes water to transform into ice. According to Kant, "the pure form of sensible intuitions in general is to be encountered in the mind *a priori,* wherein all of the manifold of appearances is intuited in certain relations."[72] As we briefly touched upon in the previous chapter, Kant argued that perceptions, which he called sensuous intuitions, are formed by a synthesis of external phenomena and the categories of the mind. To Kant, "our cognition arises from two fundamental sources in the mind, the first of which is the reception of representations (the receptivity of impressions), the second the faculty for cognizing an object by means of these representations. . . . Neither of these properties is to be preferred to the other. Without sensibility no object would be given to us, and without the intuitions, no object would be thought. Thoughts without content are empty, intuitions without concepts are blind."[73]

In other words, human cognition depends on the synthesis of a priori categories that organize perceptual experience into comprehensible patterns. Thus, in order to understand our experiences, our perceptions must depend upon pre-existing concepts. In our discussion of perception in the last chapter, we examined how perceptions, while not completely separable from sensations, were nevertheless not completely separable from cognition, either. This is because we experience far too many sensations every second for us to notice, so we therefore have to filter some out and bring others closer to our attention. Kant calls this the manifold of phenomena and describes how "all appearances are not things by themselves, but rather the mere play of our representations."[74]

Kant gave the name "schema" to what he thought linked sensibility and the a priori categories. Schemas were a mediating process that made the application of a category to a specific appearance possible. Kant describes, for example, how you might recognize this particular brown, furry creature that appears before you as a "dog" because the a priori category of substance is already present in your mind. "The schema is in itself always only a product of the imagination."[75] The schema mediates the relationship between the concept and the appearance—or what the ancients called the ideal and the real. The concept is a generalization (a generalized law) that the schema makes specific. As we will discuss later in the chapter, today's cognitive scientists and psychologists use "schema" to refer to the habitual patterns of thoughts and category systems that we use to make sense of the world.

Around the same time that European Enlightenment scholars were beginning to think with greater sophistication about mind and reason, European missionaries and fortune seekers were encountering the philosophies of the East. The result of this was a significant but largely unacknowledged influence of Indian philosophical perspectives on European thought. According to Shastri's history of classical Sanskrit literature, the translation of ancient Sanskrit into European languages began with the missionaries in the seventeenth century, when Abraham Roger published a Portuguese translation of none other than Bhartṛhari.[76] The next major translations were of Sanskrit legal texts into English by Warren Hastings and William Jones, beginning in 1776. Great works of classical Sanskrit literature began to be translated into English and then German in the 1780s and '90s. In 1808, the German philosopher Friedrich von Schlegel published a highly influential volume of translations of sections of the Indian classics the *Ramayana,* the *Mahābhārata,* and the *Manusmṛti* in his *On the Language and Wisdom of the Indians.* Latin translations of the Upanishads, along with German translations of the *Rig Veda,* followed. It has been documented that European poets, thinkers, and philosophers, such as Goethe, Herder, Kant, Schiller, and Henry David Thoreau, to name but a few, read and were influenced by these translations.[77]

And there is little doubt that these translations were key to the development of the European science of language study, which began as what was called "comparative philology." [78] Originated in 1820 by the German scholar Franz Bopp, who published the philological classic "Analytical comparison of the Sanskrit, Greek, Latin and Teutonic languages, shewing the original identity of their grammatical structure," philology took an atomistic view of language. One early result of philology was the discovery of what these philologists called Indo-European language, an antecedent language from which many other (principally Indian and European) languages emerged. The study of Sanskrit then became the foundation for the emerging "science" of philology. According to the nineteenth-century scholar Max Müller, in midcentury "in almost every continental university there is a professor of Sanskrit who lectures likewise on Comparative Grammar and the science of language."[79] Yet even today most studies of language and linguistics give a minimal nod of acknowledgment to the Sanskrit grammarians and their contribution to the study of language; most—including Leonard Bloomfield—begin the history of language study with the Greeks. But the historical record bears witness to a tremendous, yet largely unacknowledged, influence of both Vedic literature and the work of the grammarians on the study of language and thought in Europe and the Americas. [80] Moreover, some scholars today argue that comparative philology may have not originated in Europe at all, but in far earlier scholarship on the relationship between Persian and Sanskrit. Moreover, as Pollock argues, "It is a source of wonder—and should be a source of no little shame—that we Indologists have provided no comprehensive picture of the great achievements of Indian philologists during the three or four centuries before the consolidation of British colonialism. In fact, the early modern period of the history of Indian philology remains, in some ways, more obscure than the medieval or ancient."[81]

As did language study in ancient India, in Europe comparative philology developed along two very different lines, one generally atomistic and one largely holistic. In brief, the atomistic perspective views language from one or more of the following standpoints: (1) Language is a kind of transportation system that we use to transmit meanings from inside our heads to others. Words are like little packages of meaning. (2) Language is essentially a system of signs and symbols that represent and stand for things the world. Words basically correspond to things in the world. (3) Language is in essence an object that can best be studied when broken down into constituent parts, each of which should be studied separately. The European atomists were principally concerned with analyzing language as an object of inquiry, and, following the Indian grammarian Pāṇini's lead, categorized the underlying structures and patterns of language. A nineteenth-century American textbook defines philology as

> the science which teaches us what language is. The philologist deals with the words which make up a language, not merely to learn their meaning, but to find out their history. He pulls them to pieces, just as a botanist dissects flowers, in order that he may discover the parts of which each word is composed and the relation of those parts to each other: then he takes another and yet another language and deals with each in the same way: then by comparing the results he ascertains what is common to these different languages and what is peculiar to one or more.[82]

Although Pāṇini's atomistic perspective on language eventually led to the science of what we call linguistics today, Bhartṛhari's holistic perspective never exactly died out, but was for the most part absorbed by other fields such as philosophy, poetics, and communication. Therefore, we trace the holist perspective on the relationship between sound and word from the ancient Indians to the European philologists, who, unlike the European atomists, were principally concerned with meaning and communication and who theorized language as a process of social and cultural interaction. Whereas the European atomists searched for mechanistic systems, objects, structures, and rules that largely revolved around syntax, the European holists sought organic forms, processes, and meanings in human speech that largely revolved around semantics.

One of the foremost European holist scholars of language was a colleague of Bopp's named Wilhelm von Humboldt, a German Enlightenment philosopher, diplomat, and minister of education who studied Sanskrit (as well as other languages) and created the first professorships and programs of Sanskrit studies in Germany. It is not clear whether or to what extent Humboldt was influenced by Bhartṛhari, but he drew different conclusions than did the atomists from his studies of comparative philology and philosophy of language. His writings articulate a holist perspective on language from one or more of the following standpoints. First, unlike the atomists, Humboldt conceived language and thought to be deeply connected, mutually interdependent, and, at times, indistinguishable.[83] According to Humboldt, "one must free oneself from the notions that language can be separated from that which it designates."[84] Secondly, unlike the atomists, Humboldt conceived of language as the universe in which human beings dwell—we live in and depend upon language and cannot live outside of it. According to Humboldt, "the bringing-forth of language is an inner need of human beings, not merely an external necessity for maintaining communal intercourse, but a thing lying in their own nature, indispensable for the development of their mental powers and the attainment of a worldview, to which man can attain only by bringing his thinking to clarity and precision through communal thinking with others."[85] The holist perspective also sees language as the warp and weft that both weaves humans into culture and with which humans weave cultural worlds. That is, like Bhartṛhari, Humboldt viewed language as a productive rather than a representational process. "The mutual interdependence of thought and word illuminates clearly the truth that languages are not really means for representing already known truths, but are rather instruments for discovering previously unrecognized ones."[86] That is, language is not simply a tool that humans use. Rather, it is a culturally based, life-shaping force that exerts power over humans; "it is language itself which restrains me when I speak. . . . It then becomes evident how small, in fact is the power of the individual compared to the might of language."[87]

The third difference between atomist and holist perspectives pertains to the way that Humboldt conceived of language as a process or gestalt that is best studied holistically in use and as a synthesis rather than analysis. For example, Humboldt understood that meaning exists not in words but in the processes of communication, and, moreover, that no communication can ever be completely or perfectly understood, as we discussed in chapter 1 and to which we will return to in chapter 6. Thus, although Humboldt's thinking created a strong impression on some European philosophers, poets, and literary scholars, very few linguists took up the humanist perspective on language in the nineteenth and twentieth centuries, and for the most part, the holistic contributions to the study of language were eclipsed by the atomist perspective. As we will see in the next chapter, in spite of the ongoing dominance of the atomist perspective, there nevertheless remains a not insignificant holistic thread to follow into the twentieth century.

CONTEMPORARY PERSPECTIVES ON
LANGUAGE AND THOUGHT

Words are full of echoes, of memories, of associations. They have been out and about, on people's
lips, in their houses, in the streets, in the fields, for
so many centuries. . . . A word is not a single and
separate entity, but part of other words. It is not a
word indeed until it's part of a sentence. Words
belong to each other.

—VIRGINIA WOOLF, *"Craftsmanship"*

In the last chapter we explored how the atomist perspective on language
developed out of a long tradition that can be dated back to the ancient Indian
grammarian Pāṇini, who first devised a systematic organization of language
into grammatical, phonetic, and morphemic categories. This category system
influenced generations of language philosophers and linguists, while the
holistic perspectives of Bhartṛhari and later Humboldt were (with the exception of a small group of scholars in Russia whom we will discuss in the next
chapter) largely abandoned in the West due to the dominance of the Platonist
tradition of cleaving language and thought. Under the influence of European
Enlightenment thinking, a science of language emerged toward the end of
the eighteenth century. By 1900, this atomistic paradigm of language studies
became immortalized by the teaching and eventual publication of the work
of the Swiss linguist Ferdinand de Saussure, who drew a great deal of (only
partially acknowledged) inspiration from the Sanskrit grammarians and
Pāṇini in particular. According to Saussure, the principal aim of linguistics
should be to "determine the forces that are permanently and universally at
work in all languages, and to deduce the general laws to which all specific

historical phenomena can be reduced."[1] Saussure's landmark *Course in General Linguistics,* published in 1916, laid the foundation for what would become structuralist linguistics.

Moving decisively away from philology and its concerns with sound, language families, and evolutionary change, Saussure's structuralism emphasized language structure and mechanisms and introduced what was to become a new field called semiotics—the study of signs in society. We will discuss Saussure's ideas more extensively in the next chapter, but what is relevant for us now is how the atomist perspective went about breaking language into separate categories. Just as Plato had severed and demoted language from thought, so Saussure severed and demoted speech from language. To Saussure, linguistics was a science, and its object of study was language, "a well-defined object in the heterogeneous mass of speech facts."[2] Notice here that language is separated from speech—language is "a product that is passively assimilated by the individual," whereas Saussure saw speech as an individual, psychological act. Although some scholars compare Saussure to Bhartṛhari, this comparison once again reveals the atomist eclipse of the holistic perspectives on language and communication. To Saussure, language, as "a grammatical system of signs that express ideas," is not to be confused with mere speech, which as "[t]he activity of the speaker should be studied in a number of disciplines which have no place in linguistics except through [its] relation to language."[3] Thus, in contrast to the Indian grammarians, for whom language and speech were not divided, Saussure's system of language as a semiotic system sundered language from speech.[4]

Atomist Perspectives on Language

[C]olorless green ideas sleep furiously.
NOAM CHOMSKY, *Syntactic Structures*

Building upon the structuralist work of Saussure, in the 1960s the American linguist Noam Chomsky revolutionized the atomistic study of linguistics with his theory of transformational grammar. Ironically, even though Chomsky allies himself with Humboldt, and particularly with the latter's insight that "language makes infinite use of finite means," Chomsky's atomist work in linguistics bears little resemblance to the holistic philosophy of Humboldt. In fact, his work bears more resemblance to the Nyāyas' linguistic calculus.

Chomsky held that underlying all human languages was a system of repeatedly occurring rules of grammar—a set of general laws that seemed to be universal.[5] Since that time, the study of syntax has been in the foreground of linguistics as the central and essential structure of language. One example of this is an invented sentence by Chomsky—"Colorless green ideas sleep furiously"—that ostensibly demonstrates how syntax (structure) trumps semantics (meaning).[6] From an atomist point of view, Chomsky argued that while semantically the sentence is a nonsensical jumble, grammatically it is absolutely correct—it contains the appropriate arrangement of subject, predicate, adverbs, and adjectives. According to Chomsky, if we shuffled that perfectly correct English syntax into a different sentence, such as "green sleep colorless furiously ideas," we would get a mess—a seemingly nonsensical sentence that makes neither semantic nor syntactic sense. To Chomsky, this fact demonstrated the centrality of syntax over semantics, because language was made up of structures found in grammar and not, as the philologists had it, in sound and meaning.

Perhaps at this time Chomsky was influenced by Lewis Carroll's famed poem "Jabberwocky," which is read by Alice in *Through the Looking Glass*. This poem, like Chomsky's sentence, conforms to all the rules of English grammar, but makes playful delight out of sound and meaning. The words themselves are unfamiliar, yet they *sound* familiar, and the poem itself conforms to a regular ABAB rhyme scheme. Here's the poem's opening stanza:

> 'Twas brillig, and the slithy toves
>> Did gyre and gimble in the wabe;
> All mimsy were the borogoves,
>> And the mome raths outgrabe.[7]

Now to Chomsky, the fact that such a seemingly "nonsensical" text might "make sense" would be explained by the syntactic structures underlying language. But what goes unasked (and unanswered) by Chomsky's atomist analysis is how and why Alice and her readers *understand* this supposed nonsense.

In the novel, Alice is confused by the poem, and we can imagine why: something's not right, she probably thinks. "'Twas" sounds like the eminently normal contraction of "It was," and "brillig" sounds an awful lot like "brilliant." Is the poem's author setting the stage for a bright and lovely day? Alas, no. Later in the story, Humpty Dumpty tells Alice that "brillig" means "four o'clock in the afternoon—the time when you begin broiling things for dinner."[8] And then those "slithy toves"—could they be slimy toads, or slithering doves? Like Chomsky's "colorless green ideas," "Jabberwocky" seems to be a jumble of orderly nonsense—or is it? While we will reserve our discussion of meaning and communication for the next chapter, it is worth noting, from a holist perspective, how Alice responds to the poem. While she thinks it pretty, she doesn't quite understand it. But at the same time, and here is the crucial thing, she says that "somehow it seems to fill my head with ideas—only I don't exactly know what they are!"[9] In other words, Alice finds the poem not meaningless nonsense, but instead a ticklishly mysterious melody that somehow makes its way inside her. Alice is willing to entertain the thought that although she might not understand the poem, she nevertheless hears *and feels* the echoes of ideas in its song. Moreover, even though she doesn't fully understand the strange ideas filling her head, she nevertheless appreciates the poem's musical play of rhythm and rhyme. Alice, in other words, is able to gather together the ideas of the poem without confining them to things or schemas she already knows. And her reaction suggests something important about the limitations of the atomistic approach to language and communication; namely, its inability to tolerate, let alone account for, those aspects of lived human experience that don't fit the standard Cartesian subject/object model.

Alice's response to "Jabberwocky" raises an important question about knowledge—*what does it mean to know something?* Do you know, for example, how many inches separate your toothbrush holder from the sink? Can you name the fifth letter from the right on the second row of a computer keyboard? How do you stay balanced on your bicycle? What? I didn't quite catch that. You say you don't really *know?* But how can that be? Don't you use a toothbrush every day? Well, you reply, I can find my toothbrush in the pitch black of the early morning. I just reach up and my hand just seems to *know* exactly where to find it. Also, you say, I may not be able to say exactly where that letter is, but I can type eighty words per minute, and my fingers *know* exactly where to find the letters without any effort on my part. And, you continue, as for staying balanced on a bicycle? Well, my body just seems to *know* how to stay upright. As we began to explore in chapter 1, knowledge and memory are relational and embodied aspects of consciousness that elude the grasp of atomist paradigms.

So, what does it mean to *know* something? From the atomist perspective, knowing is a mental act of cognition that takes place in our minds. We conjure facts from memory, calculate sums, demonstrate proofs with logical reasoning, and build mental models that Walter Lippmann called "the pictures in our heads." Atomists like Chomsky, Lippmann, and Descartes see the mind as the center of thought and the essence of being human. In contrast, a holistic perspective on knowledge and meaning rejects the idea that we are what the eighteenth-century German philosopher Leibniz described as "windowless monads": individual solitary minds thinking privately to ourselves, who are, like Descartes, confident only of the thoughts in our heads. Consider for a moment. What is *reason?* Is it the same as *a reason?* And what makes a reason or reasoning *good?* Is it something we can point to outside, like a rock or a river? Can we create an experiment to prove, once and for all, that we are awake and our dreaming selves asleep? Can you construct an algorithm to predict who you will fall in love with, and why?

Today, we know that one of the strengths of scientific reasoning is that it is an excellent means for understanding the natural world and has enabled us to do all kinds of things, from building machines that fly to the moon, to curing diseases and creating robots that can compute millions of equations per second. But, as described in chapter 1, these achievements come at a cost which is largely ignored by atomist perspectives. When it comes to understanding the interactions and interrelationships among the many parts of complex phenomena such as human societies, global weather systems, or complex financial markets, atomist science and logic only appear to take power, belief, and politics out of the search for knowledge. Something more, something *other,* is needed to explain the vast ocean of oddities that make up human existence. And that other, as Bohm, Pribram, and others have argued, is holism.

Holistic Perspectives on Language

If speaking, as the listening to language, lets Saying be said to it, this letting can obtain only in so far—and so near—as our own nature has been admitted and entered into Saying. We hear Saying only because we belong to it.
—MARTIN HEIDEGGER, *On the Way to Language*

Perhaps Humboldt's greatest inheritor of the holistic perspective on language and thought was the twentieth-century German philosopher Martin Heidegger, whose insights turned the entire Cartesian perspective on its head. Rather than viewing the thought of human *being* as an isolated mental phenomenon occurring privately in inner minds, Heidegger theorized thought as inseparable from our actions in the world. To Heidegger, knowing isn't a mental phenomenon conducted by internal computer-like minds; instead, knowing is something we do as we are existing in the world—holding a hammer, walking through a door, talking to strangers on a bus. "Knowing is a kind of Being. . . . The perceiving of what is known is not a process of returning with one's booty to the 'cabinet' of consciousness after one has gone out and grasped it."[10]

Just as Alice feels the rhythm of "Jabberwocky" without really understanding it, Heidegger's meaning is not located solely "in the head" but in the interdependent totality of interactions in the world with which we concern ourselves. Heidegger perceived a danger in the atomist Cartesian subject-object perspective, which mistook logical thinking for the only kind of thinking. Heidegger considered his work "beyond philosophy," that is, beyond the limits and rules of atomistic perspectives on human being.[11] In a 1955 speech commemorating the anniversary of the composer Conradin Kreutzer's birth, Heidegger distinguished between two kinds of thinking, which he called *calculative* and *meditative*. Calculative thinking is understood by Heidegger as a kind of instrumental thought governed by a mechanical concern for goals and outcomes. Meditative thinking, in contrast, is a pondering and a questioning that is not attached to a particular perspective. As he writes: "Meditative thinking demands of us not to cling one-sidedly to a single idea, nor to run down a one-track course of ideas. Meditative thinking demands of us that we engage ourselves with what at first sight does not go together at all."[12] Heidegger warns that the dominance of language governed by mechanical reasoning leads to an objectification of the world (including ourselves), which limits the possibilities of meditative thought. "In this way language comes under the dictatorship of the public realm, which decides in advance what is intelligible and what must be rejected as unintelligible."[13]

This is not unlike David Bohm's insights discussed in chapter 1 about the problems that arise when we mistake habitual thoughts for reality. "It is thus quite easy," Bohm writes, "through inadequate attention to the actual process of one's thought, to 'slip into' a form of conditioned response of memory, in which one is not alert to the fact that [it] is still only a form of thought, a form that aims to give a view of 'the whole of reality.' So, 'by default' one falls into the trap of tacitly treating such a view as originating independently of thought, thus implying that its content actually is the whole of reality."[14] Bohm says we have a problem with thought: we break things up into fragments, we don't pay attention to how our thoughts work, we mistakenly think our thoughts are "ours," and we think the things we think about are "out there."

Another example of how our perceptions are shaped by unconscious thoughts, linguistic preconceptions, and schemas is given by the Jewish philosopher of dialogue Martin Buber, a contemporary of Heidegger who shared a holistic perspective on thought. Using the example of looking at a tree, Buber illustrates the many ways we can be blinded by language and cognition:

> I consider a tree.
>
> I can look on it as a picture: stiff column in a shock of light, or splash of green shot with the delicate blue and silver of the background.
>
> I can perceive it as movement: flowing veins on clinging, pressing pith, suck of the roots, breathing of the leaves, ceaseless commerce with earth and air—and the obscure growth itself.
>
> I can classify it in a species and study it as a type in its structure and mode of life.
>
> I can subdue its actual presence and form so sternly that I recognize it only as an expression of law—of the laws in accordance with which a constant opposition of forces is continually adjusted, or of those in accordance with which the component substances mingle and separate.
>
> I can dissipate it and perpetuate it in number, in pure numerical relation.[15]

As Buber notes in his text, each description of the tree may be perfectly accurate, but it will also be partial and incomplete, stressing only those aspects of the tree that conform to the expectations of our schemas and overlooking those that don't fit. The danger of habitual schemas blinding or misleading us is demonstrated by the question that the Indian philosopher Krishnamurti once asked his students, "When we say we see a tree or a flower or a person, do we actually see them? Or do we see the image that the word has created?"[16] With this question Krishnamurti was trying to point out how our life experiences and expectations condition us to see, think, feel, and act in habitual ways without our awareness. To Heidegger, meditative thinking was not just a way to get beyond habitual calculative thinking, but was itself a quintessentially human inheritance and experience and also the very ground of being.

"Thinking accomplishes the relation of Being to the essence of man. It does not make or cause the relation."[17]

One of Heidegger's students, the French philosopher Maurice Merleau-Ponty, describes how speech is not a *representation* of thought, but what *accomplishes* thought. "Speech is not the sign of thought," explains Merleau-Ponty.[18] But, because it becomes so utterly transparent, speech "loses sight of itself" and "provides us with the ideal of thought without words."[19] Like Carey, Shotter, Stewart, and other scholars discussed in chapter 1, Merleau-Ponty describes the ways in which speech "constitutes a linguistic world and a cultural world."[20] Like Heidegger, Merleau-Ponty rejects the atomistic separation of mind and body, language and thought, subject and object; he considers the idea of thought without words as nonsensical as the idea of music without sound. Like Bhartṛhari and Humboldt, Merleau-Ponty argues against a static and unchanging perspective on word and meaning. "In truth, a language is not made up of *words,* each of which is endowed with one or several meanings. Each word has its meaning only inasmuch as it is sustained in this signification by all the others. The same holds true for these others. The only reality is the *Gestalt* of language."[21]

Atomist Perspectives on Thought

And yet, despite the power of these compelling insights, many scholars studying the relationship between language and thought atomistically narrow their search for thought and understanding to the brain and neurology. Indeed, just this morning I opened the mailbox to find that a new alumni magazine had arrived. Its cover trumpeted the lead article, "The Science of Love: It's More About the Brain than the Heart," and the back cover posed the question "Maybe Valentines should be brain-shaped." Freed from any troubling confusions about the connection between thought and language, mind and body, or brain and heart, the study described in the alumni magazine, like most research on thought today, proceeds from Descartes's *cogito* and divides thought into three separate functions of the brain—attention, memory, and schema. But take a moment and consider the following: Where is your attention right now? On the words on this page? On the music in the background? On planning your evening? Reviewing yesterday's argument with your beloved? We are all too familiar with the challenge of maintaining attention while studying or listening to a lecture or a sermon. The mind tends to wander on a course of its own—flitting from here to there like a butterfly or, more likely, jumping from tree to ground to rock to stream to tree, like a monkey—what Buddhists call "monkey mind."

Today cognitive scientists, who largely take an atomist perspective, hold that there are two systems governing where we direct our attention—a supervisory system and an automatic habitual system.[22] The supervisory system kicks in when we need to focus, switch, or divide our attention, like when a car cuts me off or when I take a sip of coffee mindful not to spill. Generally speaking, most of the time we live our lives in a habit mode that relies less on intentional attention than upon environmental cues, knowledge, past experiences, and familiar patterns to make our way in the world. I've driven to work hundreds of times, so the task requires little supervisory attention and I can turn my mind to other things. But last week, when one of the highway bridges needed repair and I had to take a detour that wound through miles of wooded back roads, autopilot just wasn't enough. I needed to pay attention.

So the mind in my body can drive the car just fine while thinking about thinking—unless some crisis erupts in the car-driving world. At that point, I can focus my attention where I like. But that's not all. Like my body driving to work, even my thinking can run along a habitual track without my awareness. As the groundbreaking American psychologist William James long ago observed, "Habit diminishes the conscious attention with which our acts are performed."[23] Our attention gets trained to expect patterns—driving home from work without thinking about it. At these times, attention can be somewhere (on something) without our awareness—as when we're daydreaming, spacing out, or reliving a memory. And what we remember has a great deal to do with where we place our attention—but not even focused attention is faultless. What did you do yesterday? What details can you remember? Do you remember what you or others wore? What you heard? How you moved? Do you remember what you thought about?

Today, many cognitive scientists believe that one of the most important elements of cognition is called working memory—"a limited capacity storage system that underpins complex human thought."[24] According to Baddeley, working memory is made up of four subsystems that underlie human cognition—the "central executive," which directs attention; the "phonological loop," an acoustic system that retains traces of sound; a "visualspatial sketchpad," which retains and integrates perceptual information; and an "episodic buffer," which integrates information into coherent episodes.[25] Of those four systems, the central executive is linked to long-term memory. The central executive uses two processes—a supervisory system that is directed by intentional attention, and a habitual system that "automatically governs most of our behavior."[26] Ironically, just as we can mistakenly assume that observation is a more or less "true and accurate" representation of reality, we can also presume that memory is more or less an "accurate" recording of what we experienced. But of course things are far more complicated than that. As we saw in chapter 1, eyewitness perception is fallible in various ways. So too is memory. Studies show that memories are strongly affected by telling and retelling and that "[o]nce witnesses state facts in a particular way or identify a particular person as the perpetrator, they are unwilling or even unable—due to the reconstruction of their memory—to reconsider."[27] In short, verbal rehearsal (re-hears-all) reinforces memory.

Other studies show how speakers' memories are affected by listeners in several different ways. First, as speakers we of course will tailor our speech to our listener—we might not tell our mother about the close call we had on the freeway the other night, but we will surely tell our best friend, using all the colorful expressions that we might keep in reserve in front of our parents. Thus, who our listeners are, their relationship to us, and the context of our interaction influence what we say, how we say it, and what details we include, emphasize, and omit. Moreover, as speakers we are also influenced by the listener's behavior. In certain cultures, for example, listeners are expected to indicate that they are listening by means of some degree of body posture, eye contact, gesture, and utterances like ums and ahs. Most people find it difficult to speak for long without these indications from the listener. Similarly, even when listeners perform all the indications of listening, but are otherwise preoccupied, speakers tend to slow down, stumble, and leave out more than they ordinarily would. In general, truly attentive listeners not only elicit more information from speakers, but they also facilitate the speaker's long-term memory.[28] And given that the primary access we have to memory is through language, it is clear that this separation is somewhat illusionary.

Holist Perspectives on Thought

From a holistic perspective, the distinction between memory and perceptual experience, or between past and present, is more complex. The holographic brain theory of Pribram discussed in chapter 1 for example, "claims that the act of 're-membering' or thinking . . . allows us to re-experience to some degree a previous perception. This is what constitutes a memory."[29] This theory has been supported by findings in neuroscience that suggest that memory is not a veridical recording of our experiences in the external world, but is instead a dynamic process that is shaped and reshaped by changing experiences as well as a variety of subjective factors. Long before the recent dizzying insights of neuroscience, however, philosophers East and West speculated on the close interconnected relationship between thought, perception, and memory.

At the end of the nineteenth century, developing theories in psychology initiated new thinking about the relationships between perception and memory, and in particular about the presumed separation between the two. "[T]here is no perception which is not full of memories. With the immediate and present data of our senses we mingle a thousand details out of our past experience," wrote the French philosopher and mathematician Henri Bergson in 1911.[30] In fact, the inextricable relationship between perception and memory seems to muddle even the distinction between past and present. As Bergson describes it, "In the fraction of a second which covers the briefest possible perception of light, billions of vibrations have taken place. . . . Your perception, however instantaneous, consists then in an incalculable multitude of remembered elements; and in truth every perception is already memory. Practically we perceive only the past, the pure present being the invisible progress of the past gnawing into the future."[31]

Today, neuroscientists understand the plastic malleability of memory, and how it is stretched and shaped throughout our lives. A key property of memory, write Edelman and Tononi, is that "it is, in some sense, a form of constructive recategorization during ongoing experience, rather than a precise replication of a previous sequence of events."[32] So the processes of attention and memory depend less on intentionality and volition than we would like to believe. The fact is that remembering, or intentionally choosing, selecting, placing our attention only explains part of the processes of perception; there are a great number of perceptions that occur regardless of our intention. Thus, James's insight that "what is called our 'experience' is almost entirely determined by our habits of attention" seems to emphasize individual choice over the holist's social and cultural processes that categorize, name, and shape our experiences.[33]

Nevertheless, as Virginia Woolf's epigraph to this chapter attests, holistic perspectives on language and thought persist, and some scholarship even carries an echo of Bhartṛhari. For example, can you tell which of the following two quotes is Bhartṛhari and which Heidegger? A: "It is words which establish things."[34] B: "To significations words accrue. But word-things [words] do not get supplied with significations."[35] In other words, words are not, or not merely, names for things that exist "out there" in the world like rocks and trees, but words themselves bestow and create "things" in our worlds. Now, we're not talking magic here—it's not like a word is a "spell" that can turn a frog into a prince. Rather, words are what give birth to things, whether those "things" are brute facts or complex conceptual schemas. "[W]hen we consider phenomenal concepts, we see that they do not exist or hold any meaning aside from the words through which they are expressed: we might say that our concepts are 'word-loaded' and from this we can infer that the word principle causes the world."[36] Perhaps the best articulation of this idea comes from the American linguist Edward Sapir, who wrote,

> Language is a guide to "social reality." Though language is not ordinarily thought of as of essential interest to the students of social science, it powerfully conditions all our thinking about social problems and processes. Human beings do not live in the objective world alone, nor alone in the world of social activity as ordinarily understood, but are very much at the mercy of the particular language which has become the medium of expression for their society. It is quite an illusion to imagine that one adjusts to reality essentially without the use of language and that language is merely an incidental means of solving specific problems of communication or reflection. The fact of the matter is that the "real world" is to a large extent unconsciously built up on the language habits of the group. No two languages are ever sufficiently similar to be considered as representing the same social reality. The worlds in which different societies live are distinct worlds, not merely the same world with different labels attached.[37]

A wonderful example of this idea comes from another American, linguist George Lakoff, who wrote a book about language and thought called *Women, Fire, and Dangerous Things*. Why this surprising title? What in the world do these three things have in common? As it happens, they are three central members of a category of things from Dyirbal, an aboriginal language of Australia.[38] According to Lakoff, all things in the Dyirbal world are classified into four separate categories. One category includes men, kangaroos, bats, the moon, storms, rainbows, and boomerangs, while another includes women, fireflies, dogs, some snakes and fishes, most birds, and anything connected with water or fire, sun, and stars. The third category includes all edible fruit and plants, as well as honey, cigarettes, and wine, and the last category includes parts of the body, bees, noises, language, and most spears. These four categories, which perhaps seem almost fictional to English speakers, make perfect sense in the Dyirbal world.

And lest you think that such farfetched categories are reserved to esoteric literature and aboriginal societies, wait a moment. Even in science, disputes reign about what goes where in the taxonomy of animal species. For example, the Harvard paleontologist Stephen J. Gould describes a fight between marine biologists over whether a lungfish (a fish with lungs?) belongs in a category related to cows or in a category related to trout. Gould says that one school of thought, phenetics, bases its classification on observable similarities like bone structure, hair patterns, and DNA. Under these criteria, the lungfish goes with other bony fish, like trout. On the opposing side is cladistics, whose proponents base their classifications on ancestral lineage and generally disregard structural similarities. So under these criteria, the lungfish is more closely related to terrestrial vertebrates (like cows) than to trout. So which is it? Well, it depends on who you ask. And perhaps more importantly, who has the last word. As Gould describes it, quoting J. B. S. Haldane, "the concept of a species is a concession to our linguistic habits and neurological mechanisms." He adds, quoting another paleontologist, that a species "is a fiction, a mental construct without objective existence."[39]

Drawing on Kant's concept of "schema," today's scholars argue about whether schemas are for the most part cultural and thereby vary by place and time, or whether they are for the most part invariant and "hardwired" into the brain. They mostly agree, however, to use the term to refer to a kind of mental template (also called a "cognitive structure" or a "knowledge structure") that can be combined and organized in patterns or sets of categories, associations, differentiations, which the mind creates out of life experiences. For example, when children are first learning language, their schemas tend to be very simple, and often, to experienced language speakers, amusingly inaccurate. When my friend's niece was first learning to speak, she called every four-legged furry animal she saw a cat. To her, everything from teddy bears to squirrels in the yard, cows in the field, and the dogs next door all fit in one single category. They were cats. It didn't take long, however, for her to learn to differentiate between these animals, and to eventually know each by a different name. It was only later that she learned to differentiate pictures of animals from living animals, and much later, to sort all these different animals into a category called "mammals" that could be further subdivided into categories such as domestic mammals (cats, cows and guinea pigs, etc.) and wild mammals (squirrels, raccoons, groundhogs, etc.). So our life experiences and language learning shape the schemas we acquire in our minds.

Although a debate between and among linguists and cognitive psychologists persists as to whether some schemas are a priori concepts or are learned along with language continues to rage on, we will here sidestep that argument and simply examine how schemas are thought to operate in relation to cognition. To psychologists, a schema is a kind of mental template or network of associations that we build throughout our lives from the threads and shards of past experiences, and that, in turn, shape our interpretations of the present. Yet, while schemas may function as a kind of shorthand to free us to focus our attention where we like, they can, as Kant noted, also blind us. The mishaps and troubles caused by expectations, assumptions, and predictions are part of the difficulties posed by schemas, as are the gross mischaracterizations of our stereotypes and the vast deserts of our selective attention. As we discussed in chapter 2, experiments conducted by the psychologist Elizabeth Loftus demonstrate how schemas influence our everyday perceptions. In one experiment, people were asked to watch a short film that contained a car crash, and then report what they saw. In the majority of cases, people reported seeing or hearing glass break when in fact no breaking glass was shown or heard in the film; viewers inferred the sound and pictures from their car crash schemas. They saw what they expected to see. According to contemporary schema theory, the four processes of perception, comprehension, interpretation, and memory are all mediated by schemas. As with attention, we acquire and begin to habituate to schemas early in life, and for the most part our schemas are shaped and reinforced by cultural patterns and expectations. "Infants must go through a long education of the eye and ear before they can perceive the realities which adults perceive. Every perception is an acquired perception."[40]

Influenced in part by these holistic perspectives, early twenty-first-century developments in cognitive science have brought new perspectives on thinking and reason that call into question the atomist separation of language and thought and explore how thought and language are mutually interdependent. For the last forty years or so, some American linguists have begun to consider metaphor as a kind of metaphor for the way we think. According to these scholars, thought and language are far more holistic, embodied, and synthetic phenomena that *produce* understanding rather than *reflect* it. The conceptual structure of thought, argue Lakoff and Johnson, authors of the groundbreaking 1980 book *Metaphors We Live By,* is metaphorical in nature—that is, we interpret the world according to metaphorical systems that "highlight and make coherent certain aspects of our experience."[41] These metaphorical systems are very much like schemas in that they organize our perceptions and experiences into familiar categories. The difference, however, is that the categories are metaphorical in that they speak of one thing in terms of another. For example, the metaphor "time is money" illustrates how time is precious— we have only a finite amount of it, and we want to "spend" it wisely. But, like schemas, metaphors also hide other ideas and suppositions (called entailments) that sneak into our thinking along with the metaphor. So, for example, "time is money" also smuggles some troubling ideas into our ways of thinking about time and money; it reinforces the idea that time is something quantifiable and that we can count it in a uniform standardized manner as we do with money. The metaphor also reinforces the idea that economics is a very important, if not essential, foundation of human life—that we best reckon our life experience in financial terms. Similarly, as Johnson and Lakoff point out, "If you *spend your time* trying to do something and it doesn't work, you can't get your time back. There are no time banks. I can *give you a lot of time,* but you can't give me back the same time, though you can *give me back the same amount of time.* And so on. Thus, part of a metaphorical concept does not and cannot fit."[42] And the danger of the unacknowledged dimensions of metaphor is that they exert such a strong influence on our ways of thinking and acting. "Metaphors may create realities for us, especially social realities. A metaphor may thus be a guide for future action. Such actions will, of course, fit the metaphor. This will, in turn, reinforce the power of the metaphor to make experience coherent. In this sense metaphors can be self-fulfilling prophecies."[43]

Importantly, the life experiences that shape schemas are not solely mental, they are also in our bodies, significantly influenced by the ways we physically interact with and inhabit the world, in what Lakoff and Johnson call "embodied reasoning."[44] According to Lakoff and Johnson, the mind is inherently embodied, and our language and reasoning are deeply embedded with our physical sensorimotor experiences, leading to metaphorical expressions like "grasping" an idea, or "dropping" the ball, or "falling" in love. Recent research in the area of psychoacoustics reveals that our responses to sound and music are also tied to embodied schemas such as balance, tension, and cyclical motion. According to Brower, "It has been found that the overtone series, having been stored in memory through repeated exposure to the complex sounds of music and speech, serves as a template for pattern matching carried out at an unconscious level. It is here that we find the most likely explanation for our perception of the major triad as more stable than the minor: its intervallic pattern forms a better match with the intervallic pattern of the overtone series."[45]

For example, consider the auditory experience of the harmonic series, discussed in chapter 1, where the triadic relationship between tonic (*do*), third (*mi*), and dominant (*sol*) is associated with first the building of tension and then, when reversed, with the resolution of tension. Conjure the British Christian hymn "Amazing Grace," which exemplifies the building and relaxation of tension between the dominant and tonic of the harmonic series. The song begins with the phrase *Ahh-May-Zing-Grace,* which starts from the dominant (*sol*) on the first syllable *Ahh,* then moves up to the tonic (*do*) on the second syllable *May* (5–1), and then up to the third (*mi*) on *Grace* and then descends back to the dominant in the stepwise "sweet the sound." Then, later in the verse, where we expect the melody to descend again, it instead ascends up an octave to the dominant at "wretch like me" (3–5). Now imagine that we stopped the song right there, on the dominant. It wouldn't feel right to most of us—not just because we're familiar with the song, but because the building of tension at the dominant cries out for resolution at the tonic—*Was Blind* (5–1), *But Now* (3–1-3), *I See* (2–1). Without the final resolution on the tonic, the song would, in an embodied way, "feel" unfinished, incomplete.

It must be stressed here that not all cultures interpret the auditory perception of harmonic movement in the same way. As we described in chapter 2, just as pitch is interpreted differently (as height, strength, or size) in different cultures, so is harmonic movement. But the important points are, first, that harmonic movement will be noticed, second, that it will be named according to an embodied metaphor, and third, that it will be culturally shaped. As Brower notes,

> In emphasizing the embodied character of our experience of movement through triadic pitch space, I do not claim that all listeners will hear changes of harmony or key as rising or falling, or tensing or relaxing, movement. Nor do I suggest that we can extrapolate from the experiences of Western subjects to those of non-Western listeners. Because such metaphorical mappings require active engagement of the bodily imagination, as well as

familiarity with the conventions of the major-minor system, individual listeners may differ markedly in the degree to which they experience such sensations.[46]

More recently, the linguists Fauconnier and Turner have developed a theory of conceptual blending to describe how we think in more detail than schema theory holds and in modes other than metaphor. According to these scholars, thought and the principles that govern it are formed through a tremendously complex process of conceptual mash-ups that are constantly creating, recreating, and expanding. Fauconnier and Turner describe *double-scope integration,* a cognitive process in which we blend attributes, qualities, patterns, and so on from two seemingly separate realms and put them together, as in, for example, the expression "computer virus."[47] Aside from analogy and metaphor, where we blend two domains (like time and money) together, Fauconnier and Turner describe how we create hypothetical realities blended from two different domains of meaning. They give the following example: "If Clinton were the *Titanic,* the iceberg would sink."[48] This hypothetical sentence advances a concealed, implicit argument (i.e., that Clinton was indestructible but his opponents were not) by constructing an alternate universe whereby the two seemingly unrelated but historically factual events are causally connected. This exemplifies how readily we can create worlds with language and thereby *do things with words.*[49]

Fauconnier and Turner describe another form of double-scope integration as what they call "action blends," a way of combining two different but in some way similar embodied actions together. They give the example of driving in a car while straining to hear the person talking in the passenger seat. In a kind of automatic trance, you reach to turn down the volume on the radio—even though it's not even on! What makes this an action blend is not simply that you make an error, they say. It's that you've blended the actions of listening to a person on the radio with conversing with a person in the car. A third kind of conceptual blending described by Fauconnier and Turner is what they call "frame breaks," where we blend elements of one kind of situation with another. For example, driving up to a window at the bank, and asking for a cappuccino. All of these forms demonstrate the ways in which language is an underlying matrix *in which* we live like a fish in water, and *with which* we create new worlds. We will return to the role of language and communication in the creation of our shared social worlds in the next chapter. Meanwhile, it's time to turn our attention to listening, which, as I have noted, has gone largely (but not entirely) unremarked in the millennia of debates over the relationship between language and thought.

Listening to the *Logos*

Listening not to me but to the Logos, it is wise to agree that all things are one.
—HERACLITUS

So how and where does listening come into all of these words about words? How does listening relate to language and thought? You may have noticed that although, on occasion, the scholarly debates discussed above characterize language as speech and speaking, rarely, if ever, do they describe it in terms of listening. Today, most research about listening takes a largely atomistic perspective that aims to improve listening processes so that we may become more effective and better listeners. Without a doubt, these are noble goals that can offer great benefit to individuals and society, particularly in relation to disabilities such as traumatic brain injuries, neurological disorders, auditory processing disorders, hearing impairments, and so forth. But unfortunately, they also, at the same time, tend to perpetuate the very mechanistic and transmission views of language and thought that keep us from understanding or engaging with other ways of being. As Heidegger warns, "the approaching tide of technological revolution in the atomic age could so captivate, bewitch, dazzle, and beguile man that calculative thinking may someday come to be accepted and practiced as the only way of thinking."[50] One of the primary motivations for me in writing this book is to present alternative perspectives on listening, thinking, and being—it is therefore both an intervention and an invitation. Take of it what you can.

As you may have sensed, a great deal of why we don't listen has to do with our atomistic beliefs about knowledge, understanding, and the relation of language and thought. In brief, the problem is that we habituate to already existing linguistic categories, concepts, and structures and then mistake these conceptual formations for the truth of the way things are. When our understandings become "securely encrusted around some conviction, justification, identity, cause, or the like, [we deny] the legitimacy of the other."[51] The cognitive structures of language are particularly dangerous when we become so habituated to them that they are automatic and invisible to us. They distort our perceptions and point us to see what we expect to see and ignore everything else. As the Catholic monk Thomas Merton described it, "The human dilemma of communication is that we cannot communicate ordinarily without words and signs, but even ordinary experience tends to be falsified by our habits of verbalization and rationalization. The convenient tools of language enable us to decided beforehand what we think things mean, and tempt us all too easily to see things only in a way that fits our logical preconceptions and our verbal formulas."[52] We become habituated to the familiar—we listen to others on "automatic pilot," hearing only what we expect to hear because we don't listen to what is actually before us.

So what would a holistic paradigm of listening include? In short, everything. Perhaps it would begin with the understanding that listening requires an awareness of our habitual categories and a willingness to go beyond them. So how does one listen beyond the schemas, categories, and dualistic thinking of the conceptual mind? One suggestion is to listen from a space of emptiness and unknowing, to be strong enough to relinquish our perceived mastery, control, and foreknowledge while remaining attentive and aware. Perhaps not surprisingly, spiritual traditions and practices are some of the last places that cultivate and preserve a holistic perspective on listening. Most religions have some form of meditative or contemplative practice for sustaining the kind of silence required for deep listening to the ineffable and the incomprehensible. Similarly, many world religions, from Vedic to Baha'i, find in listening a means of spiritual development.

A story from the Taoist tradition conveys something of this idea. A third century B.C.E. story recounts a teaching by a mentor named Kongzi to his student Yan Hui, who wants to deal with a troublesome situation in the state of Wei, where the prince is completely careless and indifferent to the suffering of his people. Yan Hui describes how "the dead fill the state like falling leaves in a swamp. The people have nowhere to turn."[53] Kongzi begins by asking Yan Hui what he plans to do, and Yan Hui catalogues a range of possible actions. Kongzi rejects each plan in turn, warning Yan Hui of the various disasters that will result because he, Yan Hui, is "still making the mind your teacher."[54] Instead, Kongzi tells Yan Hui to conduct a fasting of the mind. "Do not listen with your ears but with your mind. Do not listen with your mind but listen with your *qi* [spirit]. Listening stops with the ear. The mind stops with signs. *Qi* is empty. . . . Emptiness is the fasting of the mind."[55]

A similar teaching comes from the Zen monk Thich Nhat Hanh, who describes how the judging conceptual mind interferes with listening to the sounding of a bell—we hear the bell and then evaluate it as beautiful or strange, which then may trigger memories or associations, analyzing and comparing. "With each such judgment the experience of pure hearing becomes fainter and fainter until one no longer hears the sound but hears only his thoughts about it."[56] Merton describes this kind of contemplative emptiness as "Being's awareness of itself in us."[57]

The difficulty of listening without these kinds of judgment is well known, but when it occurs, the impact is powerful. Buddhist teacher Tara Brach describes such a moment when Jacob, a seventy-year-old meditation student with Alzheimer's disease, is giving a talk to an audience about Buddhism when he goes absolutely blank. He has no idea where he was or what he was supposed to do. Drawing on his years of meditation experience, he begins to convey everything he is aware of, moment by moment:

> "Afraid, embarrassed, confused, feeling like I'm failing, powerless, shaking, sense of dying, sinking, lost." For several more minutes he sat, head slightly bowed, continuing to name his experience. As his body began to relax and his mind grew calmer, he also noted that aloud. At last Jacob lifted his head, looked slowly around at those gathered, and apologized.
>
> Many of the students were in tears. As one put it, "No one has ever taught us like this. Your presence has been the deepest teaching." Rather than pushing away his experience and deepening his agitation, Jacob had the courage and training simply to name what he was aware of, and, most significantly, to bow to his experience. In some fundamental way, he didn't create an adversary out of feelings of fear and confusion. *He didn't make anything wrong.*[58]

Another untapped reservoir of holistic thinking about listening comes from the grammarian tradition of *sphota,* discussed earlier in the chapter and developed in Bhartṛhari and Patañjali, for whom speech, hearing, and knowledge are interrelated. "*Sphota* entails a kind of mental perception which is described as a moment of recognition, an instantaneous flash . . . , whereby the hearer is made conscious, through hearing sounds, of the latent meaning unit already present in his consciousness."[59] Bhartṛhari's listener is not a passive absorber of words but an active creator of meaning—the understanding of *sphota* does not "burst forth" until all the sounds of an utterance are apprehended by the listener. "Simultaneously with the last sound, the word is apprehended by the mind in which the seed has been sown by the (physical) sounds, and in which ripening (of the speech) has been brought about by the telling over (of the sounds)."[60] To Bhartṛhari, it was not so much that the sequence of words had to be completed as that meaning only arose from the whole gestalt of the integrated nondualism of speaking and listening.

Although few contemporary scholars have noted philosophy's historical neglect of listening, there are a few rare exceptions, with Heidegger being, of course, the foremost. In his later remarkable studies of language, Heidegger argued that the conception of *logos* that undergirds most Western philosophy is so dominated by an emphasis on speech and speaking that we have forgotten not only how to listen to others, but how to listen to the being of language itself. To Heidegger, Western philosophy has entirely neglected the being of beings, that is, the experience of being's being—not being as a noun or object, but being as a verb, as pure experience. To Heidegger, "being's poem, just begun, is man."[61] In his analysis of a fragment from the Pre-Socractic Heraclitus, Heidegger foregrounds not so much speaking as listening and finds in the fragment an injunction to listen to language itself. Heraclitus fragment B 50 is typically translated along the lines of "Listening not to me but to the account, it is wise to agree that all things are one."[62] In contrast, Heidegger translates it as "When you have listened, not merely to me, but rather when you maintain yourselves in hearkening attunement, then there is proper hearing."[63] And what is proper hearing? Like the spiritual practices discussed above, proper hearing arises from what Heidegger calls "openness to the mystery," a calling forth of what is gathered before us at the present moment. And this kind of listening demands what Corradi Fiumara calls "a kind of inner abnegation. Without this inner renunciation the individual can only hold a dialogue with himself."[64]

Of the few scholars to follow Heidegger into the elusive mysteries of listening, two in particular stand out: Corradi Fiumara and the American scholar David Michael Levin. Corradi Fiumara calls listening "the other side of language" and describes the courage required for listening "with sufficient strength to sustain blows of any kind and still remain alert."[65] That is to say, listening "could actually come across like a storm and overwhelm us . . . listening involves the renunciation of a predominantly molding and ordering activity; a giving up sustained by the expectation of a new and different quality of relationship."[66] Similarly, Levin stresses the embodied character of listening in his four stages of self-development.[67] We will explore these issues and the relation between listening and ethics in much greater detail in chapter 7.

Meanwhile, we will conclude this chapter with a few more thoughts on what we might call the creative, or constitutive, power of listening.

"When does hearing succeed?" asks Heidegger. His answer: "We have heard when we belong to the matter addressed. . . . To belong to speech—this is nothing else than in each case letting whatever a letting-lie-before lays before us lie gathered in its entirety."[68] One way of thinking about this is that listening is a shared gathering. In other words, social community does not arise just because of speaking, but because of listening. We become one when we listen together—to an opera, to a politician, to the wind blowing through the trees, or to God. In Judaism, the daily prayer called the *Shema* calls worshippers to attend to unity by way of listening: "Shema, Israel, adonois elohein, adonois echod" (Hear, Israel, the Lord is God, God is one). This prayer is not simply an assertion of monotheism but, more plainly, is an injunction to listen. For it is in listening that we become, together. Not that we will come to agree, or to see things the same way, or even come to understand in the same way. But we share the experience of *being* listening—and up from the listening bubbles a speaking. "Every word of mortal speech speaks out of such a listening, and as such a listening. Mortals speak insofar as they listen."[69]

In this way, listening can be understood as a kind of dwelling place from where we offer our hospitality to others and the world. It is an invitation—a hosting. I don't have to translate your words into familiar categories or ideas. I don't have to "feel" what you feel, or "know" what it feels like to be you. "Were our hearing primarily and always only this picking up and transmitting of sounds, conjoined by several other processes, the result would be that the reverberation would go in one ear and out the other. That happens in fact where we are not gathered to what is addressed. . . . Hearing is primarily gathered hearkening. . . . We hear when we are 'all ears.' But 'ear' does not here mean the acoustical sense apparatus."[70] This kind of listening is perhaps what is called in Quakerism the "gathered meeting," where the assembled silent worshippers cease being individual selves and instead join together in "gathered hearkening." But what might such a listening be like? Perhaps it might be something like *listening being,* where when you are listening, really listening as opposed to hearing or interpreting, *you are* that listening, such that listening constitutes the very being of your being. Listening is what we are: *Homo audiens,* listening being. But this mode of listening being is dangerous because it is otherwise. It resists certainty, closure, categorization, and the imperatives of narrative flow: *chronos, logos,* and our insatiable appetite for the familiar. By interrupting our habitual conceptual systems, listening being enables us to step outside of the quotidian order of things, of knowledge, conviction, and fundamentalisms of all kinds. In this way, listening being involves a dangerous encounter with alterity, outside of understanding, beyond temporality. It twists free of the double helix of past and future and travels the Möbius plane of unknowing like a nomad, with no home except the present moment. The nowhere of the here and now. Listening being: a contingent discontinuity of incongruities and faith that opens a space of being in which we may hear things not otherwise audible: the absent, the broken, and the radically strange. So in contrast to rhetorical eloquence, which is itself a form of mastery, to *be listening* is to refuse to control or master. It is to hold lightly, if to hold at all. Actually, it is not to hold, not to grasp. No grasping, no holding. Being.

We began this chapter with a quote from Virginia Woolf's essay on words and craftsmanship, and we will leave it with quotes from one of her novels, *To The Lighthouse*. Published in 1927 (the same year as Heidegger's magnum opus *Being and Time*), the novel follows a family and their friends in a stream-of-consciousness fashion where the thoughts and speech of the characters blend, merge, and diverge in a musical chorale of listening, speaking, and being. In one scene, the various characters are at dinner together, and their thoughts and words are reported as if spoken aloud. What is interesting for us is the ways in which Woolf makes listening itself audible in the text. "Lily was listening; Mrs. Ramsay was listening; they were all listening."[71] As the characters alternate between speaking and listening, their inner words are examined, teased, and worried by one another. The main character, Mrs. Ramsay, floats in and out of the dinner conversation listening not merely to her companions' words, but to their tones and silences as well. The combined melody and rhythm of her companions' voices form a kind of open sky into which Mrs. Ramsay could, "like a hawk which lapses suddenly from its high station, flaunt and sink on laughter easily, resting her whole weight upon what at the other end of the table her husband was saying."[72] Later in the scene, one of the characters begins to recite a poem that brings a temporary pause in the babble of dinner conversation. Woolf's description of the space that opens up in the absence of table talk reminds me of a Mary Oliver verse in which the poem is likened to a flower "that wants to open itself, / like the door of a little temple, so that you might step inside and be cooled and refreshed, / and less yourself than part of everything."[73] It is just how, at this moment in the novel, that

Woolf describes the ways in which the poem gathers the listeners together in what Heidegger would call "hearkening attunement," a listening beyond the boundaries of self and other, inner and outer, meaning and nonsense:

> [T]he voices came to her very strangely, as if they were voices at a service in a cathedral, for she did not listen to the words. . . .
>
> The words . . . sounded as if they were floating like flowers on water out there, cut off from them all, as if no one had sent them, but they had come into existence of themselves. . . .
>
> She did not know what they meant, but, like music, the words seemed to be spoken by her own voice. . . . She knew, without looking round, that every one at the table was listening to the voice. . . .
>
> . . . [It was] as if this . . .were their own voice speaking.[74]

In conclusion, the holistic perspectives on language, thought, and listening described in this chapter offer us an opportunity for going beyond (but not dispensing with) a representational view of language that keeps us tied to atomism and the hierarchies of knowledge that make the everyday ordinary processes of communication seem obvious, if not entirely trivial. In the next chapter, we will begin to situate listening in relation to dialogue and social interaction by extending our inquiry to an examination of the phenomena of "inner" and "outer" speech.

COMMUNICATION AND A NICE
KNOCK-DOWN ARGUMENT

"I don't know what you mean by 'glory,'" Alice said.

Humpty Dumpty smiled contemptuously. "Of course you don't—till I tell you. I meant 'there's a nice knock-down argument for you!'"

"But 'glory' doesn't mean 'a nice knock-down argument,'" Alice objected.

"When I use a word," Humpty Dumpty said, in rather a scornful tone, "it means just what I choose it to mean—neither more nor less."

"The question is," said Alice, "whether you *can* make words mean so many different things."

"The question is," said Humpty Dumpty, "which is to be master—that's all."

—LEWIS CARROLL, *Through the Looking Glass*

Pathetic and bedridden with fever, I absorb the ringing voices of children at play in a land some seventy-five hundred miles from my own bed at home. Their shouts and hollers come from a dusty field just over the ivy-covered wall enclosing the guest house in Delhi, where I stay while teaching in India. Intermittent car horns, dog barks, screaming babies, and bizarre birdcalls punctuate the sound score throughout the day. At night, though, you would hardly know you were in a city of some 17 million souls, the quiet is so startling. Lying there listening in a feverish daze, I wonder if the chaotically joyful rumble of children at play sounds similar all over the world. The bubbling lightness of their laughter, the piercing staccato of high-pitched shouts and cries, the melodic rise and singsong fall of their teasing and play echo with the sound of all the other playground hijinks I've ever heard. But whether it is or isn't, one thing is certain: unlike the babbling music of children at play, the speech of adults will inevitably burst any illusion that "it's a small world after all."[1] Adults violently police the linguistic and physical boundaries of identity, nation-state, and tribe, and world history is saturated with wars, genocides, and occupations that legally and often violently banish the languages of the oppressed.

Whether it is by means of burned books, forced reeducation of children, banned or mandatory tongues, or the invisible death rays of shame and ridicule, the unholy alliance of language, identity, and power has been subject to repressive political machinations the world over. The ancient Greeks briefly banned Hebrew in the second century B.C.E., and in the twelfth century C.E. the pope prohibited vernacular (i.e., non-Latin) translations of the Bible. From the eighteenth to the twentieth centuries, the United States banned indigenous languages such as Diné, Hawaiian, and Lakota Sioux, among many others, in schools and government. In the mid-twentieth century, Franco's Spain forbade all tongues but Castilian. Throughout the world, the history of languages once or forever banned is astonishing: Armenian, Basque, Catalan, Gaelic, Irish, Korean, Kurdish, Parsi, Sami, Tamil, Turkish, Ukrainian, Warlpiri, Yiddish—and the list goes on and on, up to and including today. U.S. history past and present is filled with examples of what Chicana scholar Gloria Anzaldua calls "linguistic terrorism": "[I]f you want to really hurt me, talk badly about my language. Ethnic identity is twin skin to linguistic identity— I am my language."[2] There's probably no place on the planet that doesn't bear some terrible scar from the never-ending carnival of linguistic cruelty. During the slave trade in the Americas, kidnapped and enslaved Africans were intentionally separated from kin and other co-language speakers, and teaching slaves to read was illegal.

The United States has a two-hundred-year history of repeated (and failed) attempts to declare English the country's official language at the federal level, and since the early 1980s more than half the U.S. states have declared English the "official" rather than "de facto" language. While seemingly a small-minded yet innocuous form of legislation, these declarations have far-reaching implications for a number of public services such as medical and legal translation, bilingual education, and bilingual voting, and could ultimately overrule federal requirements for providing bilingual services in multilingual or majority non-English-speaking communities in places such as Brownsville, Texas, and Los Angeles, California. Another example of the lengths to which language can be employed as a political weapon was revealed when, in response to the fact that France did not support the United States in the hurry to war after 9/11, Congress ordered all House cafeteria menus to change the name of French fries to "freedom fries." Similarly, China, France, and Germany have recently forbidden the use of English words in certain contexts. And, as we will discuss later in the chapter, when a public school district in California with a majority black population called for the largely white teaching staff to learn to interact with students in African American Vernacular English (AAVE, also known as Ebonics), a national hullabaloo ensued. The idea that "street slang" or, at best, a "mere dialect" should have the same status as English in an American classroom rocked the nation. It was for many people impossible to accept the fact that languages are forever changing, let alone that AAVE is a legitimate language variety produced by historical forces and the social conditions of diaspora—comparable to the relationship of Yiddish to German, or even French, Spanish, and Italian to Latin.

But here another question emerges: what is the difference between a language and a dialect? Typically, so-called *languages* are mutually unintelligible—Spanish speakers don't understand Swahili and vice versa—whereas so-called *dialects* are more or less mutually intelligible. Whether you speak English in an AAVE or Jamaican dialect or with a Bronx accent, you're still speaking English. But it's really not that simple. For one thing, not all dialects are mutually intelligible. For example, a conversation between three native English speakers from, say, Ireland, Singapore, and Samoa may or may not be mutually intelligible. On the other hand, a Dane speaking Danish can converse quite comfortably with a Norwegian speaking Norwegian—even though they are speaking two entirely different languages. So what gives? Well, it's all about power, and as the Yiddish linguist Max Weinreich once said, "A language is a dialect with an army and navy." Adults use language at every level to mark status and reinforce hierarchy. And of course it's not just whether and how one speaks that describes who you are, but whether anyone even listens at all. There is, as described in chapter 1, a politics of listening.

One day I was at a large picnic party in Lodi Gardens, a beautiful public park in the middle of Delhi. Groups of families playing games and sitting together talking dotted the lawns surrounding ghostly ruins of an ancient Mughal fort. Our party was composed of about three dozen families, mostly Indian with a few foreigners mixed in, who were gathered around picnic blankets loaded with food. All of a sudden a hawk swooped down out of the sky to raid a plate of ham sitting on a picnic blanket that was also crowded with people. Then it happened a second time. A huge gray hawk just careened down out of the sky, skimmed the blanket, and then shot off upwards with a chunk of ham in its grip. Yes, in Delhi. In the middle of a party. One of the park's wild dogs, who had been feigning a snooze in the grass while secretly guarding the plate of ham, barked and charged at the hawk. Most of us went "Ohhhhhhh," marveling at the audacious daring and graceful athleticism of the bird. No one seemed mad or frightened. It was, apparently, a rare but not unheard of occurrence in Delhi, where hawks thrive in the city environs. For me, though, it was some kind of ominous precursor of what was to come next.

A little while later a small boy with dirty clothes and a grease pencil mustache approached our party to beg for money. He was a street performer, maybe five or six years old at most. At the time, I was standing talking to an American woman I had just met. Pretty much everyone ignored the boy, and no one gave him any money.[3] But when he approached the pair of us, the woman handed him her piece of chocolate cake. He wasn't happy, but he didn't refuse the food; he took it and glumly shuffled away. Perhaps distracted by the cake, the boy stumbled a bit too close to the wild dog, who barked, charged, and bit him. The boy screamed and then stood crying and rubbing his leg. But here's the thing. No one moved. Yes, everyone in our party stopped what they were doing and turned to look; but nobody did anything. When the cake giver and I ran over to check that he wasn't seriously injured (he wasn't) and to offer some comfort, the people in our party stared at us in frank disbelief.

At that moment I realized I was transgressing a social norm, but I went ahead anyway—he was a child, after all. But what struck me later about the situation was that, for most of the people at the party, *who* the boy was spoke louder than *what* he said—he was a beggar and hence someone largely unseen and unheard, and certainly untouched. To me (an American who had been in India all of two weeks) he was a little boy, and simply because of that fact he deserved the care and concern of adults. For most of the other people at the party—Indians and acculturated Europeans and Americans—he was a beggar, who, for that reason alone, did not warrant the care and concern of adults. But for every single one of us adults at the party, our actions were basically automatic and unquestioned, shaped by the values and assumptions of our culture. For an American woman, the boy's identity as a child took precedence over everything else. For the Indians and acculturated foreigners, the boy's identity as a beggar was foremost. And these reactions testify to the ways in which culture is so much more than values, ritual, custom, and belief—it lives inside us as we live it out in our everyday activities: communication *is* culture.

From the holist point of view of this book, there is an inescapable fiction behind the idea that one can carve up culture, language, thought, and communication into independent and separate phenomena. This way of thinking (or of organizing chapters in a book!) reflects the challenges of how speaking and writing unfold successively in linear time—one word, one phrase, one turn after another. As with other fields of inquiry, to make things more manageable, "logical," or "reasonable," we treat what we study atomistically as an object and break it down into separate parts to describe and understand them. But this creates an illusion that they are in fact separate—otherwise why would we need to separate them in the first place? So instead of thinking about culture, language, thought, and communication as independent processes, perhaps we can think of them as interdependent facets of a crystal prism. Seen from one angle, the color of "culture" radiates as iridescent blue. Twist the crystal slightly, and the color of "speech" glows with a fiery red. Thus, while the prism is "one" thing, each of its facets offers something different and unique. But the facets are not independent. They share a home in the whole of the crystal. So dividing this book into chapters as I have done, and leading from one to the next, creates an illusion that these processes are independent: that listening is separate from speech, that thought is separate from language, and that culture is separate from communication.

Communication

What is communication? Once again, it depends on who you ask. If you ask the linguist Noam Chomsky, you'll get an answer that denies any relationship between communication and language whatsoever. To Chomsky, language is a kind of mental organ, or innate "language faculty," that is distinct from and independent of communication. Chomsky flatly rejects the "view that the purpose of language is communication"[4] or that "the essence of language is communication."[5] To Chomsky, "Successful communication between Peter and Mary does not entail the existence of shared meanings or shared pronunciations in a public language (or a common treasure of thoughts or articulations of them)."[6] If you ask the philosopher Heidegger, on the other hand, you get something quite different: language and communication are the very ground of being itself. "Communication is never anything like a conveying of experiences, such as opinions or wishes, from the interior of one subject into the interior of another."[7]

But Chomsky and Heidegger aside, if you look in the dictionary today, you'll find communication defined as "an act or instance of transmitting," "information transmitted or conveyed, and "a process by which information is exchanged between individuals through a common system of symbols, signs, or behavior."[8] Thus, communication is largely conceived, both in everyday parlance and among scholars in many fields, with what in 1979 Michael Reddy called "the conduit metaphor," which envisions language in terms of a "sealed pipeline" or "conduit, transferring thoughts bodily from one person to another; . . . in writing and speaking, people insert their thoughts or feelings in the words; . . . words accomplish the transfer by containing the thoughts or feelings and conveying them to others; and . . . in listening or reading, people extract the thoughts and feelings once again from the words."[9] Reddy catalogues dozens of examples from everyday speech that reflect an underlying metaphorical structure of the conduit, such as "you can't get your concept across that way," or "that's a loaded statement," or "that sentence was filled with emotion."

In the United States, one of the first models to exert influence on succeeding generations of scholars was what is called the mathematical model of communication, first published in a paper written by the Bell (telephone) Labs engineer Claude Shannon in 1948. Basically, the model depicts communication as a systematic transmission of messages from a sender to a receiver through a channel. Originally published in a technical journal, the paper dealt with engineering problems such as information redundancy, entropy, error, capacity, noise, bandwidth, and feedback in the rapidly developing technologies of computers, telephones, and teletype machines.[10] And even though the paper contained many mathematical formulae, vectors, probability scores, logarithmic measures, and mathematical theorems which were clearly suited for machines rather than human beings, the mathematical theory of communication (expanded and republished in a book in 1963) came to influence not only the newly developing field of information science, but the fields of education, sociology, and psychology, as well as the newly burgeoning academic field of communication.

But the conduit metaphor did not originate in response to Shannon's mathematical model. In fact, Saussure's classic turn-of-the-century *Course in General Linguistics* contains a diagram that depicts communication as a conduit between two people facing each other, A and B, with one dotted line going from the middle of A's head, out his mouth, into B's head, and on to his brain, and a similar line going from the middle of B's head to A's head.[11] On the next page, Saussure includes a similar diagram, this time of a circuit, with speech as the transmitter and audition as the receiver.[12] Moreover, although Saussure distinguishes between language (*langue,* the system of signification) and speech (*parole,* the spoken utterance), the word "communication" does not appear in the index of his course. Communication seems to be simply presupposed.

Although both Saussure's semiotic and Shannon's mathematical models became templates for theory and research into a broad range of communication phenomena, such as broadcasting, public relations, mass persuasion, face-to-face conversation, debate, and public oration, by the late 1980s scholars were beginning to question the mechanistic approach to studying communication and the ideas that were smuggled in tacitly along with the conduit or transmission metaphor. Principal among these was the idea that communication is like a train on a track carrying "content" that can be measured, packaged, predicted, and controlled. Scholars began to question the many suppositions embedded in the conduit metaphor, such as the idea that content and meaning are relatively stable "objects" that can be sent and received with varying degrees of skill and success. It was not just that the metaphors described only one side of the highly complex social phenomenon known as communication, but also that they brought along a troubling set of ideas and assumptions.

For example, thinking of communication between people in terms of machines brings us before long to thinking of people as machines. Paulo Freire, the great Brazilian educator, wrote a critique of what he called "the banking model" of education—a double-scope integration that blends the metaphorical domains of finance and the conduit. In this model, it is assumed that teachers "deposit" information into the minds of students, who "retain" it at greater or lesser "rates"—some accumulate lots of interest, some little, some lose it entirely—and then go on to use that information in profitable ways. One problem with this metaphor, says Freire, is that it depicts students as passive recipients rather than active investigators, making the teacher "the Subject of the learning process, while the pupils are mere objects."[13] Further, Freire describes how the banking model not only undermines the agency of learners, but functions propagandistically to conceal how reality is not "contained" in the information deposited, but "is really a process, undergoing constant transformation," in which both students and teachers have agency.[14]

Drawing on the history of communication technologies ranging from the telegraph, the steam-driven newspaper press, the telephone, and radio and TV broadcasting, the American communication scholar James Carey gleaned important insights into the social dimensions of communication, particularly its role in sustaining community. As described in chapter 1, Carey noted an unnamed undertheorized aspect he called the "ritual view of communication," which "is directed not toward the extension of messages in space but toward the maintenance of society in time; not the act of imparting information but the representation of shared beliefs."[15] To Carey, communication is not a conduit but "a process whereby reality is produced, maintained, repaired, and transformed."[16] Consider, for a moment, a map of your home state. What information does the map provide? What activities are presumed? Does it tell you anything about the beauty of sunsets, the majesty of trees, or the colors of birds and flowers in the area? And if you are traveling on foot, or by horse, bicycle, or train, does the map tell you what you need to know? Or does the map presume that cars are at the center of our world? Does a provincial map in Indonesia describe different features than a map in Italy? As Carey says, "[T]here are no lines of latitude and longitude in nature, but by overlaying the globe with this . . . symbolic organization, order is imposed."[17] Thus, maps, as a human construction, are a means of bringing a shared world into existence. What would a map of your neighborhood look like drawn by your six-year-old neighbor? How about your grandmother's neighborhood when she was a child? Now consider the map of the world that hung on the wall in your elementary school classroom. What landmass is in the center of the map? Is north at the top of the map, toward the ceiling, or at the bottom, down toward the floor? What is the largest continent? How about the largest country? If you've ever seen a world map from a country far from your own, the likelihood is great that the map will look quite different from the one you are accustomed to seeing, because what a map of "the world" looks like depends on the culture. For example, Australian world maps look upside down to most Americans. As the semanticist Alfred Korzybski said in the 1930s, a map is not the territory—it says as much about the maker as it does about the territory it presumably depicts. The map we draw reflects and creates the world we live in. As we described in chapters 2 and 3, categories aren't objectively existent in the external world; they are human, and as such, they are culturally specific.

Thus, our maps, like our definitions, categories, metaphors, and concepts, situate things in relation to other things, thereby invoking a skein of associations, background assumptions, understandings, values—in essence, whole theories about the world. In other words, communication is far more than a semiotic or transmission system of signs and symbols that represent objects and concepts in the external and internal worlds. Rather, the human "world" comes into being in communication—it is the way humans collaboratively construct our shared social worlds. What this means is that whatever might really and truly exist on the planet, in the skies, and below the seas, there is no human vantage point outside of communication with language—anything and everything we can say about the world, or about language and communication, must be said with, within, and through language. Thus, communication is not a tool or an instrument that "reflects" or "represents" or "stands for" objects and concepts "out there" in the world; it is a creative event, not a thing-like object. It is a process, not an object, or tool. Communication, in other words, is not merely an instrument for accomplishing goals, it is the way we do human being. As Hans Georg Gadamer, one of Heidegger's students, wrote, "wherever words assume a mere sign function, the original connection between speaking and thinking . . . has been changed into an instrumental relationship."[18] That is, we no more use language than it uses us. It is how we dwell in the world, and we cannot live outside it. As Humboldt noted nearly two hundred years ago, language "[i]n itself . . . is no product (*Ergon*), but an activity (*Energeia*)."[19] And, as the communication scholar John Stewart more recently put it, "Languaging is the way humans 'do' understanding, and in the process collaboratively 'build,' 'remake,' or 'modify' worlds."[20]

Okay. I hear you, dear reader. You're not yet convinced. So let's take something specific—say the stars in the night sky. Late one warm summer night, two people are out walking along an open country road, and one of them points and says, "Oh look, there's the Big Dipper." The pair stop to marvel at the sky, and the other person says, "Did you know that American slaves called the Big Dipper the Drinking Gourd and used it to navigate their way north?" And then the first speaker replies, "Oh, so that's what the phrase 'the Drinking Gourd' stands for. I never knew that." So what is the "Big Dipper?" From a semiotic atomist perspective, words are signs that stand for things in the "real" world. You might concede that whether you call it the Big Dipper or the Drinking Gourd, at the end of the day it's a symbol of freedom, or an index pointing north, or just the name for a constellation of stars up in the sky, or you might note that many cultures have created whole theophanies out of it. You'd say that at bottom, no matter what you call it, the words are simply linguistic signs representing some nonlinguistic stars up in the sky, casting language and reality as two separate entities—language being a tool that we use to stand in for objects in the world.

A holist perspective, in contrast, might note that for several millennia at least, people have been picking out patterns in the sky that can be seen from their particular vantage point as human beings on planet earth, identifying them as objects, and then calling them things like the Big Dipper or the Drinking Gourd so they can navigate in the dark on their way to freedom in a new world, tell stories about the ancestors, teach children astronomy, or do lots of other great stuff. But whatever way you look at it, you would note that the "idea" of the Big Dipper is a human invention, it is a "world" brought into being through language. After all, what is a constellation? It is a group of stars—we recognize Sirius in the constellation Canis Major, Betelgeuse in the constellation Orion. But what is a star? It is the name we give not to the thing, but to the idea of the thing, and this idea is woven into a fabric of stories, constructs, and metaphors, a whole interconnected web of meanings that make up a culture. We cannot really separate the name from the idea. Orion, Cassiopeia, Big Dipper, Drinking Gourd. Lots of bright lights. Patterns are observed and named and thus connected to stories, meanings, ideas, relationships. So what happens when the names disappear? What is lost is not the thing "out there," but a thread in the layered tapestry of meanings that make up a culture. And when the threads are unwoven, the tapestry is changed. Consider the "threads" of an online electronic discussion—if a link is broken, the whole fabric of the dialogue changes: responses to prior statements are lost, references are obscured, and definitions and clarifications disappear. And this doesn't just happen online. In 2009, the artist and writer Barbara Bash noted that the *Oxford Junior Dictionary* had replaced several dozen words in its newest edition; gone were words such as "acorn," "beaver," "bramble," "cheetah," "gerbil," "heron," "lark," "minnow," "newt," "piglet," "panther," "raven," "sycamore," "thrush," "willow." Disappeared. Replaced with "words they feel our technology-driven children need more—like *database, chat-room, analogue, broadband, bullet point,* etc."[21]

But, we might wonder along with John Shotter, "Why are we so blind to these processes? How do we continually fail to notice our own hand in the creation of our own worlds?"[22] Perhaps it is because we have become so immersed in the atomist representational view of language that we cannot see, or hear, our own doings. We have frozen language into a thing, making it a system, or a machine, and ourselves its hapless "users." And, by the way, what's the difference between a drug "user" as addict, or a social media "user" as consumer? Is there really a difference? And just who, incidentally, is using and consuming who? As Humboldt inveighed: "One must free oneself of the notion . . . that language can be separated from that which it designates."[23] Thus, any answer to the question, What is communication? will contain background ideas about meaning, human agency, and culture. Which brings us to the question, What is meaning and where does it come from? Is meaning *in* the words we speak? Or is it in our heads and transported across to others in words? Or is it something that we invent, improvisationally, creating what Humboldt called infinite uses from finite means?

Consider a conversation at a dinner party where one of the guests utters the phrase "I'm cold" and wraps her arms around her chest. What could it mean? Is she merely reporting her subjective state to the other guests? Or is it something else—perhaps a complaint or even a request to close the window, turn up the heat, put another log on the fire, or turn down the air conditioning. Or perhaps the two words are a covert signal to her host, indicating "It's time for me to go," or perhaps a more nuanced "Move a little closer, won't you?" Needless to say, "it is probably impossible to utter anything in conversation that has only one interpretation."[24] Instead of seeing meaning as a content contained in language, an object carried by words, a constitutive holistic approach to communication sees meaning as a collaborative creation of interlocutors employing what Roberts and Bavelas call semantic collaboration—a creative activity that we do together to make our shared social worlds: "'language' is an abstraction; it is realized only in its actual and dynamic form, communication."[25]

This holistic view of communication as a generative and creative process can be traced back to the ancient Indian grammarians, who, while espousing a different metaphysic than contemporary communication scholars, nevertheless theorized something close to what we might call a constitutive rather than representational view of language and communication. As we discussed in the last chapter, "ancient India developed . . . a profound theory of speech and meaning: the universe is not a thing but an expression; it is itself a kind of act of speech, perpetually sounding forth the nature of the unchanging God. Human beings experience sound and meaning as separate phenomena, but they are really just two branches, artificially divided by the limitations of everyday consciousness, of that unending Reality."[26] And the Euro-American idea that communication constitutes culture—that it is not merely an instrument or symbolic tool—can be traced back at least to Humboldt, who describes how "languages are not really means for representing already known truths but are rather instruments for discovering previously unrecognized ones."[27] And although at any given moment we may have a finite set of the colors of our culture and language to paint with, we are free to create not just new designs, but new colors as well. And although communication is infinitely variable, every word is inextricably related to the whole and "causes the whole of language to which it belongs to resonate and the whole world-view that underlies it to appear. . . . All human speaking is finite in such a way that there is laid up within it an infinity of meaning to be explicated."[28]

That is to say, communication, meaning, language, and thought are public and social because they are inextricably bound up with the history of every utterance ever spoken. As the Russian literary theorist Mikhail Bakhtin wrote, there is no biblical Adam, and as we discussed in chapter 3, at least since Humboldt linguists have made much of the fact that language is a finite resource from which humans can create infinite creations—anyone can, at any time, create a sentence that most likely, no one has ever heard before. But there is a residue of atomism in the way this idea of infinite linguistic generativity takes hold of our imaginations, to conceal the profoundly social dimensions of the shared worlds that all languages create. What is lost is the noninstrumental *Energia*, "this living, reactive, responsive, function of our talk that has been ignored in our representational, mechanistic approaches to meaning."[29]

In the last chapter we explored how language shapes thought via schemas, cognitive constructs, categories, relationships, and so forth, just as thought, in turn, shapes language through metaphor, framing, double-scope integration, and linguistic invention and change. Thus, meaning making does not just happen privately, but rather it is always in dialogue with language and thereby culture. In this sense, as Heidegger notes, language speaks me as much as I speak it. And, as Humboldt noted, "however internal language may altogether be, it yet [it] has at the same time an independent outer existence that exerts dominion against man himself."[30] Thus, meanings are never fixed or final; their discovery awaits. And this brings us to the second aspect of communication, its dialogic nature, which is always in conversation with inner and outer voices and past, present, and future talk. All language, whether spoken aloud or silently, whether written as literature or as history or science, is inherently dialogic. "The word is not a thing, but rather the eternally mobile, eternally changing medium of dialogical intercourse. It never coincides with a single consciousness or a single voice."[31]

The Dialogic

We have become accustomed to hearing, in the English word "dialogue," *dia-* as dual or two and *logos* as speech or argument. Hence we typically think about dialogue as two or more people speaking together, exchanging observations and ideas back and forth. But an etymological listening also hears in *dia-* the Greek prefix for through, across, or by way of, and in *logos* the Greek for speaking and listening, language and thought. Thus, if we listen closely, we may hear an echo of an idea about dialogue as the way through, or by way of, listening, thinking, and speaking. And something like this way of thinking emerged with early twentieth-century Russian scholars who were highly influenced by Humboldt. When the holistic model of language study was left behind in European and American linguistics, it briefly flourished in early twentieth-century Russia among an innovative and interdisciplinary group of scholars who explored topics including philosophy, poetics, psychology, art and literature, language, and politics. Although the school lasted only a brief period due to Stalinist political oppressions, the ideas planted during this time have influenced generations of scholars. Most relevant to our interests here are the ways in which some of these scholars, mainly Bakhtin, Voloshinov, Vygotsky, Luria, and Jakubinsky, launched a thoroughgoing critique of atomistic linguistics (which they called "objectivist"), developing a set of ideas about the inherent dialogicality of language.

Bakhtin theorized that all speakers are always already engaged in social dialogue with other speakers, arguments, claims, and conversations and that, moreover, no utterance is or can ever be disentangled from the "thousands of dialogic threads" that make up the social dialogue.[32] Thus, all speakers and listeners are, without exception, always in conversation with past, present, and future speakers and listeners. "In short, dialogism's utterance is far from an isolated act of a sovereign individual. It isn't even a duet between two speakers. It is more like an ensemble in which the simultaneous interplay of multiple, different discourses—distant and proximal, already spoken and not-yet-spoken—produce meaning at the moment."[33]

As communication, the dialogic word is not an object, it is an energy, a living vital force, *élan vital*. Because of these always already existing and infinite future meaning possibilities, all communicative acts are always already vibrating with traces or echoes of the resonance of other relations. That is, the universe of communication processes look not like empty space so much as a network of crisscrossing lines (like the traces of thousands of airline jet plumes overlapping in the sky, or perhaps like a densely woven spiderweb with millions of connections), any one of which might be drawn into a new set of relations at any moment. Furthermore, like Indra's web, the nodes of intersecting relations vibrate or pulsate as new nodes of connection arise and pass away, though none ever truly pass away, some echo always remains. Thus, the "saying" of language always already "is." "Every participant in the conversation arrives there with a repertoire of textual elements, as a result of learning to speak his or her own language—a conceptual scaffolding made up of words, phrases, turns of speech, metaphors, anecdotes, all of which are there because of the distillation, stored in language in the memory of participants, of their personal and collective history of previous interactions."[34]

Consider how one of the greatest pleasures of friendship is the invention of a special language of inside jokes, references, and shorthand. One of the marvels of communication is the delight we take in shared references, be they to literature, politics, music, or even stupid television jingles. Are any of these phrases familiar? What images do they conjure? "I am not a crook," "ROTFLMAO," "All happy families resemble one other. Each unhappy family is unhappy in its own way," "Straight outta Compton," "It depends on what is is," "Oll Korrect," "I can haz cheeseburger?," "Families is where our nation finds hope, where wings take dream," "I love you like a fat kid loves cake." Regardless of whether these phrases make you yawn, cross your eyes, laugh, or cry, there is a kind of fellowship created when we share a language with others, and for some people, the more obscure the shared referent, the greater the pleasure; for we are everything we have heard, said, and read throughout our lives. And these cultural memes influence us no less than our ancestral genes. But when we think of dialogue from a representational perspective, we lose sight of these dimensions of communication. And when we think of dialogue as call and response, question and answer, speaking and listening, we are employing a linear spatial model that conceives of speech acts as a series of separate individual utterances that we volley back and forth like a tennis ball: utterance A is followed by utterance B, and if by chance one of us misunderstands or misspeaks, we pick up the ball and resume the volley.

In this way, the transmission view depicts dialogue in spatial terms, wherein not just content, but time itself, moves in one direction at a time—from past to present to future. Echoes of spatiality can also be heard in metaphors for dialogue such as "point," "position," "foundation," and "floor," as well as in "face-to-face," "taking sides," "back channeling," "uptake," and "triangulation," to name but a few examples. But these distinctions between "positions" lose some of their relevance when we think about dialogue from a more holistic perspective that can twist free of simple binaries such as speaker/listener or inner/outer or before/after, which confine our thinking and limit our understanding of the complex phenomenon we call communication. For a dialogic perspective also allows for the displacement of time and place. Bakhtin invented a term, the "chronotope," to describe the complex interrelationships between time and space in literature. Bakhtin's portmanteau combines time (*chronos*) and place (*topos*) to describe the temporal power of place—be it a road, a castle, a threshold, a square—each "space" reverberates with echoes of historical contingency. The dialogicality of communication means that our words with others stretch far into the past and into the future, and into worlds both familiar and strange. In this view, language reverberates with the echoes of every utterance ever spoken, or what Bakhtin calls "the internal dialogism of the word."[35]

Today, even contemporary scholars who are developing new and innovative theories of collaborative joint dialogic action appear to be confined to a linear spatial model of communication. In this scholarship, listeners and speakers are understood to be conarrators who, moment by moment, collaborate to mutually make meaning together. But even these newer models remain limited by linear spatial conceptions of speaking and listening, wherein, for example, utterance is followed by response, which is then followed by confirmation—back and forth in the space between speakers and listeners. But the metaphor of spatiality is perhaps nowhere more firmly embedded in our thinking than in relation to inner thought and outer speech. Consider, for example, this clever scene from the 1977 Woody Allen movie *Annie Hall*, where two mutually attracted and newly introduced single New York intellectuals are standing on a balcony drinking white wine together. Leaning back against the railing, Annie and Alvy banter nervously, while at the same time their thoughts are projected on the screen as subtitles. Thus, the audience, but not the characters, is given privileged access to each interlocutor's internal and external speech. Table 2 transcribes an excerpt from the soundtrack alongside the subtitles projected simultaneously on the screen.

This amusing scene depicts how the two characters maintain an interior dialogue with themselves as well as an exterior dialogue with each other. It is as if there are at least three conversations going on simultaneously—Alvy with Annie, Alvy with Alvy, and Annie with Annie. But even this is too limited, for there are many absent others also addressed in Annie and Alvy's speech and thought. Moreover, the characters' thoughts are depicted as "inner"

Table 2 *Annie Hall* balcony scene

Spoken words	Written subtitles
Annie says: Well, I—I—I would—I would like to take a serious photography course.	*While Annie thinks:* He probably thinks I'm a yo-yo.
Alvy says: Photography's interesting, 'cause, you know, it's—it's a new art form, and a, uh, a set of aesthetic criteria have not emerged yet.	*While Alvy thinks:* I wonder what she looks like naked?
Annie says: Aesthetic criteria? You mean, whether it's a good photo or not?	*While Annie thinks:* I'm not smart enough for him. Hang in there.
Alvy says: The—the medium enters in as a condition of the art form itself.	*While Alvy thinks:* I don't know what I'm saying—she senses I'm shallow.
Annie says: Well, well, I . . . to me—I . . . I mean, it's—it's—it's all instinctive, you know. I mean, I just try to uh, feel it, you know? I try to get a sense of it and not think about it so much.	*While Annie thinks:* God, I hope he doesn't turn out to be a schmuck like the others.
Alvy says: Still, still, you need a set of aesthetic guidelines to put it in social perspective, I think.	*While Alvy thinks:* Christ, I sound like FM radio. Relax.

speech (talking with themselves) and their spoken words as "external" speech (talking with each other). Thus, the boundaries between inner and outer are neatly, though whimsically, drawn. And if we're paying attention, it leads us to ask different questions about listeners and speakers, such as, Are they one and the same? How are they different? Is the inner voice in my head the same as the one outside? How about my thoughts? Are they the same as speech, or different? And when I'm "talking to myself," who is listening?

Inner Speech

From an atomist perspective, inner speech is often characterized as "self-talk," "hearing oneself think," or "silent speech." But from a holist perspective, the distinction between inner and outer speech is, not surprisingly, quite a bit

blurrier than we might first imagine. Scholars in the Soviet school of psychology theorized both the existence and the dialogic nature of what Lev Vygotsky
identified as inner speech. Vygotsky demonstrated how inner speech develops
first as an egocentric self-talk that children address to themselves and that is
essential to the development of their minds and their acquisition of language.
As Frank E. X. Dance writes, "[S]poken language has present in it an active
residue of the functions of the communication, vocalization, and speech behaviors that developmentally precede spoken language in the child."[36] Vygotsky
also demonstrated the ways in which children learn language through an
"outside-in" process that begins with listening in the womb. First when we
are neonates, and then we are infants and later children, our minds develop
as we gradually "internalize" the utterances of others' language such that it
becomes "ours." In experiments with children, Vygotsky found that when
problem solving, younger children aged three to five tended to talk to themselves, externally verbalizing questions, ideas, and suggestions as a means to
orient their thoughts and solve problems.

But as children develop their cognitive and linguistic skills, their external
self-talk (which Vygotsky calls "egocentric speech") becomes increasingly
elliptical and rare. "The decreasing vocalization of egocentric speech denotes a
developing abstraction from sound, the child's new faculty to 'think words'
instead of pronouncing them."[37] Thus, "inner" speech is born of the child's
"external" speech, making the boundaries between inside and outside perme-
able and, at times, indistinct. Consider, for a moment—when an infant in the
womb listens to the vibrations of her mother's voice, is the sound coming from
"outside" or "inside" the infant? Is the mother's voice "inside" or "outside"? As
with a hologram, the vibrations from the mother's voice ripple throughout her
body and that of her baby—each waveform containing a part of the whole. In
a beautiful image of the holistic perspective on the dialogic dimensions of
mind and language, Vygotsky writes, "Consciousness is reflected in a word as
the sun in a drop of water. A word relates to consciousness as a living cell
relates to a whole organism, as an atom relates to the universe."[38]

Thus, even the "innermost" thoughts in our head are permeated with
words from "outside," and these "exterior" voices echo and resonate in our
most "interior" thoughts. This is what James Carey means when he describes
how thought is public and social—that our "innermost" thoughts can only
be revealed by way of language that derives from "outside," forever obscuring
the boundaries between inside and out. There is, in each of us, an internal
Greek chorus that speaks silently but is "completely dialogic, totally saturated

with the evaluations of the possible listener or audience, even if the speaker has no idea whatever of this listener."[39] Returning to the *Annie Hall* balcony scene, we can hear layers of this chorus, when Annie first performs a doubtful voice ("I'm not smart enough for him") and then follows with encouragement ("Hang in there"). Thus, there is now not merely one "inner" Annie, but two—a critic and a fan. We hear a similar "inner" duet when Alvy first critiques his "outer" speech ("I sound like FM radio") but responds with an encouraging word ("Relax"). Thus, if we consider the dialogicality of all speech, when we move from the exteriority of the room to the interiority of the two people, we might hear something altogether different and more complex—a blending of inner and outer. This is what leads Voloshinov to describe the "double-sided position of the word . . . [A]ll intonation is oriented in two directions."[40] Voloshinov continues, "Human speech is a two-sided phenomenon . . . always oriented towards another, a listener, even if, in reality, the other person is not present."[41]

One question that might arise at this point pertains to the relationship between inner speech and thought. Are they one and the same, or different? If different, how so? Basically, inner speech is similar to, but at the same time different from, both thinking and external speech. "Inner speech gives rise to verbal thought and its process may augment nonlinguistic thought, but thought can exist apart from inner speech."[42] Voloshinov describes inner speech as a process by which "[i]n understanding a word or combination of words we, as it were, transfer these words from the external (heard or read) speech of another person into our own internal speech; there we produce them again and again, surround them with other words, and find for them a particular place in [the] general speech flow of our consciousness."[43] Furthermore, inner speech in adults does not consist only of self-talk, it also plays important roles in directing, structuring, or planning our activities—both speech and nonspeech. Russian theorists such as Vygotsky, Jakubinsky, and Luria make a point of differentiating thinking and verbal thinking. "For Vygotsky and Luria human thought is always *verbal,* but it is not literally thinking in words. It is dependent on language in that it draws upon word meanings and the organizing principles of language, but it is not constrained structurally to *words* only."[44] That is to say, much, but not all, of our thinking is linguistic thinking, and just how much is or is not linguistic depends partly on the individual person and partly on the culture. To the French phenomenologist Henri Bergson, inner speech is the motor accompaniment of speech, but is not identical with it: inner speech "is to speech itself what the rough sketch is to the finished picture."[45]

Vygotsky's model of inner speech stipulates two additional and important points. First, just as inner speech is not identical with thought, neither is it "the interior aspect of external speech—it is a function in itself."[46] "Inner speech . . . is closer to thought than external speech, so it encompasses more rudimentary levels of verbal processing than those forms of external communication that have been encoded for another person."[47] And one of the crucial functions of inner speech, according to Vygotsky, is to bring thoughts to completion, or, to put it another way, to give birth to thought. That is to say, that speech is what makes thoughts possible. "But while in external speech thought is embodied in words, in inner speech words die as they bring forth thought. Inner speech is to a large extent thinking in pure meanings. It is a dynamic, shifting, unstable thing, fluttering between word and thought."[48] The transition from thought to speech is, according to Vygotsky, "no easy matter."[49]

If, by now, you have noticed a resonance or some similarity between Vygotsky, Humboldt, and Bhartrhari, you are not far off. Like inner speech, Bhartrhari's "[s]phota leaps into consciousness with an unaccountable burst."[50] Similarly, Humboldt theorized that "thought, like a lightning-flash or concussion, collects the whole power of representation into a single point, and shuts out everything else."[51] But how does this actually happen? How do words come to be? Building on Vygotsky's work, the Soviet psychologist Alexander Luria developed a five-stage process to describe the transformation of thought to speech that is uncannily similar to Bhartrhari's three-stage process.[52] Both Bhartrhari's and Luria's models describe the speech process as a "transformation of consciousness," wherein the initial stages of speech are an integrated gestalt without temporal sequence or differentiated parts. And they both resonate with Vygotsky's observation that "in inner speech, words die as they bring forth thought."[53]

In short, neither Luria's nor Bhartrhari's model of speech production depicts a simple conversion of thoughts into words, but rather, both involve a complex transformation from nonlinguistic conceptual intuitions that are gradually transformed into full-blown, grammatically correct speech. Thus, rather than merely reflecting pre-existing thoughts, the process of speaking actually brings thoughts to fruition. As Luria writes, "There is every reason to agree with Vygotsky that thought is completed, rather than embodied in speech and that the transition from thought into speech involves several stages."[54] Luria's five-stage transformation process moves through three intermediate stages that become increasingly grammatically complex before arriving at the last stage of the expanded utterance.[55]

In the first stage of both models, speech as we would know it is latent and as yet unborn. Bhartṛhari calls the first stage *paśyanti,* wherein *sphoṭa,* as an undifferentiated whole, initiates the transformation to speech. "[P]aśyantī, speech is the speech-principle in which the capacity for revelation is inherent, but not explic[i]t. . . . It is only identical with consciousness or perception in its intrinsic form."[56] Bhartṛhari writes, "The inner principle called 'speech' which exists egg-like, evolving into speech-activity, assumes sequence through its parts."[57] Luria's model begins with an initial motivation, such as "a demand . . . , a desire for informational communication . . . , and a desire for clearer formulations of one's thought."[58] Table 3 outlines the stages of Luria's and Bhartṛhari's process. A textual description of the remaining stages follows.

Like Luria's first and second stages, which he describes as "a psychological structure that still remains largely a mystery," Bhartṛhari's *paśyanti* is in non-linear and nonsequential form; it is "neither a 'previous' nor 'a subsequent,'" and is, moreover, 'without parts." According to Coward, because *paśyanti* is "beyond the level of differentiated cognition, it is impossible to define it in word-sentences. It is at the level of direct intuition and therefore must finally

Table 3   A comparison of Luria's and Bhartṛhari's models

Stages of speech	Luria	Bhartṛhari	Description
1st/1st	Motive	*Paśyanti*	Motivation, curiosity, desire for information, connection, or expression. Undifferentiated gestalt. Nonlinear, nonsequential.
2nd/1st	Semantic set	*Paśyanti*	Intuition of pure meaning. Holistic integration. Inexpressible semantic relationships such as causality, inception, function.
3rd/2nd	Schema	*Madhyamā*	Elementary elliptical grammatical forms. Subject/object relationships.
4th/2nd	Syntax	*Madhyamā*	Sequential ordering of grammatical structures.
5th/3rd	Utterance	*Vaikharī*	Gramatically correct speech. The word is revealed through sound.

be understood through experience."[59] This is similar to Luria's stage two, which he calls the semantic set, and which begins with an integrated gestalt of semantic relationships such as causality, inception, and function that is as yet inexpressible. Like Luria, Bhartṛhari also stipulates a motive (perhaps instinct, perhaps desire) as the origin of this "intuition of . . . pure meaning. . . . [T]here is present at this [paśyanti] level a kind of 'going-out' or desire from expression."[60] Pillai describes the holistic integration of this stage: "while an object is perceived, one feels that its perception is through its parts. However, in all these, apprehension of parts, or of subject-object difference in cognition is only apparent, it is only an aid to an integral perception."[61] A wonderful example of this process is given by Vygotsky, who describes seeing a boy in a blue shirt running down the street. "Thought, unlike speech, does not consist of separate units. When I wish to communicate the thought that today I saw a barefoot boy in a blue shirt running down the street, I do not see every item separately: the boy, the shirt, its blue color, his running, the absence of shoes. I conceive of all this in one thought, but I put it into separate words."[62]

Bhartṛhari's second stage, madhyamā (the middle), shares much in common with Luria's third and forth stages, which begins the sequential ordering of grammatical forms and the elementary subject/object relationships, followed by the penultimate stage, which generates elliptical grammatical structures. In the madhyamā stage, "speech has already become a dynamic process, and is mental. It is linked to an object or an idea, and has already reached the stage of concretization on the level of the mind. But it has not yet been uttered."[63] Similarly, Luria describes his second and third stages as where "the subject begins to understand what it is that is to be transformed into an utterance."[64] This transformation process is a mystery, still little understood. To Bhartṛhari, the word in the mind "causes" speech sounds. But this is not a mechanical, but a kind of chemical, or energetic, cause. Bhartṛhari employs the metaphor of fire to describe the process by which the word "causes" speech. "Just as the light which is in the fire-stick acts as the cause for further lights, similarly the Word which is in the mind is the cause of speech-sounds."[65] But this "cause" is a transformation, not a transfer—the way water transforms into ice, or vapor, or fire transforms wood into flame.

As you may have noticed by now, one has to deliberately strive not to use words that express the conduit metaphor when speaking of communication—words such as "transmission," "transfer," "convey," and so on. It is difficult because of how saturated our thinking is with transmission and conduits.

But it is possible to think of communication processes as a kind of sharing rather than as a kind of sending, just as we might think of sharing (but not sending) a bowl of soup, a poem, or a beautiful sunset. To think of these things—soup, poem, sunset—in the conduit mode of transfer reduces all of it, the beauty, the harmony, the sharing, to the barest possible minimum, over-simplifying and reducing everything to the physical/spatial dimension and ignoring everything else. It obscures how both integral and gestalt-like the processes of sharing and communication are. Vocate describes Luria's third stage as "that phenomenon we have all experienced of knowing what we mean or intend as a gestalt, but are unable to express because we have not yet given it a linear or sequential ordering, that is, the structure of syntax."[66] For Luria, "the thought, which includes meanings that are comprehensible to the speaker but are not yet expanded enough to be understood by others, is con-verted into a schema through the apparatus of inner speech." [67]

Bhartṛhari calls the third and final stage of speech *vaikharī*, "when speech is an uttered realization. It is articulate speech."[68] *Vaikharī* is comparable to Luria's fourth and fifth stages of motor speech and expanded speech utter-ance. Bhartṛhari describes how the conceptualized *sphoṭa* is "fixed to a spe-cific meaning and then through the instrumentality of the speech-sounds produced [*sic*] through (their) causes."[69] As with Vygotsky's conception of the utterance as a completion rather than a reflection of thought, Bhartṛhari describes the word as being "revealed" by sound. "A speaker often takes sev-eral minutes to disclose one thought. In his mind the whole thought is pres-ent at once, but in speech it has to be developed successively. A thought may be compared to a cloud shedding a shower of words. Precisely because thought does not have its automatic counterpart in words, the transition from thought to word leads through meaning."[70]

Now let us return to the balcony scene where Annie and Alvy are talking together in dialogue. Notice first how the characters' thoughts are projected on the screen as if they were full-blown, grammatically correct sentences. It is as if their thoughts were a kind of inner speech minus vocalization. The con-tent of the thoughts is not implausible (who among us hasn't had such inse-cure thoughts), but they are depicted as having utter syntactic clarity. Part of what makes the scene funny, and so familiar, is how absurdly contradictory the "inner" and the "outer" voices are—the vocalized outer "Alvy" is smooth and sophisticated, whereas the silent inner "Alvy" swings from puerile curios-ity to scathing self-criticism. In other words, this scene describes how the "I" itself is multiple, forever occupying two and often more positions at the same time. It also demonstrates how a conversation between just "two" people invariably involves multiple and often competing perspectives.

But at the same time, the *Annie Hall* scene also reflects the atomist perspective that thoughts are represented by speech, rather than given birth to in speech. And this brings us to the matter of time. At any given moment, our thoughts, actions, and interactions are swirling with eddies and currents from past, present, and future time. As we will examine more carefully in the next chapter, once we are born, everything we experience is filtered through what we have already experienced, and thus the river of our lives grows wider, deeper, stronger as we age. Alvy's reference to FM radio, for example, bore a significance in 1977 when the film was released that is hard to imagine in 2014. Though it began in the 1940s, commercial FM radio only really began to compete with the more popular AM radio in the early 1970s, and it had hitherto been associated primarily with class, prestige, and sophistication. So Alvy's self-criticism that he sounded "like FM radio" (meaning that he sounded pretentious, as if he were putting on airs) would have been addressed to an audience from the past who still held, or even inherited, those earlier associations from others, such as working-class parents and neighborhood friends. Similarly, Annie's memories of other boyfriends as "shmucks" call up a past previously shared with others, now being projected into the future.

And as we discussed in the last chapter, some memories cling to us in the form of embodied habits—the way your hand and arm curve to reach the mouse on the left, forgetting that you are at that moment at a public computer, where the mouse is on the right. Your bodyself has lost track of the present and has instead been pulled by a strong current of the past. Sometimes we will react to some small criticism by a spouse, friend, or coworker as if we were three years old and being chastised by our angry mother. It all filters together, in and out of the past and present, into the future, and back to the past. And this process begins at the moment of perception, when, as we described in chapter 4, the very categories, schemas, and associations required for perception are social—they are acquired through learning the language and ways of our culture, where "every concrete perception . . . is already a synthesis, made by memory, of an infinity of 'pure perceptions.'"[71] And the learning never stops. As long as we live, we are constantly acquiring new and revising, reinforcing, or transforming older perceptual patterns, memories, and associations. These accumulated memories were called by the Russian scholars the "apperceptive mass," and they shape how we perceive and understand the world. Like a jumbled attic of long-lost toys, books, pictures, and memorabilia, our apperceptive mass is filled with things forgotten, yet still present. "[O]ur reception and understanding of another's . . . speech are apperceptive—that is, they are determined not only . . . by our actual momentary stimulation by another's speech but also by the entire range of our antecedent internal and external experiences and ultimately by the entire contents of our psyche at the moment of listening."[72] Thus, time is not a linear movement but a recursive spiral that draws from the past to create the future. We will examine these ideas in far more detail in the next chapter, but for now it is enough to note how when anyone, from everyday folks to artists and even scholars, talks about "dialogue" we tend to think of time in linear spatial terms where speaking and listening happen separately as distinct and temporally separated phenomena.

For example, let's go back to Annie and Alvy talking on the balcony. The camera follows the audio soundtrack as the conversation moves back and forth almost like a tennis match, serve, return, lobby, and so forth. No interruptions, no overlaps, just a simple fluid movement back and forth—the dialogic process appears to be a relatively straightforward process of succession, wherein one person speaks at a time and each utterance is followed by a responding utterance, and so on. But of course dialogue is rarely so neat and tidy. Often people speak at the same time, interrupt one another, think about something else while others are speaking, refer to earlier points or memories. But the spatial back-and-forth image is deeply engrained—even forward-thinking figures such as Bakhtin and Voloshinov, while launching brilliant campaigns against the tyranny of monologic positivism, nevertheless frequently employ spatial metaphors to theorize dialogic interaction. The spatial bias in our investigations into dialogue continues today. For example, even in their critique of the speech-centricity of speech act theory, Roberts and Bavelas employ a spatial metaphor to describe dialogic interaction. They write, "Our criticism is that the hearer is still a minor player . . . who simply catches (or misses) the ball that is thrown."[73] Similarly, DeSouza, DaSilveira, and Gomes contend that "dialogical relationships are brought to a spatial dimension, emphasizing simultaneity, juxtaposition and discontinuity of the voices,"[74] while the media theorist Ong describes the temporal experience of sound as a spatially linear phenomenon that "exists only when it is going out of existence."[75]

But here's the question: does it ever really expire? Leaving aside questions about how far sound waves can travel and echo across space in time, does the sound of language in fact die? What are you hearing right now as you read/

hear these words? And what are those voices from the past that speak, from time to time, in your head? And what about the thoughts and music one hears while silently riding the bus or sipping a coffee? There is, in sonic resonance and sympathetic vibration, a kind of simultaneity—sound does not abide alone, but gathers other voices with it. Sound has a kind of inevitable polyphony created from the sound itself and the vibrations it triggers around it. And, as a wave form, it lives in time. So if we are to take the ideas of akroatic thinking and communicative dialogicality seriously, we will have to think more carefully about time—for if the dialogic means we are always in conversation with past and future speakers, then the tennis model of dialogic temporality is not enough. Thinking of dialogue in terms of nonlinear time rather than as linear spatiality enables us to contemplate the vast interlacing of time in terms of past, present, and future in the communication process. Our past lives inside us, nested like the Mandelbrot fractals discussed in chapter 1, where the seeming chaos of thoughts, reveries, and unconscious memories swirls in an unaccountably random fashion until deep structures of self-similarity are revealed. The accumulation of these patterns and memories is what makes us who we are. But just as past, present, and future voices blend and interact to make us who we are, so do the inner and outer conversational selves and other selves that we inhabit and which inhabit us.

Intersubjectivity

Just as the idea of inner speech blurs distinctions between inside and out, so the idea of intersubjectivity blurs distinctions between the idea of self and other. From a holistic orientation, meaning resides neither in our individual intentions nor in words themselves, but in the shared cocreated space of intersubjectivity, where "the utterance always binds the participants of the situation together, as co-participants."[76] These ideas were developed in the school of Russian poetics as well as in phenomenology. For example, French phenomenologist Merleau-Ponty calls dialogue a place of "dual being," wherein the speech and thoughts of both parties are "interwoven into a single fabric . . . of which neither of us is the creator."[77] Intersubjectivity is thus a concept used to describe the space of shared understanding, or common ground, between persons, wherein people, as individual subjects, collaboratively create and share meaning. Originating in the field of phenomenology, intersubjectivity was originally associated with the work of German phenomenologist

Edmund Husserl, who explored how the intersubjective world of shared social objects, constructs, and meanings must, by necessity, transcend the clearly bounded separation between selves. According to Husserl, the consciousness of the experiencing subjective self, or "I," requires other subjective selves, or other "I's," to mediate and confirm the self's understanding of the world.

Martin Buber, a contemporary of Husserl, developed these new insights about intersubjectivity into a philosophy of dialogue that centers on a study of the I-Thou relation and the constitutive power of the between. For Buber, "real living is meeting," and in meeting one suspends egocentricity for an opening to intersubjectivity, the unpredictable and foreign land of the *between*. Buber describes how, in every interaction between human beings, there exists a *between,* a real place located not in individuals or in the general world, but in a space between self and other. Buber's relation between self and other is foundational to human existence because the self can only come into being when it is in dialogic relation with others. "I become through my relation to the Thou; as I become I, I say Thou."[78] Thus, the self does not exist as a "person," let alone think, until it encounters another person through the saying of Thou. To Buber, the I-Thou relation is itself a pronoun—not a combination of two pronouns, but a whole in and of itself. "Being, lived in dialogue, receives even in extreme dereliction a harsh and strengthening sense of reciprocity; being, lived in monologue, will not, even in the tenderest intimacy, grope out over the outlines of the self."[79] Moreover, the idea of a precommunicative human being who exists prior to language is impossible. "A precommunicative stage of language is unthinkable. Man did not exist before having a fellow being, before he lived over against him, toward him, and that means before he had dealings with him. Language never existed before address."[80]

Recent research in the fields of psychology and psycholinguistics is shedding light on how intersubjectivity begins in infancy, if not in the womb itself.[81] Trevarthen reports research that demonstrates that even in the womb, the fetus recognizes and responds to the voice of the mother, and Nagy reports that infants only two days old respond differently to a friendly expressive face than to a completely still one. Trevarthen discovered how in their earliest interactions, infants and their mothers engage in "protoconversations" that do not simply involve a form of call-and-response mimicry or imitation, but reveal sustained rhythmic repetitions and coordinated interactions where mother and child interact in a synchronized dance of gaze, body movement, and sound. These researchers have found that infants arrive on the scene of life as inherently poetic and musical beings "moving and hearing with pulse and rhythm, immediately sensitive to the harmonies and discords of human expression."[82] Remarkably, Powers and Trevarthen have found in the earliest interactions between parent and child, regardless of language and culture, "similar rhythms, melodic accents, repetition and rhymes."[83] Trevarthen describes how infants possess an innate intersubjectivity and musicality where "[a] loving proto-conversation . . . is a kind of musical performance of recipro-cal imitation in which adult and child cooperate."[84]

Other studies in the area of social cognition are demonstrating the crucial role played by intersubjectivity in both thinking and in communicating. What is slowly being revealed in these studies is the degree to which self and other begin to lose their centrality as twin gravitational masses in favor of a shared bidirectional center located in between the conversational partners that exerts its own gravitational force. "When two individuals interact in this way, the coordination of their body movements, utterances, gestures, gazes, etc. can gain such momentum that it overrides the individual intentions, and common sense-making emerges."[85] This overriding of separate individual intentions is what Roberts and Bavelas describe in their collaborative theory of meaning making, wherein the sharp edges between self and other as source of meaning are dissolved.[86] As Fuchs and De Jaegher put it, "Meaning is co-created in a way not necessarily attributable to either of the interaction part-ners. Mutual incorporation opens up potential new domains of sense-making, i.e. domains of sense-making that were not available to me as an individual. In terms of participatory sense-making, in these situations we speak of truly *joint* sense-making."[87] The magnetic force of the *between* draws the self out of itself as a pure and distinct form, creating a new, generative, and shared col-laborative process in which self and other are less differentiated. These kinds of interactions have been observed in research within engineering teams, in math classrooms, and in narrative storytelling. The findings repeatedly dem-onstrate the ways that communication is a shared joint activity that generates a between which shapes meaning with a momentum of its own as "the 'in-between' becomes the source of the operative intentionality of both partners."[88]

Thus, communication cannot be reduced to an instrumental tennis match where the back-and-forth exchange transports meanings, but is instead an unfolding process that carries its participants through a shared ocean of meaning. We will examine these issues in further detail in the next chapter when we investigate a concept we will call "interlistening." In the meantime, suffice it to say that intersubjective listening involves what Kaplan means when he says, "If I am really talking to you, I have nothing to say."[89] That is,

I come to the conversation empty—not empty of my experience or history, but empty of the belief that my experience or history defines the limits of possible meaning and experience. Thereby, I am empty of all intentions other than that of engaging with the what-will-happen. The coordinated rhythmic patterns of gesture, vocal inflection, and gaze in intersubjective interaction are similar to those found in improvisation, in particular, that in improvisational jazz, where players begin with a shared context of a "tune"—a familiar melodic and harmonic structure—and then, one by one, or perhaps in tandem, push beyond the boundaries of rhythmic, harmonic, and/or melodic structure. Truly gifted players can take the melody and bend it around the key or time signature, lifting it beyond what they already know. When they are really playing—really improvising—they *have* nothing prepared to say, but generate it spontaneously out of the musical between. Thus, in order to improvise, players have to "listen"—they have to follow the familiar structure, that is, be aware of it at all times, where they are in the song, where the others are, and they have to listen beyond, what might come newly, originally, to them. A jazz trumpet player might sew a quote from Miles Davis's *Sketches of Spain* into her solo during the jazz standard "Sometimes I Feel Like a Motherless Child." An improvisational pianist might throw a quote from a familiar TV advertisement into his performance of "My Funny Valentine." Each player abides entirely in the present—listening, or, as Heidegger would say, meditatively thinking about "what at first sight does not go together at all."[90]

This kind of listening takes place in linguistic forms as well, such as improvisational comedy and spoken word poetry, where the same tango of listening and speaking, of finding the pulse of the familiar structure and pushing beyond it, occurs. The listening involved in writing poetry is similar; in order to say the unsayable, a poet must break through cliché and familiar structures of knowing and naming, and this can only be achieved with both an awareness of the shared structure (the familiar story, image, tune, category, etc.) and a willingness to go beyond it—that is, both to listen and to speak beyond, outside the confines of the shared familiar structures and of the always already "known." This intersubjective improvisational dance arises from the fact that for the participants the center of gravity is not the soles of their feet, but the whole group, and as such, players, like listeners, are never merely doers but "always and at the same time a sufferer." As Arendt describes it, these infinite interconnections are the very thing that conditions what we experience in all arenas of human action: "To do and to suffer are like opposite sides of the same coin, and the story that an act starts is composed of its consequent deeds and sufferings. These consequences are boundless, because action, though it may proceed from nowhere, so to speak, acts into a medium where every reaction becomes a chain reaction and where every process is the cause of a new process."[91]

Constitutive Listening

In this chapter we have described communication from an intersubjective, dialogic perspective far different from a linear transmission-oriented model, where sequences of words are thought to depart from one self and enter another. Rather, we have examined the ways that communication is a mode of creation, not merely one of representation. Communication is the way we make the world and take up residence in it, as Carey says, whether that is through taking a vow, making a promise, or naming a star. We have also described how even the most lonely and isolated monologue is fundamentally dialogic, because it is always in response to prior speech or in anticipation of future speech. "Generally every given utterance is not *final* from the speaker's point of view: the utterance presupposes *continuation* following the encountered response."[92]

Thus, words reverberate with meanings far distant from their utterance in any given moment in time, and will continue to do so on into the future. Consider, for example, proverbs, the wisdom literature of the Bible. Some of the biblical proverbs derive from more ancient Egyptian texts,[93] and some of them show up in rap lyrics. For example, compare the following third millennium B.C.E. Egyptian *Instruction of Ptahhotep* with a not quite as ancient biblical proverb, and then fast-forward to a 2007 rap song. *Instruction:*

> Useful is hearing to a son who hears;
> If hearing enters the hearer,
> The hearer becomes a listener,
> Hearing well is speaking well.[94]

Proverb:

> My son, listen to my speech;
> Incline your ear to my words;
> Do not lose sight of them;
> Keep them in your mind.[95]

For a more current version, you can also hear echoes of these texts in the rap song "Rewind" by NaS. These three examples are not just calls to listen, but offer commentaries on listening itself that resonate over more than four millennia. Or consider the thundering beauty of the Reverend Martin Luther King's famous 1963 "I have a dream" speech, whose opening lines, "Five score years ago," echo the 1863 words of President Lincoln's Gettysburg Address, "Four score and seven years ago," and Lincoln's speech, in turn, resonates with echoes of the 1776 Declaration of Independence. The numerous quotes and allusions in both Lincoln's and King's speeches resonated with audiences then as they do now, and undoubtedly will continue to do far into the future.

And this brings us to a third way human communication is about so much more than simply information transmission. It does not take place only in sequenced linear time, but rather in a spinning spiral motion that combines past, present, and future. We have shown how our very perceptions are shaped by communication practices, and how "if there be memory, that is, the survival of past images, these images must constantly mingle with our perception of the present, and may even take its place."[96] Our words and thoughts constantly shift between verbal tenses, creating a past for a future that has not yet become. Our imaginations project a future that we remember and thus becomes our past. Our inner ears stitch and sew meanings outside of linear time as the first words we hear inevitably become the last, and the fragile cloth of understanding unfurls in a flash of comprehension. These displacements in time are not unusual or uncommon, they are built into the grammar of all languages, and we use them daily to recount stories, to ponder imponderables, or to shift between subjunctive worlds. If I only . . . It might be possible . . . If he had had a . . . Would she but . . . They must . . .

In this chapter we have explored how communication creates a space for movement beyond the horizon of self and other, and into a *between* with a power of its own to generate, transform, and invent meaning. Because of the ways this intersubjective space creates a fissure in the sharp boundaries between self and other, it creates new possibilities for peaceful means of being with others. This space, when authentically freed from the control of any plan or agenda, can move us toward unimagined possibilities that far exceed the capacities of the individual participants. The whole is always greater than the sum of its parts, and, when permitted to flourish, can impart a wisdom that typically goes unheard.

That said, you have no doubt noticed by now that, for the most part, this chapter on communication and a nice-knock down argument has had much to say about speech and speaking and next to nothing about listening. We will remedy this omission in the next chapter when we build upon these insights about communication to fashion a new model for thinking with listening—one that enables us to move past spatial, atomistic models and draw upon akroatic thinking and harmonic attunement, which we will call *interlistening*.

INTERLISTENING AND THE *TOUT ENSEMBLE*

> Do I contradict myself?
> Very well then, I contradict myself,
> I am large—I contain multitudes.
> —WALT WHITMAN, *"Song of Myself"*

When I was a teenager, I tried to read James Joyce's impossible novel *Finnegans Wake*. For about three weeks running, I would pick it up, read a paragraph or perhaps even a page, and then put it down. Pick it up, put it down. I didn't understand it *at all*—and, sadly, I didn't know that I wasn't expected to. But the crazy words made me laugh and want to memorize some of the tongue-trippingly musical lines, like "all the hoolivans of the nation" and "their duodisimally profusive plethora of ululation."[1] I was especially intrigued by the novel's opening line, which begins in midsentence and flows like the very water it describes: "riverrun, past Eve and Adam's, from swerve of shore to bend of bay, brings us by a commodius vicus of recirculation back to Howth Castle and Environs."[2] But eventually the pain of not understanding, and the nagging insecurity that it left in its wake, was too much for my young ego, and I laid the novel down.

It's terrible to not understand something that you want to, or feel you should, understand. It's so difficult in fact that we have lost (if we ever had it) the ability to *not* understand—to simply stay with some something, be it a poem or a painting, music or someone's words—and just be with it, experience it, appreciate it, without having to fit it into some tidy box of "understanding." And there is something about *Finnegans Wake* that seems to enact the ways that misunderstanding is woven into understanding, braided together like channels of a river, an integrated whole that can merge and diverge, separate and converge, or even change direction and course like the mighty Mississippi River. In defiance of seemingly rational laws of order and linear sequence, the Mississippi routinely violates the will of the U.S. Army Corps of Engineers, which works so hard to keep the river on a predictable 2,320-mile course from the northern cold of Minnesota down to the southern swamps of the Mississippi Delta at New Orleans. Nevertheless, there are predictably unpredictable times when the river bursts its banks and forges an altogether different path, sometimes one so crazy that it makes stretches of *downstream* run *north* of upstream. That's right. The river wanders off into curlicues such that a riverboat traveling downstream (from north to south) will, in some places, be winding its way north (backwards, toward upstream) in a countermovement not unlike the first and last sentence of *Finnegans Wake,* where the second half of the book's final sentence is the first line of the book!

Even more than the seemingly irrational course of the Mississippi, Joyce's novel disrupts the ordinarily orderly progression of things that move in sequence from start to finish, before to after, past to present to future, or beginning to end. This is time con-fused, that is to say, past fused with present fused with future. And all the silly yet erudite language of Joyce's novel, its puns, riddles, and polysemies, "the shebby choruysh . . . that would black-guardise the whitestone ever hurtleturtled out of heaven," work to confuse the ordinarily orderly progression of language, bringing sound, meaning, language into a confused cacophony, at once dialogic, polyphonous, and nonlinear. It is as if language were not carved up into three separate processes of thinking, speaking, and listening, but was rather an organic whole, a confused multiplicity that echoes, vibrates, and pulses in nonlinear time. But how is one to understand such a poetic and scholarly mélange that interleaves hundreds of literary references as well as allusions in Sanskrit, Greek, Dutch, and Italian into a magnificently awesome chorale? Well, perhaps we're not. Or, perhaps, understanding is not what we think it is. Even aside from the fact that understanding is inherently political—as Upton Sinclair once wrote, "It is difficult to get a man to understand, when his salary depends upon his not understanding it!"[3]—understanding itself is not well understood. It's kind of a shadowy ghostling that thrives on mystery, obliqueness, confusion. Try to hold it still in the palm of your hand and it will flutter free. Understanding makes a gift of itself, only to later take it back again—like the pre-Copernican era we discussed in chapter 3, when the Ptolemaic earth-centered understanding of the universe only came to be replaced by the heliocentric understanding as a result of scientific, social, and political developments.

Understanding is thus always partial and incomplete—it may take minutes, weeks, or even centuries, but eventually what we thought was knowledge firmly planted and incontrovertible shifts, however slightly, into something else. At the same time, understanding does not always follow misunderstanding in such a linear progression—often they are nested inside each other, like yin and yang, where bits of understanding are seeded in a field of misunderstanding, each containing the other. At times the relation between understanding and misunderstanding is like a dream world where creatures asleep are awake, everything that was not suddenly is, and the snake at the beginning of the world eats its tail in the end. But we rarely have a sense of this, for just as the atomist perspective fractures speaking from listening, so it splits understanding from misunderstanding, never coming to how each requires the other, how each is inextricably bound to the other, like the Ouroboros.

Consider: I'm driving down a busy street and hear a siren wailing. What do I "understand" by that sound? Perhaps a dozen things at once—Where is it? What direction is it traveling? Should I move over? Are the cars behind me moving over? If not, is it because they don't need to or because they're too self-absorbed to care? Is the approaching vehicle a fire truck or an ambulance? Is there just one? Who is hurt? How badly . . . And on and on. Perhaps my understanding is tinged with worry or fear from a memory, or the loss of a loved one. Or perhaps I'm a newspaper stringer down on my luck and the siren sound means hope: a story, potential employment, and perhaps even a scoop. Or I'm a fireman from another city wondering where the firehouses and hospitals are, how many alarms have sounded, how can I help? Or perhaps I'm on the phone with a friend who just lost a spouse and is in deep grief, needing my full attention. Or perhaps I finally got the baby to sleep and now the siren will wake her up. Or perhaps I'm trying to focus on this chapter, and the sound is nothing but irritation, frustration, distraction—and then I catch myself and am disappointed by my selfishness . . . And on and on. In each of these scenarios, my understanding comes not from the sound itself, but from the situation and my place in it. When we mistake understanding for something fixed and final, something out "there" rather than something accomplished between and within a situation, we create a wall around possibility and limit the living creativity of our learning and being. For the myth of perfect understanding, and its high-handed renunciation of misunderstanding, deafens us to the ongoing birth of understanding. In any given context, there are thousands of possible understandings, and to insist on one is to kill the living movement of understanding.

Consider again, for a moment, the word "understand" and its synonyms. To stand under. Something is "there" above, us and we are below, underneath, looking up. We reach "up" and try to "grasp" it, "catch" it, "capture" it. The origin of the synonym "comprehend" is to seize or lay hold of, to hang on to. And similarly, the word "apprehend" carries this sense. Elusive criminals, like subtle meanings, can be quite difficult to apprehend. In each of these synonyms, the idea of understanding is linked to capture and containment, to a break in an ongoing flow of movement. As if understanding were a great tiger that we must take into custody and keep enclosed and tightly controlled. But what if it weren't so? What if we were able to give up this way of understanding understanding and see it not as a captured stillness or singularity, but rather as a momentary pause in an ongoing movement of unfolding, like a rest in a musical score, or a pause in a story, or a swirling eddy in an inexorable, ongoing river of meaning? What if, to change metaphors, understanding were something like an electron cloud, swirling with possibility instead of certainty, or a mysterious quantum wave of possible associations and connections, some more likely than others but none entirely predictable? This is understanding as mystery, uncertainty, ambiguity, rather than as facticity, certainty, or precision. It is understanding as an evolving movement of balletic grace that entails both holding on and letting go—both understanding and not understanding at one and the same time.

In Greek the word *pharmakon* is used to express something that is both poison and remedy.[4] In our communicative interactions with one another, misunderstanding is often thought of as a kind of poison, as a "mistake" that stains the beauty of our convictions. But misunderstanding can also be a powerfully healing medicine that engenders new possibilities for transformation, learning, and growth. For example, several scenes in the novel *The Sixth Lamentation* suggest these ideas beautifully. In one scene, the narrator illustrates the rich fertility of misunderstanding when he observes, "As with all misunderstandings, Cathy was on to something."[5] Later, near the end of the book, the prior warns a junior priest of the dangers of too much understanding by cautioning, "You never will understand, fully; and in a way, you mustn't. If you do, you'll be trotting out formulas."[6] Thus, as with *pharmakon,* both understanding and misunderstanding can be poison or remedy—each to each, and at the same time. Contrary to popular wisdom, then, there is great strength in not understanding—in giving up our convictions and certainties to let understanding evolve. Just as a cup filled with tea has no room for more, a mind filled with certainty is unable to grow and discover. "In order to arrive at what you do not know / You must go by a way which is the way of ignorance."[7]

As we will examine much more closely in the next chapter's examination of ethics, in our everyday communicative interactions with one another, one way we can make room for understanding is to clear a space in which we can tolerate the painful ambiguities of not understanding or knowing and, in turn, of being misunderstood. For when we assume that understanding is contingent upon continuity, similarity, or agreement, we leave little room for discovery or for others. In his work on the difficult dialogue between Palestinians and Israelis, Z. D. Gurevitch finds that the ability to not understand is essential for any peace, let alone understanding, to arise. Gurevitch argues that strangeness, rather than familiarity alone, is essential for dialogic understanding to arise. When we encounter another person in dialogue, unless we disrupt our everyday familiar and taken-for-granted understandings and "make the other strange," we will never truly know or understand the other *as other*. "The birth of dialogue, then, is contingent on the emergence of otherness."[8] But this birth is a difficult one because our dialogic encounters are typically governed by a search for shared connections and familiarity that confirm our already shaped understandings of ourselves and others, and the world. Thus, by "making the other strange" and suspending our already familiar understandings, we must be able to withstand the discomforts and tensions of *not understanding*, which Gurevitch calls *the ability to not understand*. "The real difficulty is how to debunk previous images of understanding—that is, to 'de-explain' rather than [to] explain, to 'de-reason' rather than to reason, to restore strangeness into the active framework of the encounter."[9] We will further explore the ethical dimensions of these issues in the next chapter, but for now we will approach communication "as a raid on the inarticulate / With shabby equipment always deteriorating."[10] Which brings us to a question about temporality—do understanding and misunderstanding occur sequentially or all at once, like Bhartṛhari's *sphoṭa,* a bursting forth, arising and falling at the same time?

On Time

For most of us, there is only the unattended
Moment, the moment in and out of time
The distraction fit, lost in a shaft of sunlight,

The wild thyme unseen, or the winter lightning,

Or the waterfall, or music heard so deeply

That it is not heard at all, but you are the music

While the music lasts.

—T. S. ELIOT, *"The Dry Salvages"*

We begin with a problem of yet more metaphors, those relating to sight. Many scholars have noted how visual dominance sits at the center of Western epistemology, wherein "seeing" is thought to be synonymous with "understanding," and words like "vision," "view," "outlook," and "perspective" engender a visual mode wherein acts of cognition such as thinking, comprehending, and understanding are translated as mental pictures to be seen by the mind's eye. Listening, in contrast, is rendered as a subordinate modality, most useful for bringing invisible events and objects to light, as when radio astronomy and ultrasound transpose sonic phenomena into visual images, making sounds into mere "anticipatory clues for ultimate visual fulfillments."[11] Scholars Marshall McLuhan and Walter Ong have illustrated the ways in which our visual bias arose historically through the introduction of writing. When words are written, both scholars agree, they become part of a visual world that silences the sound of language, "splits thought and action," and cleaves speaker from addressee.[12] Ong writes, "In this economy . . . everything having to do with speech tends to be in one way or another metamorphosed in terms of structure and vision."[13] As touched upon in the previous chapter, one of the things that gets left out in spatial and visual conceptions of speech and its relation to communication is time, or rather, a nonlinear, nonspatialized conception of time.

What is time? We typically think of time as an indistinct but insistent river flowing eternally from past to present to future. But this view obscures the many ways the lives of our minds are a tangle of braided streams, currents, shallows, eddies, and swamps of memory and anticipation, sparkling with an occasional visit to the present moment. It also obscures the rich dialogicality of every moment, echoing eternally with words from the past, often below the surface of awareness. Just now as you were reading, perhaps a thought or memory arose in your mind and your thoughts wandered away from the page for a moment or two until you were drawn back into the text. And just as each moment is laden with moments from remote distances of our lives, so our communicative interactions with others create new synchronies of nonconscious coordination.

As we have previously discussed, Bergson was concerned with our thinking about time and memory, and in particular with the fact that time was rendered only in terms of mechanistic quantification. According to Bergson, Western thinking about time has been dominated by spatiality, wherein we describe time as a kind of continuous linear movement in an unbounded homogenous medium, similar to how we envision space. Thus, like space, time is something we measure, and the measurement is produced by movements in space—when the earth completes one revolution on its axis, we call it twenty-four hours of time, when the moon orbits the earth, we call it a month of time, and when the earth circles the sun we call it a year of time. In this way, we imagine time as a series of equally spaced intervals that can be isolated from one another and arbitrarily divided into discrete entities. But human consciousness is not experienced this way.

In contrast to a spatial view of time, Bergson asks us to think time without space, without quantification and measure—he asks us to consider temporal experience (which he calls *durée*) as a confused multiplicity rather than an ordered homogeneity to calculate. Counting, argues Bergson, requires and implies space and infinite divisibility. *Durée* is time without measure, differentiation without quantification. "Pure duration is the form which the succession of our conscious states assumes when our ego lets itself *live,* when it refrains from separating its present state from its former states."[14] Bergson describes, for example, how, when listening to a symphony, the notes of a musical phrase are not heard as discrete spatial intervals, but as sounds melting together into an organic whole. He writes, "[E]ven if these notes succeed one another, yet we perceive them in one another, and . . . their totality may be compared to a living being whose parts, although distinct, permeate one another because they are so closely connected."[15]

In the Euro-American tradition, the beginning of the conflation of time and space may be traced back to the Greeks' inquiry into the relationship between time, motion, and change. Time became important for the Eleatics when the question of whether, how, and why things change led to an argument between Parmenides and Heraclitus about being versus becoming—is the universe always in flux, in a state of ever-changing becoming in time, or is the universe and everything in it a vast, unchanging, and timeless still point? This argument was never decisively concluded, but the distinction between homogenized clock time and individual human experiential time was appreciated by Socrates, who in Plato's dialogue *Theaetetus* takes a backhanded slap at lowly speech and language when he distinguishes between the freedom of the philosopher, who "always has time at his disposal to converse in peace at his leisure," and the enslavement of the orator (rhetorician), who "is always talking against time, hurried on by the clock."[16] Eventually, however, the conception of time settled into the spatial mode for Aristotle, for whom time was "merely the way we 'measure motion,' the way we 'measure the difference between before and after,' that is, reduce our descriptions of motions to statements of the sequence of change."[17] And with the invention of calendars and sundials that measured time by movements in space, the spatialized model of time was complete.

For Kant, however, the question of time was perhaps more complex. As we discussed in chapter 3, for Kant time and space were not simply mere concepts like Aristotle's twelve categories (quantity, quality, relation, etc.), because each and every one of the twelve categories presupposes the concepts of space and time, which are the formal conditions of all phenomena and therefore cannot be derived from external experience. Time, according to Kant, was not merely clock time, but the inner experience of consciousness, while space dealt with the empirical world of objects. Because both time and space were presupposed in the core "pure" concepts, Kant argued that time and space were super pure concepts upon which everything else depended. He wrote, "[I]n order that certain sensations should be referred to something outside myself, i.e. to something in another place of space from that where I am . . . the representation (*Verstellung*) of space must already be there."[18] Similarly, Kant argued that "[t]ime is not an empirical concept deduced from any experience, for neither coexistence nor succession would enter into our perception, if the representation of time were not given *a priori*."[19]

Kant gives the example of how the a priori concept of causality could not exist without a prior idea of time in the form of a before and an after. According to Sherover, Kant was perhaps influenced by previous conceptions of time—such as Newton's differentiation between an absolute and a relative time and Descartes's 57th principle, which distinguished time and duration—when he suggested a third form of time that was neither quantifiable nor systematic. As Sherover explains, Kant's third form of time was "temporal human perspective within which [objects] appear and within which cognitions are sought; for objects appear to us in our anticipations, memories, plans, and recollections and it is only within this non-quantifiable range of temporal experience that the attempt for systematic and mathematical cognitive description may arise."[20] In this way Kant associated time with freedom and denied the "kind of spatializing linear temporality of postulated moments used for quantitative description which serves physicists and other clock-watchers as indexes of true duration."[21]

Anyone who has ever been "lost in thought" or caught up in a passionate activity, in that state which the Hungarian psychologist Mihaly Csikszentmihalyi describes as "flow" and the poet T. S. Eliot calls "unattended time," understands that time's relationship to attention and memory is not simply a matter of mechanical calculation. Our experiences rarely conform to clock time. We find, of course, that painful experiences last too long and pleasures are far too fleeting. And intentionally focusing our attention on a single phenomenon (whether of mediation or study or speech) even for ten minutes can either seem like forever or be a short-lived blur. Similarly, a conversation may seem to take forever or go by in a flash. The relationship of time to human experience becomes important for our thinking about listening when we consider how most theories of communication theorize a linear process in which speech is followed by listening. But, as we discussed in the last chapter, not only may speech and listening be simultaneous, as *sphoṭa* theory holds, but the notion of a unidirectional sense of time may not be relevant at all. As Bergson writes, "The truth is that memory does not consist in a regression from the present to the past, but, on the contrary, in a progress from the past to the present."[22]

Bergson attributed the spatial dominance of our conceptions of time to a problem of language, wherein multiplicity without quantification is unthinkable, unspeakable. We are "betrayed by the deeply ingrained habit of setting out time in space."[23] According to Bergson, our experience of duration is betrayed by language, which freezes, isolates, and segments the flow of consciousness. This is reminiscent of Bhartṛhari's and Luria's description of the transformation of thought to speech discussed in the last chapter, which moves from a nonlinear gestalt to an ordered sequential pattern of words. According to Luria and others, the human brain is capable of both simultaneous and successive synthesis. So in place of, or in addition to, the linear spatialized model of time, I wish to develop a distinction between what we might call "synchronic" and "diachronic" time. Although these terms have been used by Saussure and subsequent linguists to describe linguistic evolution over time (Saussure's "diachrony") as opposed to the underlying structures of linguistic systems at any given point in time (Saussure's "synchrony"), we will use them here quite differently by building upon insights from Luria's and Bhartṛhari's models of the speech process.

But first we must attend to Saussure and his model, which is built upon the fact that language appears, paradoxically, as both an enduring and a transitory phenomenon with both collective and individual dimensions. Because language is both interior and exterior, it can be shared aloud or hummed in solitary silence. These contradictions are in part what led Saussure to separate language into two separate parts—what he called language (*langue*) and speaking (*parole*). To Saussure, *langue* is "the true and unique object of linguistics," while the activity of speaking (*parole*) has "no place in linguistics except through their relation to language. . . . Language and speaking are then interdependent; the former is both the instrument and the product of the latter. But their interdependence does not prevent their being two absolutely distinct things."[24] Thus, the fleeting and ephemeral aspects of speech were seen by Saussure as a performance, distinct and separate from the systematic solidity of language. "Language is speech less speaking. It is the whole set of linguistic habits which allow an individual to understand and to be understood."[25] Having expelled speaking from the school of linguistics, Saussure then turned his attention to language as "a system whose parts can and must all be considered in their synchronic solidarity."[26] And, as a good atomist, he considered this very systematicity to be the proper aim of linguistics. Not that language did not change, in Saussure's view; indeed it did, as the studies of philology and historical linguistics attest. But language had both stability and change, which brought Saussure to his second bifurcation— between synchronic and diachronic linguistics, which, once again, were absolute distinctions: "The opposition between the two viewpoints, the synchronic and the diachronic, is absolute and allows no compromise. . . . It is obvious that the diachronic facts are not related to the static facts which they produced. They belong to a different class."[27]

Synchronic language to Saussure was a largely static immutable system of rules, laws, and regularities, and it gorged upon the whole enchilada of grammar, morphology, semantics, and phonology. To Saussure, diachronic language, in contrast, was mutable and dynamic—it changed over time. Thus, diachronic linguistics, like philology, deals with the evolution of languages and "the substitution of one element for another in time," whereas synchronic linguistics analyzes the "relation between simultaneous elements."[28] And, speaking like the true father of structuralism, Saussure held that synchronic language was of course the more important, as it discovered the fundamental principles underlying a given language system.

Ironically, because Saussure chose not to pin the butterfly wings of speech to his structural wall of language, we are free to return to the *langue/parole* division and take up where Saussure left off. And one of the first things we notice is how Saussure's synchrony and diachrony binary reinforces a linear, spatialized notion of time: diachrony as a horizontal x-axis that moves from left to right, and synchrony as a vertical y-axis that ranges from up to down. Thus, Saussure's synchronic time is a stillness; there is no movement because its simultaneity is frozen in stasis. But, as we described in the last chapter, speech moves in nonlinear time—successive words shape the meaning of future and previous words in an eternal blending of past, present, and future. The latter words shape the meaning of the previous words, just as the former words shape the meaning of the successive words. In speaking, diachronous time is a river moving from past to future, while synchronous time is an ocean that contains all time from past to future and cycles in rhythmic waves and vibrations. So one problem with Saussure's version of the synchronic dimension of language is that it is, for all intents and purposes, a frozen, unmoving, static kind of time. And this spatialization of language cannot be applied to *parole* because, among other things, it distorts the gestalt of synchronous *sphoṭa,* the bursting forth of language, which moves in simultaneous time. Saussure's synchrony is a freeze-frame photograph rather than the swirling, nonlinear ocean of reverberations, voices, and meanings that seems to be the partner to the river of diachronic time. So even were we to accept Saussure's twin dichotomies of *langue/parole* and synchrony/diachrony, we would nevertheless note how Saussure's notions of time for language completely ignore speech and speaking, not even to mention listening. So let us begin to imagine synchronic and diachronic time as they might pertain to speaking and listening.

Diachronic Time

According to an outworn caricature, time in the East is circular and time in the West is linear. We will dispense with that distinction right now.[29] Why? Because both of these systems are diachronic in that they set out to calculate and measure what we might call diachronic linear time, the unfolding of time in succession, be it in the shape of a circle (cycle) or of a line, straight or curved. But diachronic time, whether experienced as cyclical or linear, is characterized by two limitations: finitude and unidirectionality. That is, diachronic time is punctuated by a still point, the end of one cycle and the beginning of the next, like the phases of death and rebirth that mark the lifespan as well as the seasons. As an example of diachronic time, consider the change of seasons. I was raised in the northeastern United States, and therefore I suffered from the absence of discernible rhythms of nature when I moved to the West Coast. Having lived most of my life in a place where spring and summer were lush green, winter a pale gray and white, and autumn blazed with glorious reds and yellows, I lacked the sensitivity to notice California fall creeping into winter, or its spring blooming into summer. The sight of Oregon's radiant red camellias blooming in February seemed somehow wrong, as did the year-round blooms of bougainvillea in Portland, the forever gray-greenish pallor of Texas live oaks in Austin and the ubiquitous fragrance of California eucalyptus in the Bay Area.

When I moved back east, the long trudge from late fall to late spring, where skeletal black trees scrape the gray skies and everything blurs in a dull, muted brown, was almost intolerable. But oh, the joy as the first traces of green skidded across the hills, an intoxicating green rush of rebirth. And it prompted me to recall how, when I was a child, I experienced a little thrill of horror each late winter when I worried about what would happen if the trees never "woke up" and returned to life? What if they slept on forever? This forgotten early encounter with the finitude of infinity, the neverendingness of the end, was heart-stoppingly incomprehensible at age six or seven, and remains now an unfathomable paradox. For despite its apparent finitude and the inexorable cycle of return, one of the secrets of diachronic time is the unresolved nature of its infinitude—its impossible incalculability. Therein lies the paradox, Zeno's infinitely divisible "arrow of time," which renders the shifting tempos of life and movement as deathless, motionlessness space.

From one point of view, size, distance, speed, and duration are all relative, and the subdivision of space is infinitely directional—things can get infinitely smaller or infinitely larger. Any unit can be halved or doubled. As in Heisenberg's quantum world, Bohm's holographic universe, and the Eames *Powers of Ten* we discussed in chapter 1. Any apparently solid "thing" can be shown to comprise millions of smaller things or can, in turn, be shown to be merely one of millions of things that make up yet another larger "thing." It's like the 1987 movie *Innerspace,* which revisits the theme of the 1966 *Fantastic Voyage.* Entering the giant (to them) human body, the miniaturized characters in these films see the vastness of the space between blood vessel and ventrical, between cilia and cochlea, between mitochondria and nuclei. It is much like how, as children, we are invited into an imagined world where atoms look like solar systems, and cells undulate with life like scuzzy ponds. What ancient Taoist philosophy understood, physics now attests: our models of the universe are relative, and the miles of space between the sun and moon are recapitulated in the miles of space between this moment and that.

> The tiny particles which form the vast universe are not tiny at all.
> Neither is the vast universe vast.
> These are notions of the mind, which is like a knife,
> always chipping away at the Tao,
> trying to render it graspable and manageable.[30]

Infinity is hard to imagine indeed. Imagining infinite space leads to Zeno's paradox—because if we can divide the distance an arrow travels toward a target infinitely in half, then, according to logic, the arrow will never arrive at the target because there will always be half the remaining distance to halve. Therein lies the paradox. But it is only paradoxical if we mistake our constructs of space for time itself. We have taken the abstract construct of extension into three dimensions (length, depth, width) and imposed it on time (past, present, future), and then gotten so comfortable with the construct that we mistake it for the thing itself, which in this case is space. We have done the same thing with time. We've taken abstract constructs such as linearity and sequentiality, superimposed them on what we call "time," and then mistaken these ideas for time itself. What complicates this even more is the extent to which we have privileged spatiality over temporality and thereby spatialized time, made time into a spatial dimension with past present and future directions extending in a linear fashion from the now of any given moment. But as Heidegger notes, our experiences belie this sequential linear expression. "Only when a man has seen does he truly see. To see is to have seen. What is seen has arrived and remains for him in sight. A seer has always already seen. Having seen in advance he sees into the future."[31]

Why do we do this? Why do we spatialize time? It has to do, perhaps, with the way we privilege vision over audition. Consider, for example, our metaphors for understanding and intelligence: *I see.* He has *vision.* These metaphors about sight take linear extension—the basis of three-dimensionality—and impose it on time, forgetting that the metaphor is a social, not a scientific, phenomenon. So-called objective time suffers from a little strain with the need for time zones to keep clock time in correct relationship with the slightly wobbly rotation of the earth. Similarly, the relativity of clock time is revealed with the needs of daylight savings time, when we turn our clocks backwards or forwards to counter the slow creep backwards and forwards of sunlight. Lastly, we see these wrinkles in time through cultural differences in time—such as in many southern climates, where time has a slower pace and looser boundaries. In some places, a noon meeting could mean 12:30 P.M. or even 12:50 P.M., whereas in other places noon means 12:00 P.M. on the dot. These kinds of differing cultural conventions also govern expectations and beliefs about meal times (is dinner at 5:30 P.M. or 10:00 P.M.?), business hours (do the shops open at 8 A.M. or 10 A.M.?), and so forth. Thus, the idea of "punctuality" is a culturally specific notion. In India, for example, the business hours signs are replaced by "timings," which offer a loosened sketch of times, the idea being that time is not a singular still noun but a plural moving event, a happening that coexists with other happenings. Certainly, we need clock time to organize and coordinate events and experiences with others, to plan, to order, to remember, to create. But clock time offers itself as a standardized and uniform totality in ways our experiences of life may not.

In much scientific and everyday thinking, spatial distance and diachronic clock time are linked—a light year, for example, is the distance light travels in a year. Clock time is thus time defined in terms of space. But also consider how spatial distance is relative to speed and how speed is relative to time. For instance, the sentence "He lives an hour away" (time as distance) could mean six hundred miles (an hour by air), sixty miles (an hour by car), or three miles (an hour by foot). That is, distance is perceived as far or close depending on the speed of travel. Depending on what you're doing and at what scale you're doing it, at a certain point of proximity, time becomes irrelevant—the grocery store around the corner, your thigh pressing against mine on the train, the infinitesimal space between the tip of Evelyn Glennie's drumstick to the surface of her drum, or two cells in her fingertip, two molecules in that cell, or two atoms in that molecule, and so forth. There is always some space, no matter how slim. Distance, conceived as space, is infinitely divisible.

But how might our thinking about time change if listening, rather than vision, became our central metaphor for understanding time? For one thing, spatiality and extension might not so dominate our ideas of time that we could, perhaps, be free to imagine sound without spatiality and space without temporality. Moreover, as with our discussion of understanding and misunderstanding in the last chapter, we might also be able to imagine both as both—sound as diachronic and synchronic, sequential and simultaneous, and always,

always polyphonous. As we discussed in chapter 2, sound, like time, has rhythm and pulsation, and its vibrations are "measured" in the musical sense of ratio, proportion, harmony, texture. Diachronous time, like sound, is "measured," but in the mechanized sense of quantification and calculation. So our conceptual categories about time and space have led to us to perceive distance and time as interwoven, as a holistic fabric of Einstein's space-time continuum.

But spatialized dimensionality aside, what is time? Certainly we experience internal subjective time that depends on a given context and our psychological state. Our sense of time while loading a cart full of bricks may feel like hours or just a few minutes, depending on our health, mood, strength, companionship. And it will feel different from our sense of time when watching a movie, making love, or falling asleep. It will also vary between individuals. Thus, the perception of time may be different from clock time. "To say that the stimulus endures is not to say that the sensation is sensed as enduring but only that the sensation also endures."[32] But, as we discussed in chapter 2, perception is itself loaded with cultural sense that becomes habitual, almost "second nature," to us; we no longer perceive—or are aware of perceiving—a piece of clothing on our body, our bare feet on the carpet, the tension in our jaw, and so forth. That is, the sensation of duration and the duration of sensation are different. But this is not to say that subjective time is wrong and clock time is right. Whether measured as a cycle or a line, clock time moves relative to space—when it's three P.M. in New York it's three A.M. in Tokyo.

Thus, clock time is measured in relation to the movement of bodies in space, be they very large bodies like planets, the sun, or the earth or very small things like photons. As we described above, a day is one rotation of the earth on its axis, one spin. A month is a revolution of the moon around the earth, and a year the revolution of the earth around the sun, and these orbits, too, are their own form of distance. So, in some sense, clock time, seasonal time, nighttime are a matter of cyclical rotation, a neverending return. This might be thought of as mythic time. But, as with other all our perceptions, the way time is measured and quantified is to some degree arbitrary. Could we not design larger or smaller categories of time—bundling five rotations of the earth on its axis into one week and thereby having seventy-three rather than fifty-two weeks a year? Or could we have three "hours" a day—a morning hour, an evening hour, and a night hour which vary in length—rather than twenty-four identically calculated hours? Or could we calculate time based on the moon, the sun, and a constellation in some kind of hybrid combination?

In the end, however, no matter which way it's done, all calendar systems involve some kind of funky calibration to accommodate the fact that there is no perfectly consistent measure of time because time is not a rational number, it is a proportion. To lose sight of this fact, to mistake a holistic proportioned relationship for an atomistic fixed quantity, is to lose contact with the rhythms and patterns of life.[33] The other limitation of clock time is the perception of its forward movement and accumulation. There is no going backward, into the past, other than through memory—recollection. There is no new doing in the present that impacts the past, other than our memories and interpretations of it. We can revisit or even discover the past in memory and dream, but, no action we undertake now will affect the past; apparently we can only change the future. The past is fixed and unchanging, even timeless, in this sense. But, as we discussed in the last chapter, the past is deeply embedded in the present and future, and the future is embedded in the present. Counting and clock time wrench the human experience out of the lived experience of a specific given context and into an uninhabited abstraction, and our lived experiences of being are subsumed by quantification. As Levin describes it, "This time-order of our social life is, as such, a cause of suffering, because it installs us in a present, a 'now,' that is essentially self-contained: isolated from 'its' past and discontinuous with 'its' future, this 'present' is supposed to be rich and full. . . . But in truth, this atomic now-point is thereby *emptied* of meaning—a present which somehow is never really present, never really lived."[34]

The restless and inexorable press of diachronic clock time thus seems to breed a sense of scarcity, so that there is never enough time, we are always running out of time, or saving time—what Gebser calls negative time.[35] The regime of the clock rules and regiments human experience into a calculable, translatable abstraction. That is, clock becomes master. And while time is expanding into increasingly smaller units, the accumulation seems to diminish rather than expand—that is, time moves faster and faster. We can observe this acceleration with technological innovations. In 1990, a standard home computer processed information at a speed of roughly five million cycles per second (5 MHz); today home computers process information at up to two billion cycles per second (2 GHz). And in television and film, the rate of changing images on the screen has increased exponentially. For example, in movies from the 1930s, the average shot was about thirty seconds, meaning that there were on average two edits per minute. Today, film shots may last on the screen for as little as two or three seconds, with perhaps as many as thirty edits per minute. This is what makes old computers and films appear endlessly slow to younger people and new computers and action films appear incredibly fast to older people.

But, when accelerated time, or rate of change, becomes the master governor of human life, ideologies of social control flourish: "Don't waste time," "Time is money," and "A stitch in time saves nine." The ubiquitous uniform measurement of continuous linear time can easily become a prison sentence, whether it be the rigidly standardized schedules for learning in school or the tedious calibrations of the punched clock at work: our lives are governed by a hidden curriculum of obedience to clock time. Forget the dry tedium of c-span—in our time-is-money world of "sound-bite democracy," political discussion has all but ceased to exist. The question now becomes, at what point in the future will the 140-character "literature" of Twitter come to be seen as a grotesquely garrulous excess? Who will have the patience to listen to the halting, labored speech of a beginner, or the ponderous ruminations of an elder? As Gebser writes, "The addiction to overcoming time negatively is everywhere evident. The previous thresholds of time are surpassed everywhere. . . . Precisely these exertions, fleeing into quantification, are a temporal flight born of the time-anxiety which dominates our daily lives."[36]

Of course, we live our lives for the most part in linear diachronous time. Our daily activities are ordered into sequences that take place in one moment followed by another—everything from raw to cooked eggs, or from crawling to walking to running, or from match to flame to smoke occurs in diachronous succession. Further, there are recurring cycles of generalized, not mechanically exact quantifiable periodicity everywhere in nature, from the monsoon season to the parturition of a fetus, and, as we discussed in chapter 2, even lifespan, which can be calculated as a ratio between heartbeat and size. So life without some measure of diachronic time is impossible. But at the same time, life is not run by clockwork and human beings aren't (yet?) machines. For the time being at least, human lives unfold with a kind of spiraling and branching recursivity and synchrony. But as we sacrifice our wonder at complexity and uncertainty (when will the baby arrive?) to the colder comforts of certainty and predictability (when the doctor induces labor!), it's all too easy to forget the nonlinear holism of temporal life.

Consider, for example, those reality TV shows that trace people's ancestry through their parents. In order to make a coherent (i.e., linear) narrative, these shows typically track a single line of *a* parent, and a parent before that, and one before that, and back and back. So that by the end of the day, Sarah Jessica

Parker can exhale with enormous relief when she learns that her great-great-great-great-great-great-great-grandmother was not in fact a witch hunter, but was, *whew,* a victim of the witch hunter's wrath. But wait a second. Do we really in fact know she wasn't also related to the witch hunter? After all, we only traced back a sequentially linear family line, when actually, by the time we get to SJP's sixth great-grandmother, she also has, in fact, 127 other great-grandmothers and 127 great-grandfathers to whom she is directly related, not to mention all the dozens of possible cousins, aunts, and uncles arrayed in the background as well. So diachronic time presents us with an illusion of linearity and finitude in what is, if you go back far enough, a nearly unfathomable branching.

Synchronic Time

To say that time is synchronous is to break the spell of diachronic linearity and speed and illustrate how every *now* is interleaved with every past and possibly future now. For synchronous time is dense, heavy, filled with memory, and the harmonic strains that can be brought to mind in an infinity of interconnections like an ocean of memory sloshing this way and that. Rather than a quantifiable spatial "object," synchronic time is a happening, a concurrence of events. These are not frozen events in stasis, for synchrony involves movement and co-occurrence, like the bursting forth of *sphota.* There is a perhaps apocryphal story about how Mozart composed his music that illustrates this idea. In a letter to an unnamed baron that has been reprinted in many Mozart biographies and in other books about creativity, Mozart describes how musical ideas (i.e., bits of melody, phrases, rhythmic processions) come to him seemingly from nowhere. He hums them to himself as he begins to think about structures, such as the rules of counterpoint or the sonority of various instruments. "All this fires my soul, and, provided I am not disturbed, my subject enlarges itself, becomes methodised and defined, and the whole, though it be long, stands almost complete and finished in my mind, so that I can survey it, like a fine picture or a beautiful statue, at a glance. Nor do I hear in my imagination the parts *successively,* but I hear them, as it were, all at once (*gleich alles zusammen*)."[37] That is, before he lays it out on paper, in the linear succession of musical notation, Mozart hears the music all at once. This *tout ensemble* of everything together all at once seems like *sphota,* a flowing, undifferentiated gestalt, that is transformed into linear sequence. But because the social world is orchestrated around diachronous time, it is hard to think of time without succession in space, so we imagine the synchronic to be like a camera still that is seen from all angles at once. But synchronous time moves the way a symphony moves—all the instruments together blending as melody, harmony, rhythm, recapitulating earlier themes, anticipating later motifs, and echoing fugue-like with memories of other music. All the voices coordinated together and apart.

Synchronic time is therefore always in the background of diachronic time, often hidden but never absent. Synchronic time speaks to us daily when our lived experiences alter our perceptions of clock time—whether through anxieties that last too long or pleasures that don't last long enough. Meditation, for example, tends to slow time down and reveal the wrinkles and folds of otherwise linear time. Similarly, aesthetic experiences, like art, music, film, can alter our perceptions. Once, after I had watched Tarkovsky's film *Solaris,* a long visual tone poem on the nature of consciousness and being, my own sense of time changed. Watching the film felt like listening to music, creating in me a way of synchronic being that was filled with fugal movements of temporality; past, present, and future merging so that the film's rhythms persisted long after it ended. As I stepped outside into the cool evening air after seeing the film, my familiar everyday world was unrecognizable; it had, for a little while, a new sense of rhythmic density of time and memory commingling and colliding, a sense of losing track of time, simultaneity, synchronicity. Thus, experienced time is not a standardized measurable unit but a concatenation of interrelationships that coalesce and divide like one of Bohm's holograms, a Bach fugue, a poem by T. S. Eliot, or a stream-of-consciousness novel by Joyce. In experienced time, everything may happen at once. It is our habit to select some events for attention and ignore others from the continuum; some sensations recede into faint echoes while others barge forth. Synchrony is thus related to infinity by virtue of being without calculation, measure, or end. It is always in process, and never complete. Even when we organize the pastiche of our experiences into coherent currents through narrative and the successive diachrony of spoken language, we remain within a synchronic movement as each retelling is woven into the fabric of our memories. Like Bhartṛhari's *sphoṭa,* listened language lives in synchronic time, it engages with the confused multiplicity of everything at once of memory, the simultaneity of past, present, future all at once, *tout ensemble, all together now.* In short, listening gives us access to the otherwise unobserved presence of synchrony. To modify a turn of phrase from Martin Buber's *I and Thou,* without diachrony we humans cannot live, but human life without synchrony is simply not living.

In many ways, everyday life already grapples with the underlying ineffability of synchrony through the distinction between what are called objective and subjective time, or clock time and psychological time, as if the former were real and the latter a distortion. But we well know how a minute can seem like an eternity while waiting for a loved one, or how an hour can disappear in an instant, but such experiences are held by the master time clock to be mere psychological illusions. So-called real, objective time is clock time, the circle of time. And this brings us to a paradox—for although cycles and circles have been dominated by linearity, there is nevertheless a holism of interconnected, nonlinear movement that radiates synchronously in a circle. When something takes the form of a circle or sphere, everything is connected to everything else. For example, in a classroom with rows of desks, all students face the teacher, and only the teacher. But move those desks into a circle, and everyone faces each other—not only do students have access to their immediate neighbors on either side, but everyone has access to everyone at the same time. The interactions arising from those movements of interconnection bring a sense of aliveness, an interpersonal dance of synchronous movement.

Another beautiful example of the idea of synchrony as simultaneous movement is illustrated by what is called "cymatics," the study of how the vibration of sound waves animates particles of matter into beautiful and complex shapes. Pioneered by Swiss scientist Hans Jenny in the first half of the twentieth century, what Jenny calls "cymatic phenomenology" reveals recurring vibrational textures and patterns that can be found everywhere in the natural world, from the Mediterranean mountain ranges to the delicate contours of a seashell. In hundreds of experiments, Jenny demonstrated the remarkable diversity of forms generated by sonic vibration. For example, if you sprinkle some sand on a metal plate and then vibrate the plate with sound waves, you will see nearly instantly the sand organizing into a complex intricate pattern, some like snowflakes, some like flowers, some like the complex lattice designs in tile or glass found in churches and mosques around the world. Change the frequency or the amplitude of the sound wave, and the sand re-forms, instantly, into a different shape. Exchange the sand for a liquid such as glycerin, and still other patterns appear. Although changes in the moving medium (sand, alcohol, water, etc.), the quantity of the medium, the source of vibration (pitch, amplitude, etc.), the surface upon which the medium sits, and so on affect the pattern produced, when all these elements are kept consistent, the same pattern is produced and again. "The more one studies these things, the more one realizes that sound is the creative principle. It must be regarded as primordial."[38]

For Jenny, cymatics demonstrated that sonic vibration was the primordial organizing principle of all life: "if we can comprehend the wholeness of vibration or oscillation, and grasp the totalities in which it is manifested, then we have caught hold of reality."[39] As we discussed in chapter 2, vibration occurs everywhere in the known universe, and "from this perspective, one can begin to perceive the world as a vast interlacing network of discreet fields of oscillation, which become 'things' as they interact with the pulsations of our perceptual senses, which are also subtle vibrational fields."[40] For our purposes in this book, cymatics illustrates how synchrony is not a stillness but movement, and that holistic perspective offered by cymatics can provide deep insights into the interconnectivity that not merely surrounds, but, in fact, *is* us. Or to put it another way, synchronic time is not "outside" us, like a river that we float upon in the boat of our bodies. Rather, time "is" our life's existence, time *is* us. We will return to this idea in chapter 7 when we examine the relationship between *kairos* and akroatic thinking, but in the meantime the idea is to stress that synchronic time, unlike diachronic clock time, is neither motionless nor does it *require* spatialized metaphors to conceptualize or express (though such metaphors are, for Westerners, difficult to avoid, as demonstrated above).

For example, there are currently indigenous cultures (such as the Ainu Japan and Russia, the Amondawa of Brazil, and the Nuer of Sudan and Ethiopia), who live, conceptualize, and speak about time without reference to space.[41] The language of "Amondawa seems to contradict the idea that there is a natural, prelinguistic conceptual domain of time whose linguistic organization is universally structured via metaphoric mapping from the lexicon and grammar of space and motion."[42] In these cultures, time is an event-based happening not tied to spatial relations or preset temporal frames. According to Sinha et al., Amondawa "speakers regularly talk about events in the past and future, but their temporal expressions appear *not* to be derived from terms expressing spatial location and motion."[43] What this research suggests is that although the metaphor of time as the fourth dimension of space has taken seemingly everlasting root in the technological mind, it is not necessarily natural or inevitable. Moreover, the very metaphor itself reveals something about the creative power of synchrony. As described in chapter 4, metaphors are themselves born when two otherwise separate words, things, or ideas move together, synchronously, at the same time. Just so it is now "time" to get back to the question of listening and its relation to time, and for that we need a new concept that can express the holistic synchrony of listening and speaking with others that I call interlistening.

Interlistening

Despite the many possible alternatives to atomistic perspectives on human interaction, we have only yet begun theorizing listening as a full partner in the communication process. Whether we employ discourse analysis, speech act theory, conversation analysis, or the coordinated theory of meaning, there are dozens of ways to name, categorize, and punctuate speech acts. We can contrast phonemes with graphemes, distinguish performatives from behabitives, or identify irony, ideographs, and anaphora. Similarly, whether we study adjacency pairs, interrogatives, subjunctives, or reported speech, our eyes are on the spoken word. But when it comes to listening, we are, ironically, at a loss for words. Sure, we have active listening, interpretive listening, and mindful listening, but nomenclature aside, it is not even clear how we would begin to punctuate the listening act: Does it have a beginning, a middle, or an end? An inside and an outside? Does it even have a form? And, come to think of it, why are all these questions cast in spatial terms? We have, it seems, confined listening and speaking to a cage of spatiality.

As we described in the last chapter, intersubjectivity describes the way communicative interactions between people transcend simple boundaries between self and other or inner and outer and, in so doing, confound the atomist subject-object perspective. Like intersubjectivity, interlistening describes the ways communicative interactions transcend boundaries around time, place, and person. Interlistening is thus a descriptive, not a normative, term. It is not an ideal toward which we should aspire; it is, in contrast, a description of the multiplicitous phenomena that arise simultaneously when we listen, speak, and think. That is to say, listening, speaking, and thinking are an integrated plural, rather than a triplet of three seemingly independent processes occurring separately from each other. From this point of view, speaking, listening, and thinking are not three separate systems, but are nested and interpenetrating aspects of an integrated communicative speech language whole. The bifurcated conceptions of communication in terms of language and speech, speaking and listening, and internal and external speech have thrown us off a bit. They have made us privilege grammar over semantics, verbal over nonverbal, spoken over gesture, speech over listening, and words over everything else. If we move out of that paradigm of language-centered study and move toward a more communication-centered study, other possibilities and understandings arise. As Humboldt wrote,

> It is precisely the highest and most refined aspect that cannot be discerned from these disparate elements, and can only be perceived or divined in *connected discourse;* which is all the more proof that language proper lies in the act of its real production. It alone must in general always be thought of as the true and primary, in all investigations which are to penetrate into the living essentiality of language. The break-up into words and rules is only a dead makeshift of scientific analysis.[44]

In this way, we can say that *languaging* occurs in both speaking and listening. The concept of interlistening expresses the dialogic simultaneity of listening, thinking, and speaking, which coalesce in the polyphonic, polychronic chorale of human communication. It is an idea to help us explore speaking and listening as irretrievably con-fused aspects of the dialogic that (a) reverberate with each word and voice previously heard, thought, said, read, or dreamt, and (b) arise from multiple modes of embodiment and temporality that center on the body, the lived materiality of the now, and the eternal circulation of pastpresentfuture time.

I have chosen the name "interlistening" in part to inhibit the indomitable speech-centricity of our long-lived perspectives on language and communication, and partly to bring the connotations of attention and awareness to the foreground. "Interlisten" expresses the simultaneity of listening, thinking, and speaking. When we interlisten together, we recognize the confused multiplicity of dialogue so that we may we understand more fully Bahktin's insight that "the word (or in general any sign) is interindividual" and Voloshinov's idea that the "word is a two-sided act."[45] Interlistening describes the ways in which listening is itself a form of speaking because each utterance and action of listening and speaking resonates (i.e., brings into a kind of sympathetic vibration not unlike the vibration of strings) with a background context where an always already existing universe of prior dialogic relations vibrates. In dialogue, interlistenings reverberate with connections to everything heard, thought, said, and read in the past, present, and future lives of each interlis-

tener. Just as musical instruments and other objects can resonate sympatheti-
cally in response to vibrations produced by external bodies, interlisteners too
can hum in and out of rhythm, harmony, and time in dialogic interaction.
Interlistening thus brings a multiple emphasis on the *inter-* of interaction,
interdependency, interrelation, intersubjectivity, as well as an acknowledgment
of the attunement, attentiveness, and alterity always already nested in our
processes of communication.

What I wish to gently suggest here is that while speaking, for the most
part, seems separate from listening and thinking (from a perspective that
abides in the spatialized diachronic time of succession, linearity, movement
from before to after, from earlier to later, and so forth), listening, thinking,
and speaking occur simultaneously in synchronic time, in the moving simultaneity of pastpresentfuture. And, perhaps more controversially, I want to
suggest that both speaking and listening are synchronous, they happen at the
same time, all the time, together. Every speaking is at the same time a listening, and every listening a speaking. In other words,

> When one talks and one listens,
> two talk and two listen.
> When one talks and thousands listen,
> thousands talk and thousands listen.
> When one talks and there is no one to listen,
> one still listens.

We can hear prior strains of these ideas when Bakhtin refers to the distinction
between speaking and listening as a "fiction that produces a completely distorted idea of the complex and multifaceted process of active speech communication" and when Bergson asks, "[H]as it not been said that to hear is to
speak to oneself?"[46] We also hear echoes of this synchronicity from Merleau-
Ponty when he describes how "[t]he orator does not think before speaking,
nor even while speaking; his speech is his thought."[47] And faintly in the far
distance, we hear this theme reverberating with Bhartṛhari's *sphoṭa*—to the
extent that we interlisten in dialogue, we also, at the same time, think.
Bhartṛhari's *sphoṭa* theory is said by some to be a metaphysics of language,
where the *sphoṭa* is a transcendent phenomenon, ungrounded in physical
reality. Whether this is the case or not is beside the point here, for we are not
describing a metaphysics of meaning, we are using the *sphoṭa* theory to account for the simultaneity and synchronicity of speaking and listening, as

well as for describing the polytemporal dimensions of thought. Whether or not the true meaning of language resides in the word or the sentence (a big debate among grammarians) is not an issue that concerns us here. Instead, we are trying to conceptualize language and communication holistically rather than atomistically; rather than breaking the various phenomena of listening, thinking, and speaking into separate analytical categories, we are trying to understand them in relational synthesis. It is a different way of linking synchrony and diachrony that we call interlistening.

Pluria and Relationality

To grasp the multiplicity of interlistening, we will use the term "pluria" to describe different dimensions of auditory consciousness—the plurality of modalities that coalesce in the ongoing gestalt of interlistening. These phenomena arise in multiple modes and forms and center on the body, the lived materiality of the now, and the eternal circulation of past, present, future, which mingle together in each moment. In this way we might say that interlistening is polymodal (occurring across multiple sensory modalities such as seeing, tasting, speaking, listening, and so forth), polyphonic (occurring through the voices of different characters such as self, other, real, imagined, inner, outer, our best friend, parents, former teachers, and so forth), and polychronic (occurring in a confused multiplicity of temporal modalities such as past, present, future, duration, and so forth). Interlistening is thus a dense pattern of movements arising and passing away within a holistic gestalt, which atomist perspectives categorize as separate and boundaried phenomena. Interlistening thus interweaves the many qualities of speaking, listening, and thinking from a relational, not a referential or representational, perspective.

The three pluria of interlistening (polymodality, polychronicity, and polyphony) offer not a typology, but a way of describing a process focused less on the content of words or language and more on the qualities of interaction. Interlistening is thus not something to do or not to do, or to do more or less, it is something we are always doing. It is not agentive or intentioned, it is there like the pitch, rhythm, and volume of music are there, and all we can do is become more aware. Interlistening is thus a wholly relational phenomenon, not unlike the proportional relationships of harmony described in chapter 2, which is not made up of separated elements, but is an epiphenomenon that arises from the interaction itself. The relationality of interlistening thus involves the multiple dimensions of embodied consciousness that vibrate in the dance of conversation between people talking, whether it is in a courtroom, a classroom, a bedroom, or a bar. That is, relationality describes the qualities of interaction, both conscious and unconscious, that occur when we communicate. These relational patterns may be in conflict or congruence, they may be in or out of sync, they may match or clash, but they are patterns of interaction that we can be more or less aware of as we communicate. As we discussed in the last chapter, intersubjectivity illustrates how "meaning originates between us not from within us," and how this process "is not just me coordinating with you and you with me, but each of us is sensitive to a continually changing 'it' between us."[48] Merleau-Ponty has a beautiful description of this process:

> In the experience of dialogue, there is constituted between the other person and myself a common ground; my thought and his are inter-woven into a single fabric, my words and those of my interlocutor are called forth by the state of the discussion, and they are inserted into a shared operation of which neither of us is the creator. We have here a dual being where the other is for me no longer a mere bit of behavior in my transcendental field, nor I in his; we are collaborators for each other in consummate reciprocity. Our perspectives merge into each other, and we co-exist through a common world. In the present dialogue, I am freed from myself, for the other person's thoughts are certainly his; they are not of my making, though I do grasp them the moment they come into being, or even anticipate them.[49]

As we discussed in chapter 5, communication is intersubjective—to one degree or another, it always creates a third space that is greater than the sum of the interlocutors. The concept of interlistening describes both the intra- and intersubjectivity of communicative practice, and takes into account not so much content as process, not the *what* so much as the *how*. Because we are working within language, the diachronic attributes of order, sequence, category are essential, but focusing exclusively upon them can be misleading. Therefore, the three categories of pluria are only aspects of one congruent whole, facets of a crystal, senses of the body. But in order to describe them, we will focus on them separately, one at a time: first physicality and embodiment, then temporality, tense and timing, and lastly, sonority and musicality.

Polymodality: Physicality and Embodiment

Physicality pertains to the embodied dimension of interlistening. It involves proprioception, the interacting and mutually influencing patterns of breathing, posture, and gesture. It also involves the sensory dimensions of smell, taste, and touch, as well as body movement and energy. Fuchs and De Jaegher describe what they call "mutual incorporation," where the interacting bodies of people in communication extend beyond each "individual's" boundary and "form a common intercorporality."[50] This is far more than a kind of *body language* conceived as a sending and receiving of nonverbal messages—it is *embodied communication* that circulates in an interdependent cycle of what Clark calls "continuous reciprocal causation," where everything, from movements to gestures to posture, affects everything else in a continuous circle of interactive complexity. Atomistically describing the interactions of players in a tennis match as "a step-wise progression (involving a sequence of discrete states) would clearly do extreme violence to the time-coordination of events and processes. The motion of the ball, the tracking (and anticipating) eye movements, and the various gross bodily actions are all unfolding in a kind of phased and interanimated parallelism."[51]

One of the early pioneers of the study of unconscious coordination, William S. Condon, used an incredibly precise frame-by-frame film analysis to observe synchronized patterns of movement between speakers and listeners. "[The] microanalysis of sound films of listener behavior led to the surprising and unsuspected observation that listeners move in precise synchrony with the articulatory structure of the speaker's speech. . . . [I]t is as if the listener's whole body were dancing in precise and fluid accompaniment to the speech."[52] Condon found that the bodies of listeners move in coordinated relation to the sounds and rhythms of their interlocutor's speech, including pitch, intonation, volume, and tempo. "With the ongoing emergent flow of each 'different' sound form in the stream of speech, there is a parallel emergence from the listener's body of sustained, organized movement."[53] "When two individuals interact in this way," Fuchs and De Jaegher observe, "the coordination of their body movements, utterances, gestures, gazes, etc. can gain such momentum that it overrides the individual intentions, and common sense-making emerges."[54]

Other forms of physical synchrony include ducking, wincing, leaning, yawning, and so forth. For example, have you ever ducked your head during a movie when some very large object hurtled toward you from the screen? Or perhaps you've winced at the sight of a friend's broken limb dangling at an unnatural angle. Other examples of unconscious physical coordination occur when people walking together synchronize their steps even though the length and frequency of their gaits differ greatly.[55] And how about those funny moments when you're walking toward someone in a narrow passage and each of you inadvertently mirrors the other's movements, continuing to block rather than easily circumnavigate one another? Our well-honed yet unconscious patterns of synchronous interactions are hard to break, even when we wish to avoid bumping into someone!

Generally speaking, the more synchrony occurs in interaction, the greater the sense of connection and empathy among participants. In a recent study of therapist-patient interaction, Ramseyer and Tschacher found that the more doctors and patients unconsciously coordinated their postures, gestures, movements, and so forth together, the greater the sense of connection and therapeutic quality both reported in the work.[56] These findings confirm Condon's insight that that "the more two interactants share movement or posture together, the greater the rapport between them. Such rapport contributes to a sense of acceptance, belonging, and well-being."[57] Thus, gesture is not just an embellishment, but can be an integral part of listening, thinking, and speaking. One of the pioneering scholars of gesture, David McNeill, describes how "gestures do not just reflect thought but *have an impact on thought*. Gestures, together with language, *help constitute thought*. . . . Gestures occur because they are part of the speaker's ongoing thought process."[58]

Beyond using gestures to point, describe spatial relationships, direct our interlocutors' attention, and so forth, research has found that gesture plays an important role in cognition. In their research into how children learn math, for example, Francaviglia and Servidio consider gesture to be a kind of "cognitive scaffolding" that emerges from dialogic interaction among students in problem-solving groups.[59] Importantly, the gestures used by a student to think through and express concepts and relationships are repeated by others in the group who use them to continue development of ideas. The gestures thus develop through the conversation, modifying and being modified by the conversation and serving as an important scaffold for learning. The gestures are not simply symbols that come to be adopted by the group, but become themselves shapers of knowledge that act upon the gesturer and the listeners, interanimating the participants in the conversation. All of which is to say that not only do "bodily actions operate both outwardly and inwardly in meaning-making activity," but "meaningfulness emerges from the ability to activate a social reaction of another in yourself, a way of reacting in your own actions similarly to the actions of others."[60] When I was in India, for example, I found myself unconsciously mimicking the distinctively Indian head movement that accompanies so many social interactions. Rather than nodding up and down or saying encouragers like "Yeah" or "Okay," many listeners in India express their attention to speakers by tilting their head slightly left and right—a gesture I found extremely difficult to resist.

Other research reveals that that speakers unconsciously rely on listeners' nonverbal movements and gestures in response to their speech for a number of things, including memory. For example, Pasupathi, Stallworth, and Murdoch found that when talking to nonattentive listeners, speakers remembered less and told their stories less well. Their findings demonstrate that attentive listeners facilitate long-term memory in speakers in ways not attributable to mere rehearsal—whether talking to distracted listeners or to no listener at all. They found that attentive listeners elicited more information, detail, and elaboration from speakers even when no questions or interruptions occurred. "Listener's attentiveness matters—attentive listeners elicit more information, overall as well as more novel and elaborative information, than do distracted listeners."[61] Other scholars have demonstrated that telling stories is a "joint activity" accomplished between speakers and listeners. As Bavelas, Coates, and Johnson describe it, "the narrator needs a listener to tell a good story; a good listener is a collaborator, a partner in storytelling."[62] These insights were also noted by scholars in the Soviet school, who observed how listener reactions influence speaking: "the tone of speech, its 'temperature' varies, depending on the extent that the speaker 'warms up' or 'cools down' by the mimicry of the listener. If the listener attends closely, the speech process is facilitated."[63]

Thought of in this way, the boundaries between self and other, inside and outside, mine and yours become indistinct as the intersubjective *between* becomes an actor in its own right. An example of this arose in a listening class I taught where students were invited to approach listening from an embodied perspective. One student described the listening experience of learning to dance the tango with a partner as "beyond words." The student was describing how attentive listening (paying attention to body movement, posture, the minutest of movements) was essential to the dance, and that thinking or reasoning about the dance would interfere. "The two people are together in one activity in reciprocrative [*sic*] sense to one another. . . . You do not try and question and reason your way out to figure out the dance. You just dance and your body naturally adapts to it." Here is Humboldt's two-hundred-year-old insight into this process: "Conversing together is never comparable with a transfer of material. In the understander, as in the speaker, the same thing must be evolved from the inner power of each; and what the former receives is merely the harmoniously attuning stimulus. Hence it is also very natural for man to re-utter at once what he has just understood."[64] Similarly, Bergson's observation that "[s]ome neuropaths cannot be present at a conversation without moving their lips; this is only an exaggeration of what takes place in the case of every one of us. How will the expressive or rather suggestive power of music be explained, if not by admitting that we repeat to ourselves the sounds heard . . . ?"[65] In sum, interlistening involves the whole being, body, heart, and mind, and it occurs within and between persons, in and out of time, which brings us to one of the most significant findings of Condon, later explored by other scholars: the temporal synchrony of speaker and listener interactions, to which we will turn next.

Polychronicity: Temporality and Tempus

Temporality involves the rhythmic aspects of interlistening, such as timing, order, sequence, coordination, syncopation, repetition, and punctuation, as well as the tensed aspect of interlistening, such as time scales and periods of past, present, and future. Much of the work on intersubjective physicality pertains to the incredibly rhythmic and unconscious synchronicity between interlocutors in conversation. As mentioned above, Condon discovered a remarkably precise synchrony of movements between speakers and listeners, which he called "entrainment" and which "tends to occur continuously during the interaction, if the listener is attending and free to move. There can be a relatively continuous and ongoing, yet constantly varying, stream of speech, which is almost simultaneously being continuously and organizationally tracked as expressed in the organization of change of the body motion of the listener."[66] That is to say, both speakers and listeners are moving in a rhythmic process that neither one is directing. "If we are moving while we are listening, our body motion organization entrains with the sound patterns of the speech of the person we are listening to."[67]

These findings have been confirmed by a number of scholars, including McNeill, who found a consistent rhythmic pulse with repetitive and periodic recurrence between gestures and speech of both speakers and listeners. He found that speech and gesture were integrated for both speakers and listeners. More recently, Loehr found that "the tempos used by hand, head, and speech during conversation are consistent with a common human tempo of around 600 milliseconds" and that "eyeblinks typically happen on the rhythmic pulse" of the speaker's speech.[68] Similarly, Bertau describes how not just specific thoughts, but consciousness and the self, come into being through the rhythmic patterning of dialogue. She writes, "Time as mutual synchronisation is the central aspect to all these types of speech, reaching into preverbal protoconversations and into exchanges and adjustments of two bodies. Self comes to be within the rhythm of intersubjectivity."[69] It is important to note that these processes are unconscious and occur without our awareness. To imagine the difficulty of these synchronizations, one need only recall the difficulty of consciously attempting to synchronize a telephone greeting with an interlocutor from another country whose ritual greeting formula differs radically from one's own. Or consider the challenge of getting a word in edgewise when speaking with conversational partners whose rhythm, speed, and inbreaths far outpace one's own.

To further investigate and describe the synchronic nonlinear dimension of time in communication, it may be helpful to return to the ancient Indian grammarians, whose concept of *sphoṭa* deals with the irrepressible movement of transformation from inner to outer and from nonlinear to linear. In chapter 4 we discussed Bhartṛhari's and Luria's depiction of external speech as the final stage in a process that begins with an undifferentiated gestalt or kernel of desire, or impulse, that may arise whole cloth simultaneously as it is transformed into a linear sequence of words that unfold in diachronous time. *Sphoṭa* takes place in synchronous time and only takes the form of orderly succession in diachronic linear time when it is transformed into the spoken word. Speech is uttered in linear time, but it is created in synchronous time. "The Word is neither a 'previous' nor 'a subsequent,' because it is the speech-sounds which are produced in sequence. But the non-sequential is revealed as sequential as if it were divided."[70] As the undifferentiated burst of prelinguistic thought, *sphoṭa* is filled with linguistic potency but is not yet itself linguistic. It is nonspatial and nontemporal, like Vygotsky's vision of the boy in blue which we discussed in the last chapter. It is a form of intuitive knowledge, as yet inarticulate and inarticulated. And just as the *sphoṭa* initially exists as an undifferentiated burst of meaning in the speaker, so it exists as an undifferentiated burst of meaning in the listener, who hears the words in an ordered, linear diachronous form, but who derives the meaning in an instant flash of interlistening insight.

Bhartṛhari describes listening as a synchronous simultaneity: "Simultaneously with the last sound, the word is apprehended by the mind in which the seed has been sown by the (physical) sounds, and in which ripening (of the speech) has been brought about by the telling over (of the sounds)."[71] Moreover, Bhartṛhari's listeners are generating as much as receiving: "Even before the vibrations of the speech-organs (which produce the word) have subsided, other sounds, are formed from the word (sphoṭa) itself, as one flame from another."[72] Thus, to Bhartṛhari, meaning is not in the utterance itself, but is something achieved by the hearer. But this transformation of *sphoṭa* to speech involves a movement of time from synchrony to diachrony. Remember Vygotsky's boy with a blue shirt from chapter 4? Once my speech gives birth to thought, it is by necessity ignoring dozens of other things about it—so much is happening in synchronic simultaneity that inevitably speech loses something that was in the bursting forth of *sphoṭa*. This loss has been described by Bergson as how we can be misled by language, which, he says, "gives a fixed form to fleeting sensations" and "is not meant to convey all the delicate shades of inner states."[73] A good example of this can be observed during a strange moment in the Michael Jackson film *This Is It*, when, during a rehearsal of the song "I Want You Back," Jackson stops singing and dancing and speaks to the director and production staff. Jackson's movements are smooth and elegant as he strides up and down the stage, using his hands and gesticulating, pointing to his ears. But he seems to be having a great deal of trouble putting his thoughts into words. Here's a transcript:

MJ: You guys, I gotta tell you this. When I'm trying to hear it feels like somebody's fist is pushed into my ears. It's really very difficult. I know you mean well, so, but it's, I'm trying to adjust to the ear, the inner ears, okay? With the love, with the love, l-o-v-e. . . . It's not easy, though.

At this point the director, Kenny Ortega, asks Michael to repeat himself because, he says, he didn't hear.

KO: Michael, one more time, I couldn't hear you, sir.

So Michael tries again.

MJ: The inner ears are very difficult for me when you're raised to use just your real own, you know, aural—oratory ears. Now it feels like somebody's fish is, just their fist is shoved into your ear. I'm trying to hear and I can't. So I'm adjusting to the situation.

This brief scene illustrates several ideas about interlistening worth noting. First, without the ability to hear himself with "his own aural" ears, it is difficult for Michael Jackson to sing—he can't produce sound without the ability to hear it at the same time. Singing and hearing must occur simultaneously. But also notice his wording—when he refers to his "oratory ears," Jackson is not (or not merely) misspeaking, but he is demonstrating how interlistening transposes the binary categories of speaking and listening into a complex modality that is experienced synchronously as "oratory ears." Lastly, it is puzzling that Jackson seems to struggle so when basically all he wants is the earphones turned down. Why can't this incredibly brilliant musician and composer find his words? Partly it may have to do with the fact that he can't hear himself—and that without the ability to listen, he is unable to speak. Another possibility is that he is in synchronic rhythmic time, not diachronic linguistic time, and in the radial rhythmic movement of music and dance the words simply escape him because the linearity of language is out of synch with the rhythmic pulsation of music. Perhaps his deep engagement in synchronic musical time makes it very difficult for him to diachronically define, explain, ask them to turn down the sound in his earphones. In this sense, we are reminded here of Bergson's insight that "imaginary homogeneous time is . . . an idol of language, a fiction. . . . In reality there is no one rhythm of duration."[74] Jackson's synchronic *durée* cannot be expressed in linear language. The experience is simply "inexpressible because language cannot get hold of it without arresting its mobility or fit it into its common-place forms without making it into public property."[75]

Insofar as the polychronic rhythms of synchronic *durée* create forms of vibrational attunement, they cross boundaries between inner and outer, self and world. The rhythmic tempos and vibrations of the voice, the body, or the seasons do not stand outside the embodied self, but intertwine with it as a holistic and participatory gestalt. In an essay that traces the etymology of the

Latin *tempus,* meaning "time," Benveniste contends that for the Romans, *tempus* was a dual concept with a concrete living and material aspect combined with an inheritance from the Greek conception of time as an abstract, objective, and inanimate succession of moments.[76] His essay reveals the multiple semantic fields of *tempus,* which resonate with embodied and material attunement: meteorological (*temps, tempestus, temperatura, intempéries*), proportion or ratio (*temperare,* "temperament," "tempestuous"), and occasional (*printemps,* "temporary," "extempore," *in tempore*). To these we could of course add others such as "tempo," "temper," and so forth. Thus does the living materiality of time as embodied, synchronic movement reveal itself in our dialogic interactions.

Polyphony: Sonority and Musicality

The musical dimension of interlistening pertains to all of the auditory and sonic qualities of the communicative interaction. It might involve the texture or timbre of the sound, its density and multiplicity, or extend to pockets of silence, or to repetition, fugue, or reversal. Or it might pertain to the volume: a whisper versus a shout; or the tonality: assonance, dissonance to the voices and their echoes with other past or present voices. We all know the sense of disorientation when the tone of someone's voice clashes with their words, or when a rising intonation indicates a question, or when a descending intonation indicates sadness. As Bertau theorizes, the voice itself is "a form of vivid materiality, it offers a meaningful structure in so far as it is always turned toward somebody. And it is meaningful because of its participation in the inter-individual interactional world it is rooted in."[77] All of which is not to say that sonority doesn't include language, for of course it does. We can hear the polyphonous exuberance of sonority in *Finnegans Wake*—as "confused a multiplicity" as ever written—where language is a stream-of-consciousness sound play, and meaning resonates with polysemous polylingual puns in Sanskrit, Gaelic, and many other languages, and allusions to texts such as the Bible, the Upanishads, and the *Egyptian Book of the Dead* abound. To read *Finnegans Wake* is to listen to the sound of the words, the rhythmic cadences of its musicality, its droning or incandescent melody. If one relaxes enough, one can get drunk from the music of these pages. "The Mookse had a sound eyes right but he could not all hear. The Gripes had light ears left yet he could but ill see."[78]

As discussed in chapter 5, the musical dimension of language is central to the development of language in children, and musicality constitutes interactions of mother and child in terms of rhythm and voice. In an empirically grounded study of the prelexical musical polyphony of self-other relations between infants and mothers, Gratier and Bertau detail what they call the "deep dialogicality" of early interaction. They make apparent how the infant is "not *facing* the world with the (referential) tool of language, but *within* the world and language, together with Other."[79] According to Powers and Trevarthen, "The main message is that normal happy infants and their mothers use their voice tones cooperatively, with 'communicative musicality' to sustain a harmony and synchronicity of emotional 'narrative envelopes.'"[80] As infants grow into languaging children, this musicality makes its way into children's play, as the singsong of teasing and calls attests, as well as the classroom. Erickson describes the importance of musicality—in terms of volume, pitch, timbre, contours, rhythm, cadence, and pitch patterns—to the learning environment created by classroom interaction. "When teachers and students share a similar implicit musical signalling system for the coordination of attention and action in talk, they tend to understand one another clearly and have positive feelings toward one another. When the mutual signalling system is not working well and interactional stumbles happen (akin to performance stumbles in dance and music), negative affect and misunderstanding often occur. . . . Our capacity to think with and feel with one another seems to be tied to our capacity to dance and sing in smooth, predictable rhythm with each other in our talk."[81]

Sometimes the importance of musicality makes its way into adult conversation as well. Principally it takes the form of humor, puns, rhythms, and rhymes. But it can take other shapes as well. So here's a confession: I have a habit of echoing what people say, which, sadly, often makes some of them irritated. They think I'm mimicking them as children do, to annoy them or poke fun of them or otherwise tease them. But that's not it. It's because the sonority of what they say is sometimes too wonderful not to repeat. It might be the pitch or intonation, or the singsong rhythmic quality, or some other musical aspect, but is not about the meaning (unless perhaps punning is involved), it's about the sound itself. Just like in *Finnegans Wake*. Here's an example from the novel when Jute (who is not, incidentally, jeff mute) interlistens with the stammering utterer Mutt (also not jeff mute). The delicious dialogue begins,

Scuse us, chorley guy! You tollerday donsk? N. You talkatiff scowegian? Nn. You spigotty anglease? Nnn. You phonio saxo? Nnnn. . . .

> Jute.—Are you jeff?
>
> Mutt.—Somehards.
>
> Jute.—But you are not jeffmute?
>
> Mutt.—Noho. Only an utterer.
>
> Jute.—Who? Whoat is the mutter with you?
>
> Mutt.—I became a stun a stummer.
>
> Jute.—What a hauhauhauhaudibble thin, to be cause! How, Mutt?[82]

The sounds and rhythms of this passage work in concert with the words to tickle, embellish, and otherwise bring the reader/listener into an ensemble of sound play that gathers together and celebrates the pluria of interlistening.

The Holism of Interlistening

As described in previous chapters, the atomistic models of communication and language have thrown us off a bit by privileging verbal over nonverbal, spoken over gestural, speech over listening, and words over everything else. And even were we to ever break free of atomism's singular lock on our conceptions of language and communication, we would find ourselves nevertheless left with the relentless drone of spatiality ringing in our ears, its monochromatic coloration, like white noise, silencing the sounds of listening. As partial antidote we have, in this chapter on interlistening, examined the verdant fertility of misunderstanding, how it is the mother and father, daughter and son, of understanding; and how, like Whitman, we are ourselves untamed and untranslatable, with the sounds of our "barbaric yawp over the roofs of the world."[83] Not beautiful or lovely, the fertilizer of misunderstanding provides the nourishment for understanding to grow. The decomposed detritus of a lifetime of words, memories, and experiences is not merely an instrument for nourishing the soil of understanding, it is the very medium in which understanding lives and grows. We have also looked into the qualities of synchronous time and sought to consider how the simultaneous movement and polyrhythms of lived experience might bear on the layered multifaceted processes of listening. Conceived solely through a linear perspective of diachronous time, our studies of listening may all too easily conform to the entailments of the conduit metaphor and the dictates of instrumental transmission. Thought of with and through the rhythmic cycles and interanimations of past/present/ future synchronic time, the tidal flow of Bergson's *durée,* and the simultaneity of interlistening, our study of listening can pursue new frameworks, directions and interconnections.

In this chapter we have further explored how, even were we to conceptualize inner speech as inherently dialogic, polyphonous, and embodied, we would still be left with the unanswered question, if inner speech is dialogic, then who listens? In the thought experiment of this chapter, we have played with the supposition that dialogic *interlocutors* were instead *interlisteners* by examining the ways in which speaking/listening are not two separate processes, but two facets of a single integrated process. We have described the ways in which interlistening involves both temporal synchronicity and diachrony, how it involves multiple modalities and subjectivities and the three pluralities of physicality, temporality, and sonority. Like Virginia Woolf's Mrs. Ramsay, we have conceived of interlistening as if whatever we heard "was like the movement of a trout when, at the same time, one can see the ripple and the gravel, something to the right, something to the left; and the whole is held together; for whereas in active life she would be netting and separating one thing from another . . . now she said nothing."[84] We have imagined communication processes as a multiplicity of interrelationships, not as a language space but as a polymodal language dance, a nonlinear flowing, never still, movement that, like a river, pulses and billows. The voices of this language dance are not merely our own, but belong to the generations of ancestors and the gatherings of our everyday experiences, the interstitial layerings of our every encounter with others and the world which make us who and what we are:

> Through me many long dumb voices,
> Voices of the interminable generations of slaves,
> Voices of prostitutes and of deformed persons,
> Voices of the diseased and despairing, and of thieves and dwarfs,
> Voices of cycles of preparation and accretion,
> And of the threads that connect the stars.[85]

Through an interlistening perspective, we have explored how speaking and listening are not separate distinct entities, but are part of an ongoing organic chorale of communication, and how, just as musical quotation, digital sampling, and mash-ups create new musical soundscapes, so too does the confused multiplicity of interlistening. The idea of interlistening presented here is thus neither an injunction nor a directive. It is an invitation, a sharing, like pointing out a sunset or a soaring hawk—we observe what is there, always knowing there is more we have missed. Interlistening is thus a descriptive and not a prescriptive term. It is not a norm, or an instrument to accomplish a goal or achieve an end, and it is not pure and good. In fact, we might even say that interlistening *is* not, but rather, that interlistening *occurs,* it is largely unintentional, uncontrollable, unforeseeable, and it occurs with a plurality of qualities that we can choose to notice or ignore, dismiss as folly, relish with delight, or simply regret. Wherever we go, whatever we do, interlistening is occurring. Whether or not we notice is up to us.

From an everyday diachronic perspective, our thought process seems so unintentional, our ideas continually floating in and out of mind seemingly at random. A worrisome thought crosses, and one can fall prey to an anxiety that courses through the body, descending from jaw to shoulder with an imperceptible creeping tautness. Only in the practice of meditation, it seems, can this incessant flashing of thought be revealed—meditation enables us to not listen to these thoughts, but to greet them with a friendly nod, as if to riders on a bus; we acknowledge their existence but don't get off the bus and follow them home. The intentionality of meditation thus sits side by side with the unintentionality of thought, both at the same time. But by electing to *not* listen to thoughts, we are in no way electing not to interlisten, for that is out of our hands. As a form of listening, meditation is perhaps interlistening made conscious, deliberate, intentional. Listening to interlistening can thus involve an exercise of intentional agency—one pays careful attention, willing oneself to focus on what is occurring and letting it reverberate with one's inner voice.

In this way, listening occurs as a form of inner speech, an unintentional speaking. Typically we understand speaking to be a volitional action involving an exercise of intentional agency—we don't imagine ourselves speaking passively, we understand speech to be a form of action. But one can also bring intentionality and awareness to interlistening; one can observe the echoes and intrusions, the fading in and out, the interplay of understanding and misunderstanding, as one intentionally places attention where one wishes it to rest—listening to one's breathing, aware of thoughts swimming in and out of the stream like flutes and cymbals weaving in and out of a melody. But intentionality is a tricky thing. So much of our life is lived habitually and unconsciously that we can lay claim to few truly intentional acts. At the same time, we pride ourselves on our autonomy and freedom—our ability to choose. And yes, of course, when I do one thing I also do, often unconsciously, a million other things. As I type these words on the computer, the screen is powered by electricity that has been generated in a power plant that is spewing hundreds of tons of poison into the atmosphere by burning coal that has been mined by workers who risk their lives and early death in the miserable working conditions of the mines. But this is so far removed that is like an abstraction—I don't intentionally harm the workers and the environment, but my intention to better understand listening involves many interconnections that do involve harm, and I can ignore or overlook that fact, or live with awareness and higher intentionality. Can I generate power for my computer using sunlight? Can I find a way not to heat my home with oil?

Because we take for granted the facile separation between listening and speaking, we overlook the possibilities offered by intentional attention. But, like the *pharmakon* discussed earlier in this chapter, these possibilities can be poison as well as remedy. For in some ways, the past is a trance from which we never escape. Like a hawk in flight, listening makes us vulnerable—we can change our position, be blown off course, sent spinning earthward, and crash. But also like flight, listening allows us to escape, if momentarily, from our tiny earthbound perspective with ourselves as the center of the world, and allows us to lift heavenward and take in a far greater view of the whole. Listening, like flight, offers unfamiliar vistas and new mis/understandings, it offers cycles of perpetual enfoldment, the coming together and coming apart, of human being. As a description rather than a recipe, interlistening offers a practicum of attention—just as a trumpet player attends to tone, color, wind, force, pause, attack, and so forth, so an interlistener attends to the plurality of temporalities and voices, to the rhythms of sameness and difference, proximity, and distance. All too often, we ignorantly punctuate our experiences with a spatialized temporality, which, like a period at the end of a sentence, signals finality and completion, and fails to account for the expanding oscillations of assonance and dissonance, fullness and emptiness, which are better expressed by the musical temporality of a comma, or a breath. In the next chapter we will begin to take up the strength of vulnerability and examine the relation of listening and ethics.

LISTENING OTHERS TO SPEECH

Listen, only listen to my words; this is the consolation you can offer me.

—JOB

In the biblical story of Job, the selfsame principled and pious resident of Uz sits atop a dungheap lamenting his misery and railing at God for allowing so many horrible things to besiege him—first he's lost just about everything he ever had, and then he's stricken with illness. Soon three friends come by to offer him sympathy and consolation. The men sit together without speaking for seven days and seven nights, offering the comfort of their silent presence by his side. At last Job speaks, cursing the day of his birth. "Why did I not die new-born, not perish as I left the womb?" (Job 3:11).[1] He rails and rails, in utter despair. In response, his friends do what comes all too easily to many of us; they tell him what to do, why he's suffering, and how he should fix things up. One brags about his own personal connection to God, while another repeatedly accuses him of being a sinner who should repent, since God punishes only the wicked. "Renounce the iniquity that stains your hands," says Zophar (11:14). Job is now doubly stricken, first by his misery and now by his friends' so-called solicitude. In particular, he is aggrieved by their lectures and their presumption to know what he's going through, why he suffers, and what he should do. At first he mockingly thanks them for their condescending and paternalistic concern, wryly noting how each is "never at a loss for a helpful suggestion" (26:3). But soon Job's sarcasm gives way to angry confrontation as he calls the friends out on their failure to listen. "How often have I heard all this before! What sorry comforters you are! Is there never to be an end of airy words? What a plague your need to have the last word is!" (16:2–3).

How many of us have experienced this situation? Those miserable times when we are knocked flat on our backs by life and seemingly well-meaning friends walk up, glance down at us, and proceed to tell us all about our problems and what we should do about them. Or else they skip right by us and go straight to themselves, recounting in tedious detail what happened to them, what they did about it, and how they felt. In these interminable conversational situations, we are left lonelier than ever. There's possibly nothing more despairing than speaking our vulnerabilities to another human being who utterly fails to listen, and merely "hears" our suffering through the lens of her own unending story. "I know exactly what you mean," says the well-meaning empath who, in fact, "knows" nothing of the kind. Frankly, one can find more comfort talking to one's dog and cat.

In this chapter we explore the relationship between listening and ethics and discover how virtue may arise from *listening*. When we relinquish control and our attempts to master other people, listening engenders something like a quickening, wherein a birth mother first begins to feel the new life growing within her womb, or "[l]ike a hawk adrift in its fine solution of clouds."[2] More than a mere metaphor, quickening, like listening, entails the recognition of another self, the startling presence of another being, a not-self. As an enactment of ethics, listening, like quickening, brings a recognition of an unknown other to whom we are bound and about whom we feel care and concern. In this way we might say that ethics speaks by way of listening; and more specifically, it speaks by way of listening *for and to* the *otherness* of others. As Virginia Woolf's shellshocked World War I veteran Septimus Warren Smith discovers in the novel *Mrs. Dalloway,* "the human voice . . . can quicken trees into life." In a reverie of joy and beauty brought on by an unnamed altered state of consciousness, Septimus hears, sees, and feels the interconnected vibrations of life as they resonate within and all around him. "[T]hey beckoned; leaves were alive; trees were alive. And the leaves [were] connected by millions of fibres with his own body, there on the seat. . . . Sounds made harmonies with premeditation; the spaces between them were as significant as the sounds. A child cried. Rightly far away a horn sounded. All taken together meant the birth of a new religion."[3]

Although Septimus's wife finds his rapt absorption in the "nothingness" of trees, birds, and sky alarming, both disturbed and disturbing, the reader vicariously experiences an ethical quickening brought on by listening to his voice. For when we listen to Septimus listening to the listening of trees, we are brought into ethical relation with our most familiar yet wholly *other* other—

the tree. Part of the everyday background of human life, trees are everywhere standing silently, seen and unseen. We encounter trees, whether as metaphor or material, objects of beauty or of shade, nourishment, and shelter, as objects to be "used" without care, without awareness. But as much as we may objectify and externalize them, trees live with us and inside us, each to each and at one with the immeasurable and undivided swirl of life. Ancient references to trees as spiritual invocations, poetic metaphors, or scientific exemplars can be found everywhere from the Upanishads to Zen koans. In the natural world, the tree-like patterns of branching recursivity are found everywhere, from the neural networks that course through the human brain to flashes of lightning in the sky, and from the winding waters of a riverbed to the repeated branching patterns of self-similarity found in Mandelbrot's binary fractal trees. According to Plato, "the first prophetic utterances came from an oak tree," and in a well-known Zen koan, the meaning of Bodhidharma's journey to China is "the oak tree in the garden."[4]

Everywhere daily, across the history of the planet, the roots, branches, trunks, and leaves of trees have surrounded and guided human thinking. Be it an olive branch, a crooked timber of humanity, or a tree of life, we unthinkingly think with trees. That bears repeating. We *think with trees.* Yes, it typically takes an unfamiliar state of consciousness—be it spiritual, aesthetic, or psychological—to hear the symphonic quickening of life in the otherness of trees, or in any of life's other strange and varied forms. For most of us, listening to the quickening of a tree is a bit beyond the pale; like Septimus's wife, we live in the ordinary realm of the social with the listening of trees out of our reach. That being the case, perhaps listening to *merely* human others is more within our reach—difficult as it may be. Certainly, we will be tempted, like Job's friends, to speak, to know, to impose and master. But perhaps we will resist that temptation so that our listening allows for an ethical quickening, a recognition in the familiar of the strange, freeing others to indeed *be other.*

Listening Otherwise

How do we respond to the suffering of others? To begin with a personal experience: some years ago as I attempted to reread Ralph Ellison's classic novel about mid-twentieth-century American racism, *Invisible Man.* But I had to stop less than a third of the way in because the text was too painful—the humiliations and degradations recounted with bitterness and irony were simply more sorrowful than I could bear. I couldn't keep reading. It was, for me, like all those war movies that rip the mythic façade off of war to reveal its true insanity and terror. "Sometimes," I told my friends, "imagination is enough." But now, facing Ellison, I challenge myself. *Who am I to turn away from the suffering of others? Why am I protecting myself from witnessing suffering? Furthermore, how can I refuse to listen when the very race and class privileges underlying the suffering Ellison depicts protect me?* By not opening to this suffering and listening to its otherness, I protect myself and my privileges with what I already know and understand. To close Ellison's book was a gesture of refusal and complicity—turning a deaf ear in order to protect the self-existing-I. And isn't this, after all, what Ellison's text made so clear, the connection between response and responsibility—how when I witness, I become responsible? And the overwhelming anxiety that emerges from this responsibility gives me all the more reason to turn away and not listen. Writing in 1952, Ellison documented the particular and excruciating horrors of racism and its denial of his humanity, his gifts, and his autonomy. But in my hands now, as it did to readers fifty years ago, his book became a call of conscience: Ellison's text called on me to witness his pain and suffering—to not turn away, but to listen and respond. To become responsible.

The issues of response and responsibility are woven into the center of dialogic ethics, and many scholars have explored the contours of the ethical response. For the philosopher Emmanuel Levinas, the self's responsibility to respond to the face of the other is infinite, unlimited. To Calvin Schrag, "The language of morality is the language of responsiveness and responsibility, and if there is to be talk of 'an ethics' in all this it will need to be an ethics of the fitting response."[5] For Michael Hyde, too, "The language of morality is the language of responsiveness and responsibility."[6] But quietly embedded in these observations about the ethical response persists a hidden but presupposed prior action—that of listening. The idea of *the response* as related to ideas of reply, answer, and reaction, as well as its derivation from the Latin *spondere* (to pledge, promise, offer, sacrifice), stress only the speaking of an ethical actor. The act of listening is itself concealed and rendered invisible. Thus, the ethical response so powerfully described by Levinas, Schrag, and Hyde nevertheless presupposes a hidden *listening*. For in order to respond, I must first listen— that is attend, observe, attune—and in doing so receive the otherness of the other. Without this listening, there may be speaking, and there may be acting, but there can be no genuinely engaged response.

So even before it ever comes to the question of ethical response, I can simply shut the book, close my eyes, or walk away. I may pretend to listen, or, even worse, pretend not to understand. This is what Hurtado calls the "*Pendejo* Game," when white people "play dumb," refusing to acknowledge racism by claiming simply not to comprehend.[7] Conversely, I can refuse to listen by claiming to understand and yet be so immersed in the limitations and presuppositions of my own prior knowledge that I fail to listen altogether. I am struck deaf and blind, in this sense, by what I *already know* and understand. For example, in *Regarding the Pain of Others,* Sontag invites readers to reflect on the ethical significance of war photography. She recounts the story of a British photojournalist during the Sarajevo siege who, during a lull in the fighting, mounted an exhibition of photographs that included both Somalian and Sarajevan victims of war. The Sarajevans were offended and, as it turned out, refused to attend the exhibition. In other words, they turned a blind eye and a deaf ear. As Sontag explains, "To set their sufferings alongside the sufferings of another people was to compare them (which hell was worse?), demoting Sarajevo's martyrdom to a mere instance. . . . It is intolerable to have one's own sufferings twinned with anybody else's."[8]

In this chapter, we will reverse the idea that understanding precedes compassion to explore how compassion (*feeling together with*) must precede understanding. Putting compassion and otherness together in the context of communication ethics, as informed by dialogic and postmodern philosophy, at first glance may appear troubling, since the ethical impulse of compassion seems to conflict with the ethical impulse to honor the other *as* other, as notself. As we will examine more closely below, our affirmation of the other's alterity—the otherness of others—is central to ethics. So the dialectical tension between compassion (which emphasizes sharing) and alterity (which emphasizes difference) might at first glance seem irreconcilable. The difficulty of placing these two terms—"compassion" and "alterity"—together is illustrated by the words of Buddhist monk Thich Nhat Hanh in response to 9/11 and the question "What would you say to Bin Laden?" The monk said, "[T]he first thing I would do is listen. I would try to understand why he had acted in that cruel way. I would try to understand all of the suffering that had led him to violence."[9]

To many people, Thich Nhat Hanh's response may seem unethical—at best naïve and dangerously sentimental, and at worst contemptuous and, if he were an American, borderline treasonous. To other people, it may express the height of ethical communicative action, which involves an openness toward the radically other, a willingness to listen, and a concern for the other's suffering. This tension illustrates the degree to which compassion is neither simple nor unambiguous, and how it must precede understanding. For example, compassion mistaken for pity robs people of dignity. Compassion mistaken for guilt expresses not our concern for the other but our discomfort at being implicated in their suffering. Compassion mistaken for paternalism expresses not our concern for the other but our desire to exercise our power. At once simple and tremendously complex, the tenderness and openness of compassion are easily trampled by the instruments of reason, desire, and will. This vulnerability of compassion (sometimes called sympathy) to the dictates and misconstruals of sentimentality has led to a predominance of rational objectivity in much contemporary ethical theory, even among those that attempt to include emotion in the process.

For example, the philosopher Martha Nussbaum roots compassion in a three-stage cognitive process that involves judgments about the suffering of others—whether the suffering is seen as significantly harmful, whether it is undeserved and out of the control of the sufferer, and whether we feel connected to the sufferer in some way.[10] For Nussbaum, compassion only arises when we value the sufferer or recognize our common vulnerability and weakness. There is a problem, of course, when we neither perceive the suffering as harmful nor the sufferer as someone like us. We might have compassion for someone with cancer, but perhaps not someone with AIDS. Or we might feel a tremendous upwelling of concern for the families of Americans killed in New York during 9/11, but perhaps not for families of Iraqis or Afghanis killed throughout the many years of war. Thus, a compassion restricted to certain kinds of sufferers and to certain kinds of suffering is vulnerable to ideological beliefs about who is deserving and who is worthy and results in policy and practices that separate the worthy poor (e.g., widows and orphans) from the unworthy poor (e.g., unwed mothers and their children).

As the previously mentioned citizens of war-torn Sarajevo were unable to *feel together with* the citizens of war-torn Mogadishu depicted in the photo exhibit described by Sontag, what underlies the failure to respond to the suffering of others is the presence of alterity—the radical otherness, difference, incomprehensibility of the other, and the simple impossibility of it being otherwise. The excesses of alterity—of difference, otherness, and strangeness—will always inevitably exceed my knowledge, experience, and understanding. Sontag's example demonstrates how suffering is both singular and universal, but it also underscores how the singularity of suffering is the singularity of alterity, of otherness. The singularity of suffering, its very uniqueness and contingency, is matched by the ubiquity and everyday ordinariness of suffering, as expressed by the Buddha in the first noble truth: "birth is suffering, aging is suffering, sickness is suffering, death is suffering, sorrow and lamentation, pain, grief and despair is suffering."[11] Suffering, like alterity, is both unique and universal, both particular and ordinary. And as if the Buddha's iteration of the sufferings of impermanence, imperfection, and emptiness weren't enough, there probably isn't much ground on the planet that has not been soaked with the blood of some being at the hands of another.

Some ethicists, principally those grounded in feminist care ethics and continental philosophy, have found a way around this conundrum. In philosopher Nel Noddings's care ethics, the caring response is fundamentally receptive, as opposed to projective. She rejects what she calls a peculiarly rational, Western, and male conception of empathy and instead describes a process of 'engrossment' as a feeling with. "I do not 'put myself in the other's shoes,' so to speak, by analyzing his reality as objective data and then asking, 'How would I feel in such a situation?' On the contrary, I set aside my temptation to analyze and to plan. I do not project; I receive the other into myself, and I see and feel with the other."[12] Noddings illustrates the idea of empathic engrossment as our response to an infant crying. We know something is wrong, and the infant's feeling becomes ours—we feel his wailing cries vibrating in our bodies, memories, and imaginations. Our response thus follows from a *feeling with* state, in contrast to which rational objectivity "is a thinking mode that moves the self toward the object. It swarms over the object, assimilates it."[13]

Noddings's move toward empathy is similar to philosopher Hannah Arendt's description of understanding, which balances the tension between the need to distance the other with the need to connect with the other. Arendt writes, "This 'distancing' of some things and bridging the abysses to others is part of the dialogue of understanding, for whose purposes direct experience establishes too close a contact and mere knowledge erects artificial barriers. Without this kind of imagination, which actually is understanding, we would never be able to take our bearings in the world. It is the only inner compass we have."[14] Other scholars, such as Bauman and Adorno, have found a way around some of these problems of compassion through a critique of rationality.[15] For example, in an essay on the ethical dimensions of Adorno's negative dialectics, Cornell describes Adorno's critique of "thoughtless rationality" and "identity-logical thinking," which give rise to "the archaic barbarism that the loving subject cannot love what is alien and different."[16] Adorno's ethics call on us to "exercise our openness to and tenderness toward otherness. . . . The focus is less on doing what is right in accordance with one's duty than on the development of an attitude of tenderness toward otherness and gentleness toward oneself as a sensual creature."[17] But in Adorno's critical ethics Levin also observes the kind of harmonic attunement we ascribe to akroatic thinking. As Levin writes, "Adorno sometimes described his style of critique as a method of listening for 'dissonance': the dissonance between thought and action, word and deed, project and reality. . . . Thus, for Adorno, the task of the social critic is to listen for sounds of disharmony, to catch the moments of discord and discrepancy, and to make audible, in as articulate a formation as possible, the contradictions, the untruths, toward which the dissonance is calling our attention."[18] Similarly, Bauman describes how moral responsibility precedes rational thinking. He writes, "Reason cannot help the moral self without depriving the self of what makes the self moral: that unfounded, non-rational, un-arguable, no-excuses given, and non-calculable urge to stretch towards the other."[19]

But tenderness is easily trampled by rationality. And when what we call compassion depends on rationality, we have a problem. For example, Nussbaum's neo-Aristotelian "eudaimonistic judgment" requires seeing the other person as "a significant element in my scheme of goals and projects, an end whose good is to be promoted."[20] And this is part of the problem. Egoism mixes easily with compassion. Many of us may send money to the Red Cross to assist the people devastated by Hurricane Katrina, but do nothing about the underlying economic conditions that facilitate and enhance the inequitable distribution of resources and wealth that led to the chronically failing public sector of New Orleans. The encrustations and illusions of cognitive rationality are what have led Buddhists to regard knowledge "as an obstacle to understanding, like a block of ice that obstructs water from flowing. . . . Understanding means to throw away your knowledge."[21]

Thus, while many of us think we must understand in order to feel compassion, the engagement with alterity instructs that I may not, in fact, be *able* to understand. Events and experience may be unimaginable to me, beyond my comprehension. They may destroy my categories of thought or violate my beliefs about the world. Alterity reminds us, again and again, that our idea of reality is not reality, and to never forget that "[t]he face of the Other at each moment destroys and overflows the plastic image it leaves me."[22] So while an enormous number of obstacles, ranging from denial and ignorance to the starker evils of complicity and demonization, may interfere with an ethical response, the insistence on making rational understanding the ground of compassion keeps us from even *listening to suffering* to begin with. And, as we discussed in chapters 2 and 3, a great deal of why we don't listen has to do with the nature of knowledge and understanding and the role of language, cognition, and belief. Thus, the problem with basing compassion on knowledge and understanding is that we habituate to the already existing linguistic categories, structures, and schemas with which we constitute the world and then take up residence in it. These structures and schemas of knowledge enable us to make worlds wonderful, or hideous.

Although of course infamously malleable and generative, language itself can be particularly dangerous when we become habituated to its structures and forms such that they are automatic and invisible to us—as when metaphors, such as those discussed in chapter 4, are seen not as *a way of thinking,* but as the *nature of things,* if not, as Bohm warned, of thought itself. These unquestioned formations can distort our perceptions and point us to see what we expect to see and ignore everything else. As Derrick Jensen says, "Those who say that seeing is believing have it all wrong. Only when we believe do we begin to see."[23] Thus, an ethics that depends on shared understanding will be a selective ethics—if it can even be called ethics at all. It will exclude from our moral consideration those who we cannot understand or who violate our understandings. Moreover, as we described in chapter 5, understanding without misunderstanding does not exist. Thus, compassion is not and never can be the fruit of our labors to understand. Compassion is instead the very ground from which listening, and ethics, may spring.

And of course this is not an ordinary listening, it is a kind of listening attuned, with great sensitivity, to the sounds of alterity and the willingness to be transformed. As Charles Husband argues, "Understanding is not, and cannot be, a fixed cognitive entity: a discrete informational bundle; a morally weighted product of listening. Understanding is a process, and as such it is a catalyst that actively, even dangerously, interacts and changes whatever it comes in contact with."[24] In short, *listening otherwise* moves compassion from the realm of maxim, principle, utility into a world where understanding and the transcendence of egoic self-interest are possible. Listening otherwise is attuned to the suffering of others in a way that derives from regarding the other's suffering as a concern of mine not because I make some kind of cognitive leap or because of some strategic need I have of you, but because I feel *with* you, ineffably and irrevocably connected but not subsumed. This for-the-other response is described by Levinas as "the suffering and vulnerability of the sensible as *the other in me*. The other is in me and in the midst of my very identification."[25]

Although, as Nussbaum argues, ethics cannot be based on empathic imagination alone, *listening otherwise* calls us to preserve our sense of the vulnerability of all beings, of the sense that everyone suffers without insisting that our sense of the other be rationally comprehensible or even imaginable to us. For instance, can a man imagine the pain of childbirth? Can a teenager grasp the finality of death? I may not understand, or even want to understand, why the battered woman returns to her dreadful husband, but do I thereby cease to feel compassion for her? The compassion of *listening otherwise* takes us beyond the self and out into the groundlessness and ambiguity of the radical alterity of the other. As Noddings describes care ethics, "We are not attempting to transform the world, but we are allowing ourselves to be transformed."[26] This openness to letting ourselves be transformed in the face of the suffering other is the central difficulty, because it involves to a certain degree, the disruption and at times renunciation of self. And the renunciation of self can be extremely threatening.

Listening otherwise thus challenges the ego and the illusion of control and sees how the distortions that arise from our insistence on innocence, certainty, and understanding damage our capacity for compassion. As Carter and Erlmann write, "To invoke 'sympathetic understanding' is still tacitly to measure the success of communication in terms of its capacity to preserve the individual ego (and its speaking position). Plunging the ego into uncertainty, dialogue is, from this point of view, always threatening."[27] The dialogic philosophies of Buber and Levinas share with Buddhism an emphasis on decentering the ego, on subordinating the egocentric will to power to the ethical relation with the other. Likewise, drawing directly on Buddhism, Schopenhauer based his ethics of pity on renunciation of the desiring self, of individualism and egoism. The truly free person, from Schopenhauer's view, is one who "takes as much interest in the sufferings of other individuals as his own. . . . All the miseries of others, which he sees and is so seldom able to alleviate, all the miseries of which he has indirect knowledge, and even those he recognizes merely as possible, affect his mind just as do his own."[28]

Thus, among the innumerable ways I can fail to respond ethically, the communicative subjection of the other to myself is perhaps among the most hidden. This is where I insist on understanding on my terms only and hold fast to my cognitive preconceptions and categories, simply assimilating what I already know, or think I know, about the other or his or her point of view. A tragic example of this occurred a few years ago in Silsbee, Texas when a high school cheerleader refused to cheer for the high school basketball player who had raped her. When her assailant, who later pled guilty to assault, went to the foul line for a shot, the cheerleaders began chanting his name. In protest, the young woman stepped back and sat silently on the bench. According to a newspaper report, she said, "I didn't want to have to say his name, and I didn't want to cheer for him. . . . I didn't want to encourage anything he was doing."[29] But when the school principal ordered her to cheer for the player or quit the team, her family sued the school for infringing on her free speech rights, and for punishing her and not the player. The case eventually made it to the Fifth Circuit of Appeals, which ruled that the young woman's silence was not, in fact, protected speech. The eloquence of her silence was simply lost on them. They did not listen. Why? Because the ethical response requires *listening otherwise* not merely for an exchange of signs or receipt of information, but for the emergent self-transcendence that involves opening and vulnerability, which Levinas would call a *trauma* and Gadamer a *fundamental openness.* That is, turning toward is an act of both opening and renunciation. In this form of open listening, we give up our attachment to our familiar and already understood certainties and cognitions about the world in order to fully re-cognize the other. Gurevitch describes this as like an "'interpersonal Copernican discovery' . . . one's sense of centrality is lost and with it the taken-for-granted meaning of all that this centrality entailed."[30] Thus, this opening to the other is a process of defamiliarization in which we renounce the familiar and embrace the strange. "When the other is perceived as strange, he or she is liberated from the image that one has projected onto the other's experience from the center of one's self. The other emerges as an independent and 'distant' phenomenon."[31]

In this sense, the answer to the call of conscience is not a speaking, but a listening. It is, moreover, a *listening otherwise* that suspends the willfulness of self- and foreknowledge in order to receive the singularities of the alterity of the other. Speaking is certainly a crucial aspect of the ethical response, and yet so is listening—paying attention, being mindful, patiently aware. This form of listening has been beautifully and thoroughly described elsewhere, but in brief, it is listening that is fully present, embodied, centered.[32] It is an internal but not an isolated state—it is fully within reach of and open to receive the other. It listens to the other's suffering as a kind of hospitality, invitation, a hosting, because, as Corradi Fiumara notes, when "perceiving one's own mirror image in others, it then becomes difficult to accept others as 'real' persons."[33] To *listen otherwise* is to welcome the other inside, but as an *other,* as a guest, as a not-me. It doesn't insist on understanding or familiarity, or shared feelings. It is what Levinas describes as a "proximity" and what Buddhism calls nonattachment: letting go of everything—my ideas, my hopes, my plans—in the face of the infinite impermanence of the present moment. In a short essay titled "Beyond Dialogue," Levinas compares persuasion to violence and repression and substitutes instead an idea he calls *beyond dialogue*—"The presence of persons before a problem. Attention and vigilance: not to sleep until the end of time, perhaps. The presence of persons who, for once, do not fade away into words, get lost in technical questions, freeze up into institutions or structures. The presence of persons in the full force of their irreplaceable identity, in the full force of their inevitable responsibility."[34]

To go *beyond dialogue* is thus to travel beyond the limitations of concepts and certitudes, beyond linguistic schemas and categories, beyond strategy and persuasion. It is to recognize that language is always already corrupted with sedimentations of conceptual thought that have a tendency to create a sense of separation and objectification. As Zen teacher Reb Tenzin stresses, "Knowing in the true sense is knowing it is not an object of knowledge. We respond before we interpret and have meaning and signification, that's where we're living all the time. A pressed finger on the skin makes a depression before we know it. [We train] to use the mind that words reach . . . to help realize the mind that words don't reach."[35] In religious traditions this is sometimes called *bearing witness*—which is not to turn away from suffering but to look at it unflinchingly, lost neither in its ubiquity nor in its singularity. It is a kind of looking and listening without objectification or appropriation, but with a kind of awareness that makes space for the unthinkable, the unimaginable, the other.

As with *listening otherwise,* the presence that arises from *bearing witness* is a refusal to turn away from the suffering of others. And it occurs because it is only when we have lost our sense of conviction and certainty that are we able to truly listen otherwise. This kind of presence is described by Zen roshi Bernie Glassman, who conducts interfaith international retreats in Auschwitz aimed at bearing witness to the sufferings of the Holocaust. Glassman describes how one group of Jews and Germans and Poles, Tutsis and Hutus, Zen and Catholic priests reacted: "[T]hey were in shock. Their usual concepts and idea failed them, they didn't know what to think. They'd lost control. They were in a space of unknowing."[36] When we bear witness and *listen otherwise*, we listen from a space of unknowing, loss of control, loss of ideas and concepts; an opening to what is, not shrinking away, *being* there. And it is from this place that the ethical response emerges. Bearing witness gives rise to a listening without resorting to what is easy, what I already know, or what we have in common. It means that I listen for and make space for the difficult, the different, and the radically strange. I turn toward rather than away, present with what Buddhist teacher Tara Brach calls "radical acceptance": a fearless acceptance and openness to what is, right now, here before us.

But importantly, listening otherwise also calls one to give attention to oneself, to heed the tumult of contradictory voices demanding to be heard, aware that our listening is itself a kind of speaking. Listening otherwise thus requires a kind of inner strength that does not collapse into a kind of "narcissistic isolation,"[37] but one that can pay attention and tolerate our own contradictory intentions and conviction. As a mode of speaking, inner listening thus allows for the possibility that "others may understand our questions and our true intentions better—that others may help us give birth to our own thoughts."[38] To *listen otherwise* with presence is to listen with all the presence of our being. It is similar to what Buber calls "personal making present," which is not about merging, absorption, or unification, but about the fundamental dialogic relation with ourselves and with others from which an ethics may arise.

Dialogic Ethics

It is tempting to say that the voice of ethics speaks when justice is served—when courts rule in favor of disenfranchised and oppressed peoples, or when groups change dehumanizing and unjust practices, such as when the Quakers of England convinced their country that the slave trade was immoral and unjust. When justice is served in these epic moments, we point to them and say they are good. As Roy Wood says, "Ethics emerges in dialogue. Ethics is not something to be applied to communication, but is produced in social relation."[39] And yet, if ethics arises from dialogue and is not an object, instrument, or technique, it is epiphenomenal and thus arises out of something else. And if ethics is secondary to something else, what is that something else? As you may have discerned, I am suggesting that that *something* is listening;

moreover, it is a listening to otherness—to alterity—while maintaining a commitment to proximity. That is, ethics arises from listening rather than speaking and is, moreover, a voice that speaks in the presence of listening when listening occurs. It is an entering into, an attending, an obedience. Thus, it's not a question of whether the voice of ethics speaks, because it is always speaking. And the question is not whether we can hear it, but rather, whether we are listening. We hear the voice of ethics speaking when our world changes, when we are drawn beyond the limits of our subjective understanding and knowing—when what we thought we knew or understood, what we thought, how the world was shaped, what people were like, what was true, what was where, changes. It's not about the acquisition of facts or information—our world doesn't necessarily change with new information. Our world only changes when there is a kind of decentering involved, when we come to question, or leave behind, shedding like a snake's skin, our old views and certainties about our world. For instance, when the Europeans discovered that their maps of the world were wrong and they encountered the North American continent rather than Asia, their world didn't change, really. Yes, they identified new lands to exploit, but they still stayed at the center of their world, their mission to conquer unquestioned; their view of themselves as righteous inheritors, emperors, and missionaries didn't shift. They didn't shed their skin.

As a subject of study with roots in many places, it does not seem terribly unfair to say that studies of dialogue have tended, by and large, to favor the voice rather than the ear, to pass over listening in favor of speaking. In scholarly as well as quotidian parlance, it would appear that both subjects are principally concerned with speech, banishing listening to the silent subservience of dialogue's other. Whichever way it is glossed—as rhetoric, dialogue, language, or argumentation—the Western conception of the *logos* emphasizes speaking at the expense of listening. And the problem with conceiving of *logos* in terms of speech and speaking is not only that it ignores the importance of listening, but also, as shall be argued below, that it obscures how listening makes the ethical response possible.

And yet, at the same time, there is something almost redundant about the phrase "dialogic ethics"—as if dialogue and ethics were two separate phenomena instead of intertwining aspects of human existence. As if dialogue did not utterly depend upon ethics or ethics upon dialogue. As if dialogue and ethics were not converging dimensions in the whorl of human *being*. Martin Buber and Emmanuel Levinas are two philosophers of the ethical who give us insight into the co-constitutive relationship between ethics and dialogue. Through Levinas's metaphor of the "face" and Buber's word pair "I and Thou," both scholars tend to blur, or at least bend, dualistic distinctions between dialogue and ethics. In the rest of this chapter I draw upon the work of these two philosophers of *self* and *other* to build a place for listening at the heart of the ethical encounter. In so doing, I aim to reframe dialogic ethics away from visual and speech-producing models of thought and toward auditory and speech-receiving perspectives that place *listening* at the center of dialogic ethics and the face-to-face encounter. Too often, philosophical reflections and quotidian discourse tend to emphasize the visual dimensions of the face-to-face and neglect, or "overlook," the role of voice and listening in our encounters with others. Similarly, our Western philosophical traditions have left us with a logocratic tendency to emphasize speech and speaking at the expense of reception and listening. In this chapter, I attempt to sketch some ways to redress this absence by theorizing communication ethics as an embodied phenomenon enacted through the process of listening.

Although Buber and Levinas were both early to mid-twentieth-century Jewish scholars and drew from similar religious, existentialist, and phenomenological intellectual traditions, they differed in some fundamental respects both philosophically and personally. Philosophically, their work is to be distinguished by the dimensions and scope of their projects. Buber was principally a philosopher of religion, and although his work on dialogic philosophy was perhaps his most well known, it did not comprise the majority of his bibliography. Further, his work is more poetic than argumentative in style. Levinas, in contrast, produced a voluminous bibliography that developed his philosophy of ethics and the other. Like Buber, Levinas was a Jewish philosopher, but unlike Buber, he intentionally kept the two projects (writing on Judaism and philosophy) separate. And although Levinas drew upon and discussed Buber in his work, Buber never engaged Levinas's project. As a result, Buber is often read through Levinas's eyes, which some scholars, including Derrida, see as a distortion.[40] There are also some important distinctions to be made between the historical experiences and religious affiliations of the two scholars as individuals. Buber, born in Vienna in 1878, wrote as a nonstatist Zionist Jew, steeped in Hasidic folk traditions of mysticism and Kabbalah, who rejected a halakahic interpretation of Torah and saw the Bible instead as a dialogic encounter between man and God. Thus, Buber's dialogic philosophy was not entirely separate from his religious scholarship and commitments. Buber moved to Israel in 1938 and lived out the Shoah within the Jewish community, there serving as a critic of Israeli nationalism and a proponent of a joint Arab-Jewish state. In contrast, Levinas was a Lithuanian Jew born in 1906 who settled in France in 1923 and later spent a year in Germany studying with Husserl and Heidegger in 1928–29. From this time forward, Levinas steadily engaged his philosophical project concerning ethics and the other and later also began to write Jewish commentary steeped in the orthodoxies of Talmud and Halakah. Levinas survived the war and the Shoah in a prison camp as a military prisoner in the French army while his wife and child were hidden in the French countryside. Nazis murdered Levinas's entire Lithuanian family.[41]

Philosophically, two overlapping but different dimensions of Levinas's and Buber's work provide the scaffolding for reframing the face-to-face from a visual and speech-centered phenomenon to an auditory and listening-centered phenomenon. The first dimension pertains to ontology and the origins of the self, and the second pertains to ethics and its place in philosophy. Through Buber's eyes we learn to see the ways in which ontology is fundamentally dialogic, and how the self arises in relational, intersubjective space. This is expressed in Buber's pronominal words "I and Thou" and "I and It," which are both figures nonreducible to a pair of pronouns; each is instead a full and complete "word." In his classic 1923 book *I and Thou,* Buber describes how subjectivity begins, is born, in the encounter with another. "I become through my relation to Thou," and "In the beginning is relation."[42] Thus, to Buber, subjectivity is itself dialogic. From Levinas we learn the ways in which ethics is first philosophy—that is, what comes first in philosophical inquiry is not a question about being, but a question about relation that is fundamentally an ethical question. "[P]reexisting the plane of ontology is the ethical plane."[43] Thus, first philosophy asks not the ontological question of whether to be or not to be, but the ethical question of whether the relation of my being to others is justified. In short, it means "to fear injustice more than death, to prefer to suffer than to commit injustice."[44] To Levinas, the self is always accompanied by the "bad conscience" of the question of whether I have usurped the place of the other. Thus, in contrast to their teachers and existentialist contemporaries such as Husserl, Heidegger, Merleau-Ponty, and Sartre, who focus on the consciousness and ideation of the self, the Buber and Levinas subject of the self is not a self-same subject, but is a relational intersubjective subject. To Levinas subjectivity is not for itself, but for the other. To Buber subjectivity only arises in and through relation to the other.

When speaking of dialogue and ethics, then, it is important to remember that we are not speaking of two separate things, but two dimensions of the same thing: *being* human together with other humans—that is, *being* in relationship with others. The ontological ground of dialogic ethics is thus an intersubjectively grounded self that is called into being by the relational encounter with the other, the face-to-face. The philosophical ground of dialogic ethics begins from the question of the relational encounter with the other, which calls the self's "right to be" into question.

The Face-to-Face

To Levinas, the face is the manifestation of the ethical exigency that is woven into the very structure of human being. As such, the face of the other calls my being into question. The face is neither figurative nor literal, but is the expression of the demand of the other. Thus, the face, like the face-to-face, is always dual. It is a relational, not an absolute term. "The facing position, opposition par excellence, can be only as a moral summons."[45] As an absolute and infinite exteriority, the face can never be grasped or possessed, or absorbed into what Levinas calls "the same." "Ethics begins before the exteriority of the *other*, . . . before the face of the other."[46] Although not a central metaphor in Buber, the face makes an important appearance in *I and Thou*. As with Levinas, Buber's face evokes an ethical response. But whereas Levinas's face expresses the irreducible alterity of the other person as a human being, Buber's face represents the ultimate Thou of God. He writes, "He who approaches the Face has indeed surpassed duty and obligation—but not because he is now remote from the world; rather because he has truly drawn closer to it. Duty and obligation are rendered only to the stranger; we are drawn to and full of love for the intimate person. The world, lit by eternity, becomes fully present to him who approaches the Face, and to the Being of beings he can in a single response say *Thou*."[47] Thus, Buber and Levinas share a notion of the face as the sign of the other that transcends social categories of identity, as well as the idea that ethics derives from the recognition of this face in all its otherness. Levinas's interest begins with the transcendence of being through ethics, through the responsibility for the other. His attempts to locate what is "otherwise than being" are not a negation of being but an effort to come to grips with it in a way that departs from the egotistical imperialism of Cartesian hegemony. Levinas theorizes that the ethical relation originates in the asymmetrical subordination of self to other, to the priority of the other always already above oneself. This sense of the ethical as abiding in the disruption of the self's presumed "right of being" is reflected by Levinas's repeated quote from Pascal's *Pensées:* "That is my place in the sun. That is how the usurpation of the whole world began,"[48] and in another favored quote from Dostoyevsky: "We are all guilty in everything in respect to all others, and I more than all the others."[49] To Levinas, ethics begins by renouncing the self's right to be, in favor, always, of the other. The self is called to responsibility for the other before it is free.

As with the irreducible otherness of the Levinasian face, Buber describes the I-Thou relation as an encounter with alterity—the other is unknown and unimagined. Moreover, the I-Thou relation is without goal and arrives on the scene serendipitously, as if by "will and grace." To Buber, dialogue arises not from prior intentions or future aims, but from the present moment. In a 1929 essay, Buber describes the relation of dialogue as one of "turning towards the other"[50] and theorizes the ways in which both separation *and* relation occur simultaneously in dialogue: "Neither needs to give up his point of view; only, in that unexpectedly they do something and unexpectedly something happens to them which is called a covenant, they enter a realm where the law of the point of view no longer holds."[51] Buber further points to the importance of one's interlocutor's alterity when he writes in a later essay that "[g]enuine conversation, and therefore every actual fulfillment of relation between men, means acceptance of otherness. . . . [E]verything depends so far as human life is concerned, on whether each thinks of the other as the one he is, whether each, that is, with all his desire to influence the other, nevertheless unreservedly accepts and confirms him in his being this man and in his being made in this particular way."[52] Unlike Levinas's, however, Buber's dialogic ethic arises not from a subordination of self for other, but in Thou-saying, and through it, the recognition of the otherness in the face of the other.

And yet, when ethics discloses itself in an encounter with a face, rather than a voice, we are placed in a visual world that privileges vision over audition. As an epistemic stance, the metaphor of the face reflects the prevalence of visual dominance in Western philosophy, wherein "seeing" is thought to be synonymous with understanding and words like "vision," "view," "outlook," and "perspective" orient toward a visual mode wherein acts of cognition such as thinking, comprehending, and understanding are translated as "mental pictures" to be seen by the "mind's eye." Listening, in contrast, is "seen" as a subordinate modality, most useful for bringing invisible events and objects to "light," as when radio astronomy and ultrasound transpose sonic phenomena into visual images and "[s]ounds are frequently thought of as anticipatory clues for ultimate visual fulfillments."[53] Even ornithologists are bird*watchers,* not bird listeners; thus, *seeing* is the ultimate aim and auditory experience merely points toward the invisible presence of birds. As Rée describes this dominant perspective, "Vision is for the most part sheer self-commanding voluntariness compared with hearing, which appears to be little more than supine passivity."[54]

Both McLuhan and Ong have documented how this privileging of vision arose historically through the introduction of writing into previously oral cultures. Their work demonstrates how each new technology—from writing, to print, to broadcast—worked to reshape everything from economics to metaphysics as societies moved toward increasingly more visual orientations. According to these scholars, when words are written they become part of a visual world that silences the sound of language, "splits thought and action," and cleaves speaker from addressee. McLuhan describes how medieval readers originally conceived of literature as "something to be listened to" and even solitary reading was done aloud. But the uniform homogeneity of literary technologies, such as the standardized typeface of printing, dampened the lively resonance of speech when "[t]ypography cracked the voices of silence."[55] Ong is quite eloquent on the implications of this transformation when he writes, "Speech is no longer a medium in which the human mind and sensibility lives. It is resented, rather, as an accretion to thought, hereupon imagined as ranging noiseless concepts or 'ideas' in a silent field of mental space."[56]

As we discussed in chapter 5, unlike the words on the page, or the face by my side, speech comes from, but is not itself, the body. As the resonating organ of speech, the voice testifies to our embodiment as speaking and listening beings. So in place of speech, I will here introduce the notion of the voice as the face's counterpart. While voice and face are both elements of the human body that can signify and express, the voice brings the *temporal* embodiment of human *being* into sharper relief. The voice moves rhythmically through time as an event, not an object, through the medium of the breath and its rhythm of inhalation and exhalation. The voice of the other, unlike the face of the other, is invisible and cannot be seen. It has not one but many surfaces, and it reverberates with the echoes of all the other voices past and present, heard and unheard. As sound, the voice of the other is a wave of energy that surrounds me, enters me. But unlike the exteriority of the face, which preserves the subject/object dualism of *the seeing* and *the seen,* the voice of the other mingles inextricably, crossing through semipermeable boundaries between inner and outer.[57] And this may be in part what deters Levinas from pursuing listening as a doorway to the ethical—for the resonating inter-penetration and boundarylessness of sound come perhaps too close to the impulses, both philosophical and political, of union that the ethical encounter with alterity must at all costs avoid. In his 1947 essay on Proust, Levinas states the problem quite directly: "But if communication bears the mark of failure or inauthenticity in this way, it is because it is sought as a fusion. One begins with the idea that the duality must be transformed into a unity, and that social relations must culminate in communion."[58]

As described above, listening is a radically different epistemic process from visual perception—vision distances and separates, while listening connects and bridges. Like light, sound has a horizon that animates space, but unlike light, sound blurs the boundaries between interior and exterior. When sound waves of speech enter me, they become a part of me by vibrating through my body. As we discussed in chapter 2, sound is embodied in its reception, rippling through skin, muscle, bone, and synapse. And as we discussed in chapters 3 and 5, speech contains both language and nonlanguage elements and can convey meaning without sound and word.

Thus, beyond the sonic vibrations of speech, listening also requires an aural eye—an eye that listens. Nonverbal communication scholars understand the importance of a listening eye that attends not only to words, but also to the sounds and sights that comprise and surround it. These scholars study visual attributes of communication such as gesture, posture, proximity, facial expression, eye gaze, and other forms of "body language," as well as sonic attributes such as intonation, prosody, pitch, rhythm, and inflection. It might be said, then, that the ethical fulcrum sits not between visual and auditory domains but between oral and literary perspectives—ethics springs not from a literal eye that speaks, but from an aural eye that listens. The voice of the other invokes *listening ears and aural eyes* grounded in the intersubjectivity of the relation rather than *speaking eyes and deafened ears* born through the sub-jectivity of objectification and domination. Speech reveals the always elusive other through a face that preserves the infinitude of alterity. At the same time, the silence of the face points to the unsaid and unsayable—it reminds us of the ineffable, inexhaustible infinity of the saying. And just as the uni-modality of vision alone cannot hinder the impulses toward mastery and domination, so the voice without a face cannot resist the lure of speech's call for merger and unification. Thus, a polymodal face, made up of voice, vision, and listening, is necessary. But when Levinas writes that "[t]o put speech at the origin of truth is to abandon the thesis that disclosure, which implies the solitude of vision, is the first work of truth,"[59] might we not go still further and put *listening,* in conjunction with speaking, at the origin of truth? That is to say, perhaps my encounter with the other manifests neither in the separation of vision nor in the invocation of voice, but in my attentive attunement to the speech of the other.

The Listening and the Heard

In his early work, Levinas was drawn to sound's ability to destabilize and disrupt the apparent mastery of vision. In a 1949 essay on the work of surrealist writer Michel Leiris, Levinas writes that "to speak is to interrupt my existence as a subject, a master, but to interrupt it without offering myself as spectacle, leaving me simultaneously object and subject. My voice brings the element in which that dialectical situation is accomplished concretely."[60] In this essay, Levinas begins with the idea of sound as word and explores the power of speech to disrupt the empire of the self and establish an intersubjective relation. He writes, "There is in fact in sound—and in consciousness understood as hearing—a shattering of the always complete world of vision. . . . Sound is all repercussion, outburst, scandal."[61] Given this early acknowledgment of the ethical importance of voice and sound, it is curious that Levinas would come to so neglect listening in his subsequent work.[62] But in spite of his earlier explorations of sound, word, and the invocation of the other, Levinas rarely references speech's other—listening. However, Levinas is not the first or last philosopher of communication to make this omission. Consider how in spite of their seminal contributions to scholarship, the orality/literacy binarism of Ong and McLuhan is itself deaf to listening. Although there is much to say about the implications of this neglect, we will here only briefly address two. Firstly, Ong's arguments rest heavily upon claims about the temporal evanescence and spatial interiority of sound when he writes, "Sound exists only when it is going out of existence. It is not simply perishable but essentially evanescent."[63] But when examined through the dialogic and polychronic perspectives discussed in chapter 6, speech's relation to time and space is less fleeting and more complex.

So the question remains, does sound in fact go out of existence, or does it move through and away, leaving a trace behind? Leaving aside questions about how far sound waves can travel and echo across space over time, does the sound of language in fact die? What are you hearing right now as you read these words? And what are those voices from the past that speak, from time to time, in your head? Or what about the thoughts and music one hears while silently riding the bus or sipping a coffee? Similarly, Ong's theory about the evanescence of sound also overlooks the simultaneity of sound. There is in sonic resonance and sympathetic vibration a kind of simultaneity—sound does not abide alone, but gathers other voices with it. Sound has a kind of inevitable polyphony created from the sound itself and the vibrations it triggers around it. And in this sense, the polyphonous simultaneity of sound is not unlike the polymodal simultaneity of the face-to-face ethical relation. Another example of the philosophical neglect of listening can be found, ironically, in the great scholar of understanding, Hans Georg Gadamer. For even while Gadamer considers hearing to be "the basis of the hermeneutical phenomenon," he nevertheless oversimplifies when he writes, "when you look at something, you can also look away from it by looking in another direction, but you cannot 'hear away.'"[64] While it is certainly true that we can literally shut out visual but not auditory stimuli, it is also true that we can *hear* but fail to *listen*. For just as *seeing* can occur in the absence of *looking,* so can *hearing* occur without *listening,* and both the communication literature and everyday life are filled with examples (ranging from "turning a deaf ear," to "selective listening") that convey the idea of what Gadamer calls "hear[ing] away." That is, hearing without listening is response without responsibility; it is a form of pseudodialogue without ethics.

A powerful lesson about listening is offered by none other than Shakespeare's Falstaff, in *King Henry IV, Part Two.* The play revolves around the ascension of the rebellious young Prince Hal to the throne of England as King Henry V. At one point young Hal's jovial but not quite savory friend Falstaff feigns deafness in order to avoid an encounter with the police (1.2). When the Lord Chief Justice wants to question Falstaff about a robbery, Falstaff first tells the Chief Justice's servant that he is deaf. But the Chief Justice is relentless and finally insists on speaking with Falstaff, who evades and avoids the topic with a barrage of gibberish about the health of the king, who "is fallen into this same whoreson apoplexy." In growing frustration, the Chief Justice perseveres, saying, "Well, God mend him! I pray you let me speak with you!" Undaunted, Falstaff persists in dodging and diving, and declares that the king's illness was caused by "much grief, from study, and perturbation of the brain. . . . It is a kind of deafness." The Chief Justice at last gets his attention with "I think you are fallen into the disease; for you hear not what I say to you," whereupon Falstaff replies, "Very well; rather, . . . it is the disease of not listening, the malady of not marking, that I am troubled withal."

As we discussed in chapter 2, etymologically the English word "listening" comes from a root that emphasizes attention and giving to others, while "hearing" comes from a root that emphasizes perception and receiving from others. Similarly, the French verb *entendre* (from the Latin *intendere*) is defined as "au sens de percevoir par l'ouïe," which translates, as does the English "to hear," roughly as "the sense of perception by hearing."[65] The French verb *écouter* (from the Latin *auscultare,* meaning to listen and to obey) is defined as "prêter attention aux paroles, au son, au bruit," which means, as does the English "to listen," to pay attention to words, sound, or noise.[66] Although Girodet stresses that *écouter* and *entendre* are not synonyms, the French verb *entendre,* like the English "to hear," also has a secondary meaning that pertains to understanding, as in "Je t'entends" or "I hear you." Nancy glosses the French distinction by playing on the double meaning of *sense* (as in sensation and as in meaning) to account for the hidden elusiveness I associate with listening. He writes, "If 'to hear' is to understand the sense . . . to listen is to be straining toward a possible meaning, and consequently one that is not immediately accessible."[67] Regardless of the ways these distinctions are interpreted, however, the distinction itself illustrates that "listen" and "hear" are not simply synonyms, but are inflected with different meanings that suggest different ways of being in the world.

This distinction between listening and hearing echoes Levinas's distinction between "the saying" and "the said," which we might call "the listening" and "the heard."[68] In his second masterpiece, *Otherwise than Being,* Levinas began to develop a theoretical distinction between "the said," or the propositional content of utterances, and "the saying," the sociality of addressing an interlocutor. Levinas describes how "the saying" "opens me to the other before saying what is said, before the said uttered in this sincerity forms a screen between me and the other. This saying without a word is thus like silence. It is without words, but not with hands empty."[69]

Perhaps in the same way that "the saying" expresses an infinite surplus of responsibility and vulnerability that precedes signification, so then "the listening" enacts an infinite surplus of attention, no matter what is said or heard. "The listening," in contrast to "the heard," is an enactment of responsibility made manifest through a posture of receptivity that can receive the other without assimilation or appropriation. "The listening" is a process of contraction, of stepping back, that creates a distance so that the other may come forward. In "the listening" I create a space to receive you, letting your speech enter me, flow through me. In contrast, "the heard," like "the said," pertains to propositional content, and it arises from taking in your words and making them mine. "The heard" thus involves judgment and distinction— seeking certainty using cognitive structures, schemas, and familiar ways of seeing and doing. "The heard" is created when I fix your words over and against mine in order to assimilate, appropriate, convince, or seek a kind of communion. Without attending to any conceptual distinctions between listening and hearing, our ethical inquiries tend to focus too much on "the heard" and miss the fact that "the listening," like "the saying," has its own meaning, if not priority. As Levinas writes, to make the stranger a familiar is to do violence to the otherness of the other, to exclude some part of the stranger. "The listening," as opposed to "the heard," does not absorb the other into conformity with the self, but instead creates a dwelling space to receive the alterity of the other and let it resonate.

As we have touched upon throughout the previous chapters, there is a politics to listening. It's not terrifically hard to notice that in every place from bedrooms to lunchrooms, in classrooms, newsrooms, business meetings, legislative sessions, and television news shows, talk breaks down because listening fails. People, typically those with the most power, stop listening, and monologue takes the place of dialogue. Speakers and listeners presume to know and understand. We take positions and refuse to budge. There are many times we don't even allow the other to speak. We turn away, shout them down, or rule their speaking "out of order." Take for example the English professor June Jordan, whose City University of New York students were unable to publish a public letter they wrote about police brutality after one of their classmates was killed. The *New York Times* refused to publish, that is, listen to, the students because they wrote in Black English.

Or consider the political scientist Jane Mansbridge, who found that women in New England town meetings, the archetypal paradigm of American democratic discourse, only speak half as often as do men. Moreover, Mansbridge found that unlike men's speaking, women's speaking tends to provide information or ask questions rather than state opinions or initiate controversies. But even as the marginalized and disenfranchised among us clamor to be heard, our very push for airtime often ends in a deafening cacophony of indecipherable voices. So many of our political ideals of justice are about speaking that we wind up downright hostile to the silence of listening. Even the AIDS awareness group ACT UP makes its crucial political insight on the back of listening by using the slogan "silence = death." And while in one sense this is certainly true (the silence around sexuality and HIV paved the way for untold numbers of dead), might we also not say that the failure to listen = death?

Listening Others to Speech

When the voice of the other calls me into question, do I listen? And what does this Levinasian invocation evoke? In contemporary English, the word "vocation" has become nearly synonymous with occupation, work, labor, career, or profession. We have vocational training and vocational rehabilitation, vocational services and vocational-technical schools.[70] Still lingering, however, is the sense of the religious vocation as something closer to a call, to being summoned. Thomas Merton describes how the religious vocation requires one "to deliver oneself up, to hand oneself over, entrust oneself completely" to the call.[71] But what is a call without an ear to listen? Might we say that it is not yet quite a vocation? The English word "vocation" comes from the Latin *vocare* (to call), which is also related to the Latin *vox* (voice) and the Sanskrit *vāc,* an "early Vedic term for the Absolute Word" and for the goddess of speech.[72] The word "vocation" also echoes in the cognate "invocation," which according to the OED is an act of conjuring. Thus, we might say that in dialogic ethics, listening is my vocation, my calling. And this vocation of listening requires an encounter with the unknown; listening draws forth something hidden, bringing something new into the world.

As I will explain below, listening can serve as a form of midwifery that gives birth to thought and speech. Corradi Fiumara calls this process "maieutic listening," wherein "the listening interlocutor actually becomes a participant in the nascent thought of the person who is listening."[73] In other words, listening, as well as speaking, is an act of constitutive communication. For example, the constitutive power of listening is demonstrated by Laub's psychoanalytic work with Holocaust survivors. Through the process of listening to untold and repressed stories, therapists and survivors were able to co-create "a record that is yet to be made." Laub writes, "The emergence of the narrative which is being listened to—and heard—is, therefore, the process and the place wherein the cognizance, the 'knowing' of the event is given birth to. The listener, therefore, is a party to the creation of knowledge *de novo*."[74]

It is of course difficult to perceive, let alone appreciate, this constitutive aspect of listening from a transmission or Platonic view of language, where thinking and speaking are synonymous with representing and signifying and where language is seen as a kind of tool that symbolizes thoughts and objects and then transfers these representations from one place to another. As we discussed in chapter 1, in this view the world of vision dominates the world of audition, and the transmission and semiotic functions of language render other aspects of language, such as the performative and constitutive functions, inaudible. In this Heideggerian sense, language speaks me as much as I speak it. But might we not also consider how language *listens me*? As with speaking, the constitutive powers of listening happen not only within and between individuals sitting face to face, but among large collectivities gathered side by side as well. One need only consider the power of public orators to constitute large groups of people into previously nonexistent communities and solidarities. It is not simply the voice of a Dr. Martin Luther King Jr., a Mahatma Gandhi, or an Adolf Hitler that can create new worlds, for good or ill, but it is in fact the gathered hearkening of those assembled communities, of what "comes to presence" when we *listen others to speech.*

When Levinas contends that the communicative action of saying takes priority over the substance of the said, it is not just a matter of situating speech in the intersubjective occurrence of dialogue, because saying precedes the said just as being precedes the being. What is as yet missing from this formulation is the ways in which the listening precedes the heard. When we distinguish "the listening" from "the heard," we are emphasizing the maieutic (that is to say the transformative and generative) dimensions of listening, which, unpredictably, can occur only in the presence of absence. As Corradi Fiumara describes it, "a listener can only 'enter' in a way which is at once paradoxical and committing: 'by taking leave,' by standing aside and making room."[75] Moreover, this mode of listening can neither be taught nor learned, "as it is a way of relating that can only function on condition that the 'learning' is continuous, uninterrupted; we are dealing with a concern which is not conducive to an ultimate 'grasp', or mastery of the issue. The whole question, therefore, lies in the constant renewal of our approach to language; in learning and re-learning how to listen to it."[76]

One provocation for relearning to listen to language is offered by the feminist theologian Nelle Morton, who illustrates the constitutive power of listening when she describes how "we empower one another by hearing the other to speech. We empower the disinherited, the outsider."[77] How resonant Morton's phrasing is here with Levinas's ethical directive that we respond to the face of "the stranger, the widow, and the orphan," who "commands me as a Master" from "a dimension of height."[78] The empowerment of *listening others to speech* reverses authoritative normative social arrangements that silence and/or refuse *to listen the voices* of the oppressed. And, as with Buber's I-Thou relation, *listening others to speech* is not a strategic or tactical practice aimed at achieving a predetermined goal, because doing so would disobey the demands of the other in the present moment. Buber's observation that true dialogue is "a matter of renouncing the pantechnical mania or habit with its easy 'mastery' of every situation"[79] is echoed by Levinas's insistence on the mastery of the other over self, and on Morton's reflection that "clever techniques seen as positive agents for creation and change are not good for the kind of hearing that brings forth speech."[80]

But now we are faced with another question about our listening to language, this time in relation to the grammatical category of transitivity. Although there is some disagreement among linguists about whether transitivity is a universal category that manifests everywhere the same,[81] the general idea is that the transitivity of verbs expresses agentive action—a subject does something to or with an object, as in the clause "she speaks the words." Transitive verbs transfer some form of energy or action from the subject to the object. Intransitive verbs, in contrast, express a nondirected action or express the action of a subject in relation to an object, but they cannot express the action of a subject on an object.

In English, many verbs are both transitive and intransitive, as in the clauses "she speaks" (intransitive) and "she speaks the words" (transitive). This is true of the verb "to hear"—we can say "she hears" or "she hears the words." The verb "to listen," however, has only an intransitive use in contemporary English.[82] Thus, we can say "we heard the words" but not "we listened the words." Similarly, we can say "she listens" or "she listens to the others," but not "she listens the others." In French, in contrast, both *écouter* and *entendre* are transitive verbs that can act on an object, as in *je vous écoute* and *je t'entends*.

The question of why the transitive form of "listen" has disappeared from English is beyond the scope of this chapter, but it is worth examining the previously concealed maieutic dimensions of listening that emerge when we transitively listen others to speech. Transitive uses of the verb "listen" convey a sense of listening as constitutive of and prior to speaking—listening is an invocation, a calling forth of speech. The (in)vocation of dialogic ethics is a giving birth to speech by listening; it is a *dwelling place* from where we offer our hospitality to the other and the world. But it is not only that the voice of the other calling requires a listener to be complete; it is that, more radically, without a listener, the speaking simply may not occur. Morton describes how as a young doctor Carl Jung worked with women who were not willing or able to speak to their doctors, who, in turn, assumed that the women had no language. With patience and perseverance Jung found a way to connect with the women by listening and imitating their gestures and movements until finally they began to speak. Morton writes how Jung "had touched the place where the connection had been broken. But he did this through their language and not the language of the doctors. He had heard them to speech."[83]

Another example of the ways our speaking and thinking about language conceal the constitutive power of listening is found in the recent Supreme Court case *Citizens United v. Federal Election Commission*. In an attempt to regulate "big money" campaign contributions, the Bipartisan Campaign Reform Act (BCRA) was passed by Congress and signed into law by President Bush in 2002. The law attempted to restrain some of the excesses of campaign advertising by applying a variety of restrictions to "electioneering communications" (political ads and/or paid programming targeted to the electorate) transmitted thirty days (and in some cases sixty days) prior to elections. In their ruling, the majority of the justices overturned the bipartisan restrictions, opening the door to a virtual tsunami of corporate funding. The majority justified their decision by maintaining that political speech is indispensable to a democracy. The question of whether, or to what extent, freedom of speech requires some freedom of listening apparently never crossed their minds. In today's age of Twitter, Facebook, and "going viral," listening is at once more difficult and less appreciated than perhaps ever before. The American epidemic known as attention deficit disorder testifies to the enormously destructive power of distraction. Every day we are assailed by an insatiable calliope of sonic stimuli, crying out to us and constantly seeking our attention. Whether we are texting on the dance floor or browsing the Web during lunch, our attention is always divided—and we are rarely, if ever, in silence. We have entered the age of the attention economy, where advertisers pay billions to the media producers who bring the attention (divided or not) of audiences to their door. That's right, our attention has become a commodity bought and sold on the open market. The quality of our attention doesn't much matter—although proprietary research in some market research firm somewhere probably shows that the more diminished, distracted, and therefore unconscious our attention, the more valuable (i.e., persuadable) it is.

In summary, a maieutic listener will keep an ear out for places of silence, erasure, and misrecognition. Such a listener must notice the gaps and fissures that occur when one voice speaks in place of another, or when another is silenced. Who speaks? Who is heard? Whose voice is rendered unintelligible? These are the questions of discourse ethics, and they are poised on the fulcrum of the communicative dynamic between speaking and listening. This chapter has explored the idea that what disrupts our communication with others is not only or even primarily our speaking, misspeaking, understanding, or misunderstanding, but our failure to listen. Beyond the intellectual mysteries of listening, at heart this book centers on an ethical concern: what are the social, political, and cultural implications of our failure to *listen for the other*—that is, to listen without stealing our interlocutor's possibilities and horizons of meaning?

Beyond warning of the danger of the failure to *make strange* and see the other as wholly other, this chapter has examined the ethical exigency of the face and its relation to primordial discourse in order to disclose the otherwise hidden ethical significance of listening and its vocation as a form of co-constitutive communicative action that can *listen persons to speech.* That is, in the view of dialogic philosophy, communication avoids reducing recognition of the other to a kind of mimetic re-cognition of the other in which we view the other solely in terms of our own precognitions and thus assimilate them into what we already know (or think we know) about their point of view. Rather, communication is a process of opening to the other, which holds the promise of making worlds. Buber called this communicative opening to the other "presence," and Levinas called it "saying." To Levinas, the focus of transcendent, ethical communication is on the saying rather than the said; that is, not on the content of signification per se, but on the exposure of opening to the other. Buber, similarly, distinguished between the act of speaking and the substance of speech, with the former illustrating an emergent, generative notion of talk as a praxis of world creation and the latter illustrating the structured symbolic notion of talk as a representation of content. According to Friedman, Buber's dialogic philosophy sees communication "not as a *dimension* of the self but as the existential and ontological reality in which the self comes into being and through which it fulfills and authenticates itself.[84]

For far too long communication scholars have taken speech and speaking as stand-ins for the *logos.* But *listening* makes a "forgetting the self" ethical response possible. Whereas vision too easily possesses, such that what is *seen* is *mine,* audition offers the opportunity to *listen others to speech.* As Corradi

Fiumara describes it, "[the] cognitive dedication to the word of the other . . . demands a kind of inner abnegation. Without this inner renunciation the individual can only hold a dialogue with himself."[85] Just as the concept of *intersubjectivity* has opened up new conceptual spaces for scholarly inquiry outside the self-other binary, the concept of *listening others* to speech can open new pathways for both ethics and understanding. But a cautionary note is in order. It might seem easy to paint speaking with the blue brush of negativity and listening with a gleaming aura of gold, but that is oversimplification. Both speaking and listening are part and parcel of one process of human action—communicating.

It should not be forgotten that there are serious limitations and misuses of listening and hearing. Like speaking, listening can act for ill as well as good. In fact, we might chronicle a veritable résumé of listening, misdeeds, which could include *secret listening, careless listening, faithless listening,* and *coercive listening.* Technologies of communication, from the secret surveillance of the fourth century B.C.E. tyrant Dionysus to the present-day data mining expeditions of corporations and government, have a long history of harnessing *listening* as a way to extend power and control.[86] The ringing church bells of medieval Europe did more than tell the time, they regulated activity and imposed a standardized temporal regime upon their listeners. Similarly, interrogations, whether from a doctor, a cop, or an agent of the CIA, enact a mode of *coercive listening* that diminishes the humanity and agency of speakers. And *faithless listening* is exemplified by a history of innumerable failures to listen and heed a warning—most recently exemplified by two wars which have caused untold ruin and desolation in Iraq and Afghanistan, the devastation imposed by the 2005 Hurricane Katrina, the 2008 mortgage crisis, and the 2010 BP Gulf oil spill, to name but a few examples. Thus, just as not all speaking constitutes an engagement with dialogic ethics, neither does all listening. In summary, listening is a form of co-constitutive communicative action fundamental to dialogic ethics. Listening is neither a secondary subordinate process that follows and flows from speech, nor is it a futile gesture. Rather, listening is the invisible and inaudible enactment of the ethical relation itself; upon it, everything depends.

TOWARD AN ETHICS OF ATTUNEMENT

We shall not cease from exploration
And the end of all our exploring
Will be to arrive where we started
And know the place for the first time.

—T. S. ELIOT, *"Little Gidding"*

When one achieves a certain age, the recurring patterns and cycles of time begin to reveal themselves. What was once fresh and new is rediscovered, again and again. There is a kind of rhythmic predictability to social life—from the newest fads and latest inventions to the most recent scandals and the next tragic wars. Perhaps the dawning recognition of this eternal return explains why it is nearly always disappointing to see the old paved over to make way for the new—farm fields plowed under for ticky-tacky subdivisions, salty old neighborhoods bulldozed for freeways, an old Japanese temple on the corner demolished for a shiny new shopping mall. Aside from social, political, and aesthetic questions (such as the fate of displaced communities, the stream of toxins leaked from growing mountains of electronic waste, the steady uglification of the once beautiful), there is something more to it. Perhaps there is a nagging realization that everything is constructed. Nothing is permanent. And progress is only a dim lie.

When we move about the world as if it were always there, we needn't think about things like the annual massacres of deer on the nation's roads or the geese losing their ancient mating places to parking lots and shopping malls. We don't need to think of all the bloody wars being fought for oil or diamonds, the thousands displaced and killed, or the ongoing catastrophic warming of the planet. We don't have to think about what was and will be no more. It is just there—the streets, the curbs, the buildings, the stop lights. They become, for us, naturalized as if they were always there. But when we witness that transformation from field to office park, from meadow to McMansion, it is always painful and disappointing. Why? Perhaps because in change we see the falsity and pomposity of our eagerness to progress amidst the scalding indifference of our inability to *listen the others*. We witness and participate in the obliteration of families, of communities, of the wildlife, of the earth, but we neither listen for nor hear the cries. We thrive as conquerors, every field our next frontier. And this trauma of denial is our guilty shadow appearing over the face of the land.

We are thus in so many ways out of tune and rhythm with ourselves, each other, and our environment. Partly it is because our so-called progress comes in such lovely, enchanting guises—strawberries in December, wireless Internet connections wherever we go, and the vast hidden food processing network that we neither see nor comprehend. So we are tone deaf to the vibrational dissonance and neglect to ask, Where are those abattoirs? What happened to the families who worked this land for generations? Who made these shoes? This computer? Do the children of these workers go to school, or are the workers children themselves? To ask such questions and listen to the response is risky. It might deafen or destroy us. Listening is a risk. But it is a fine risk. As Corradi Fiumara describes it, "the inability to listen . . . can only result in a surrender to the pull of benumbing trends. . . . [A]n alternation of 'praise' and 'crucify' seems to emerge, exempting us from those 'deeper' transformations that are unique in permitting renewal."[1]

In this final chapter, we will end the book by returning to the beginning and then, perhaps, "arrive where we started and know the place for the first time." In this recirculation, we will weave together threads from preceding chapters (e.g., *akroasis*, harmonic vibration, interlistening, *sphoṭa*, maieutics, and synchrony) in order to listen toward an ethics of attunement that may "make us aware of the undertow dragging us towards benumbment and, in so doing, offer us a better position from which to avoid falling into one of the many forms of torpor."[2] In fact, we might call this kind of listening an ethics of attunement.

The *Oxford English Dictionary* defines "attunement" as a "bringing into harmony" and connects it etymologically to the noun "attune" (tuneful accord or harmony) as well as the obsolete "atone" (agreement, reconciliation, as in "at one"). Modern usage also relates to the semantic fields of broadcasting (as in "stay tuned"), mental attention ("don't tune me out"), social control ("he calls the tune"), restoration (as in "give the car a tune-up"), and so forth.

In addition, a variety of fields, including phenomenology, psychology, spirituality, and theology, have employed the term "attunement" to express forms of interconnection, congruence, and attention. For example, Michael Fishbane's recent book on Jewish theology is titled *Sacred Attunement,* while psychologist Heinz Kohut uses the term "empathic attunement" to refer to a kind of "vicarious introspection . . . the capacity to think and feel oneself into the inner life of another person."[3] Similarly, Purdy describes empathy as "the imaginative attunement of our own world to the world of another."[4] With an altogether different valence, Heidegger employs the term to mean a state of mind, "the most familiar and everyday sort of thing; our mood, our Being-attuned."[5] Although glossed differently with different emphases, these various inflections on the meaning of attunement share something in common—a relationship to an idea of vibrational resonance and its relation to time and timing.

Two concepts from ancient Greek give us insight into an idea of attunement as the relation between resonance and temporality: the words *kairos,* most superficially understood as "right timing" or the "opportune moment," and *akroasis,* translated as listening and invoking the idea of secret, esoteric teachings.[6] Although both terms were important to the Pythagoreans and other pre-Socratics and both are related to ideas of harmony and balance, only *kairos* remains a part of the Western rhetorical apparatus. But, as we will explore below, both concepts are useful for describing a listening attunement that can transcend binary oppositions and the presumed linear progressions of past, present, and future. From this perspective, *kairos* is a nondual way of synchronous listening and speaking, a dialogic midwifery that can give birth to speech. Thus, we can think of the ethical relation as a temporal and embodied process; an achievement accomplished by weaving the weft of *kairos* into the warp of *akroasis.*

Attunement = *Kairos* + *Akroasis*

The pre-Socratic concept of *kairos* seems to have originated in the context of two ancient art forms: archery and weaving.[7] The former use of *kairos* pertained to a narrow passage or opening for an arrow, and the latter pertained to the passage of threads (the weft) through strands of fiber (the warp) in the making of cloth. Perhaps not coincidentally, a hymn in the *Rig Veda* employs metaphors that combine music and weaving to describe the ritual of sacrifice:

"The sacrifice that is spread out with threads on all sides. . . . The Man stretches the warp and draws the weft. . . . [T]hey made the melodies into the shuttles for weaving."[8] In the Greek context, *kairos* is first found in the ancient poets, who use the term to mean, variously, "'symmetry,' 'propriety,' 'occasion,' 'due measure,' 'fitness,' 'tact,' 'decorum,' 'convenience,' 'proportion,' 'fruit,' 'profit,' and 'wise moderation,' to mention some of the more common uses."[9]

In time, the term made its way into the heart of rhetorical theory, first through Isocrates' and later Aristotle's schools of rhetoric, where it is widely understood to mean "the right or opportune time to do something, or right measure in doing something."[10] And here we might pause for a question: just what is that *something* that is to be done by way of *kairos?* The answer turns out to be surprisingly simple: *kairos* concerns the *doing* of speech and speaking. As Poulakos claims, "Clearly, the notion of *kairos* points out that speech exists in time; but more important, it constitutes a prompting toward speaking and a criterion of the value of speech. In short, *kairos* dictates that what is said must be said at the right time."[11] As depicted thus, listening seems to hold little importance to *kairos* specifically and rhetoric generally—as if speakers speak and only speak and listeners listen and only listen. But we know this is not necessarily so.

Like *kairos,* the term *akroasis,* as discussed in chapters 1 and 2, also received attention from the Pythagoreans. Although it received far less attention than did *kairos* from either classical or modern rhetoricians, a stray trace of its existence is preserved in several *Progymnasmata,* early preparatory manuals of classical rhetoric.[12] According to Pernot, "the rhetorical exercises are an ancient practice" that can be traced to the Sophists.[13] One extant *Progymnasmata* dates from the first or second century c.e. and is attributed to Aelius Theon. In addition to exercises in such familiar forms such as narrative, topos, encomium, and so forth, there are an additional five supplementary exercises that include reading, listening (*akroasis*), and paraphrase. Although there is little written about the listening exercises, there is evidence that attention to the sonic and musical dimensions of speech were emphasized at this same time by professors such as Dionysius of Halicarnassus, who instructed students on matters of melody, rhythm, and harmony and "the placing of words and clauses so that the flow of sounds produces a striking auditory impression. Style is seen as a succession of phonetic and even musical effects."[14] Similarly, Swearingen traces pre-Socratic rhetorical styles that move in the liminal soundings between song and speech, and Hermogenes' system of style includes attention to musical aspects such as order, cadence, and rhythm.[15] Thus, the ancient concept of *akroasis* can be seen to regard harmonic and rhythmic attunement as central aspects of rhetorical practice.

While little is found of *akroasis* elsewhere in antiquity or present-day rhetorical study, the lack of evidence does not certify a thoroughgoing absence. After all, the words *acroamatic* and *acroama* both pertain to esoteric oral teachings heard only by initiates and held in secrecy. And as we discussed in chapter 2, the Pythagorean schools were built upon a discerning ear, and it is here where attunement as the relationship between *kairos* and *akroasis* may be found. Although it probably goes without saying that calling *kairos* an "opportune moment" seems at first glance to cultivate an ethos of opportunism that certainly runs counter to an ethics of attunement, deeper reflection suggests otherwise. On one level, *kairos* is related to ethics by virtue of its relation to the *prepon,* the ideas of propriety and decorum, as evidenced by Isocrates' injunction to "always monitor your speech and actions so that you make the fewest mistakes possible. It is best to make use of perfect opportunities (*kairoi*), but since these are hard to identify, elect to fall short rather than overstep the mark."[16]

Interestingly, however, if we go back to Pythagoras, we find another possibility for *prepon*—the idea of *harmonic attunement,* derived from proportion itself. As discussed in chapter 2, Pythagoras discovered the relationship between sound and number vis-à-vis proportion or ratio. In the Pythagorean cosmos, number had two forms—quantity (count) and quality (tone). In other words, number could be heard as tone, and tone could be expressed as number. Moreover, "the ancients knew that the laws of tone and of rhythm were one and the same. . . . Any rhythm, through increasing its frequencies, may be transformed into a tone or an interval of two or more tones."[17] Thus, both aspects of number were equally important to a vibrational and harmonically attuned standpoint.

Unfortunately, however, the atomist perspective has left us with a largely quantitative view of Pythagorean number that underplays the holistic and relational view expressed by the Pythagorean theorem, $a^2 + b^2 = c^2$, leaving us with Kayser's question "why was the 'qualitative' side of Pythagorism, even as early as the time of Aristotle, either no longer understood or frankly rejected, and only its 'quantitative side' pursued?"[18] And this neglected qualitative side is directly related to the embodied holism of *akroasis,* for although a proportion can be expressed numerically, the number is only the expression of the relationship, not a quantity itself. An example is φ (*phi*), the Greek letter used to depict what is called the "divine ratio"—i.e., $(1 + \sqrt{5})/2$—which can be expressed numerically as 1.62. Thus, in contrast to an atomist perspective that tends to view *kairos* as a singularity, we might instead see it as a kind of harmonic attunement tied to the polychronic dimensions of interlistening discussed in chapter 6. Hill describes the beauty of such a nonlinear *kairos:* "In a Pythagorean cosmos, a kairotic event is an instantaneous now that embeds the whole episode. Every circumstance has its own continually transforming moments that resonate with others, so kairotic openings are indeed points of present time tied to all other moments, past and present, which have unfolded qualitatively in the time of this situation. . . . Kairotic happenings are single events containing multiple ones."[19] Hill's holistic description of *kairos* perfectly depicts the fractally nested nature of polychronic temporality previously discussed. This is not *kairos* governed by a spatialized diachronic temporality and achieved by the act of a sovereign individual, but instead is a form of interlistening attuned to the polyrhythmic, polyphonic, and polymodal movements of temporality. Figures 4 and 5 represent how one might conceive the nonlinear and fractal nature of kairotic time. The timeline in figure 4 illustrates how resonance (e.g., vibrations producing a harmonic series) can generate multidimensional shifts of scale and patterning across various planes.

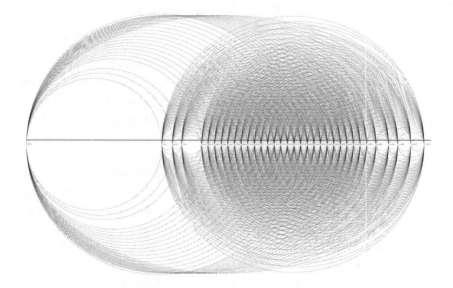

FIG. 4   Timeline. Pen-and-ink drawing by architect Manijeh Verghese, AADipl(Hons) 2012. Courtesy of the artist.

For example, although the timeline itself may be linear, each of its nearly infinite "points" both contains and is contained by an infinite series of harmonic circles that expand beyond the two-dimensional plane of the line. In this way, each circle could itself be thought of as an individual universe or memory echoing with reverberations.

Figure 5 expands the timeline by introducing new iterations of harmonic temporality. Like a nested set of fractals, each circle is an expression of infinite generativity and recursivity that contains within itself, like a hologram, the seeds of the whole. Each new iteration of the circle may coalesce into new circles or morph into new harmonic forms like the golden ratio *phi* discussed above. As depicted in figure 5, these nautilus shell–like forms blend, merge, and span the shifting series of circles across multiple dimensions. Thinking akroatically, we might liken these relationships to the temporal shifts of interlistening wherein consciousness circulates, like Bergson's *durée,* in a "confused multiplicity" of past, present, and future. Another example of the fractal-like nature of nonlinear temporality is beautifully captured in a line from Ann Patchett's debut novel, *The Patron Saint of Liars.* In the final scene of the book, one of the central characters describes a moment of reverie in which she

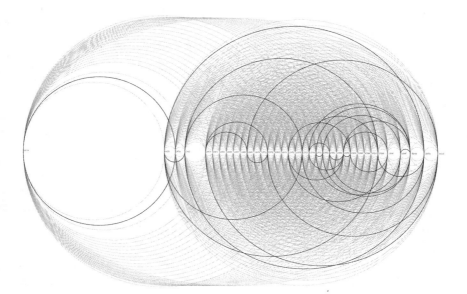

FIG. 5   Timecircles. Superimposition of nonlinear proportional relationships upon the timeline. Pen-and-ink drawing by architect Manijeh Verghese, AADipl(Hons) 2012. Courtesy of the artist.

imagines a possible future for herself and remarks, "It all looked so real in my mind, not like it was going to happen, but like it had already happened and I was only remembering it."[20]

For the most part the Pythagorean idea of the *prepon* as harmonic attunement was lost to time, replaced by the more efficacious idea of propriety. According to Isocrates, *kairos* was difficult to learn because the goodness of speech stems from its having "a share in what is opportune (*kairos*), appropriateness of style, and originality."[21] This dependence upon context and exigence is what has perhaps led some scholars to conclude that *kairos* is a kind of pragmatic or relativist ethics.[22] Pernot, for example, describes *kairos* as a Greek idea of situational ethics, which varies depending on context.[23] This is perhaps what leads Pernot to lament a lack of "truth or justice defined once and for all" for rhetoric in the classical age.[24] In later antiquity of the Roman era, *kairos,* like so many rhetorical concepts, took on an ethically questionable formalism as a form of strategic instrumentalism as a techne or skill to be honed.[25]

Some thousands of years later, toward the later mid-twentieth century, however, American scholars of rhetoric came to develop a more nuanced conception of *kairos* as "a concept far richer and more complex than 'saying the right thing at the right time.'"[26] To Carter, for example, ethics was crucial to the *kairos* of the pre-Socratics, who sought to produce ethical judgments in "a relativistic world. . . . Gorgias and the other sophists were not the skeptics and opportunists that the Platonic tradition has painted them."[27] Similarly, Helsley describes "a generative *kairos*" that "exhibits rich ethical implications in addition to its epistemological and rhetorical facets."[28] To Harker, "*kairos* is a term that reminds us of the ethical responsibility that accompanies the project of evaluating context."[29] Because of its improvisational and generative dimensions, some scholars link the concept of *kairos* to Bitzer's concept of exigence in the rhetorical situation, which "calls the discourse into existence" in a way not unsimilar to the idea of listening others to speech.[30] But for the most part, however, rhetorical discussions about *kairos* and ethics tend to eschew the relational and vibrational in favor of an emphasis on individual agency and action. Sipiora, for example, emphasizes how *kairos* reflects ethics by quoting an excerpt from Aristotle's *Nicomachean Ethics:* "Know the critical situation in your life, know that it demands a decision, and what decision, and train yourself to recognize as such the decisive point in your life, and to act accordingly."[31] Similarly, Kinneavy and Eskin link *kairos* with an ethics of equity that stems from Aristotle's ethics.[32] Following Kinneavy, Harker connects *kairos* to pedagogy and the ethical dimensions of argument with the rhetor as agent.[33]

One exception to this relatively individualistic approach to *kairos* can be found both in Bertau's reflections on *kairos* and in Hawhee's idea of kairotic bodies.[34] Drawing on the generative dimensions of *kairos* and taking a cue from Sullivan's notion of inspiration, Hawhee develops a rhetorical perspective that underscores the relational, nonlinear, and embodied dimensions of *kairos*.[35] She writes, "[I]f the notion of inspiration is considered somatically as the act of breathing in, or a commingling of momentary elements, kairotic inspiration may be usefully figured in terms of *kairos* as aperture, except this time the opening may not necessarily lie 'out there' in circulating discourses or on the body of a foe. Rather, the rhetor opens him or herself up to the immediate situation."[36] While never so explicitly stated, Hawhee's description of *kairos* suggests itself as an ethical relation enacted through an openness that cannot be anything other than a listening. This is *kairos* as a relational opening where the synchronic movement of inspiration emerges not from an individual speaking into the correct moment of a succession of moments, but from a rhythmic conjunction that bridges the in-breath of listening with the out-breath of speaking. In this way, it may be possible to return to the akroatic musical and relational aspects of *kairos,* and listen more closely to the ways in which "rhythm is carried on the waves of the blood circulation from the heart to the limbs, and in the limbs it is arrested as willing. From this you can see how the musical element really pervades the whole human being."[37]

So how do listening as *akroasis* and temporality as *kairos* relate to an ethics of attunement? Here we must connect a few dots. To Levinas, time is accomplished by the ethical encounter with alterity. "The 'movement' of time understood as transcendence toward the Infinity of the 'wholly other' does not temporalize in a linear way. . . . Its way of signifying, marked by the mystery of death, makes a detour by entering into the ethical adventure of the relationship with the other person."[38] If we can transpose Levinas's time as nonlinear transcendence of alterity into our topos of listening, then perhaps we can begin to hear the harmonic strains of *kairos* and *akroasis* and contemplate time as accomplished in relation to the other, wherein "time is not the achievement of an isolated and lone subject, but . . . is the very relationship of the subject with the Other."[39] Thus, we might say that *kairotic* temporality requires harmonic attunement and thereby involves the embodied rhythmic aspects of timing, coordination, syncopation, repetition, punctuation, and so forth, as well as the tensed aspects of grammar and narrative time, and the nonlinear psychological movements where "past and present lie 'all at once' in temporality."[40] Thus, *kairos* is an ethical virtue inextricable from *akroasis*, it is an attunement to others and the dance of circumstance. It is not timely in the mechanical sense of efficiency or serendipity, or as a well-timed shot into the goal, or timely as an intervention in the future "just in time." Instead, *kairos* is the tangle of a braided nonlinear moment choosing us—speakers and listeners—as we move rhythmically together in harmonically attuned, responsive movement.

Epilogue: A Commodius Vicus of Recirculation

So now we come to the end. Some of you may have arrived here wondering what the book's main point is, others may have found the absence of such an "ah ha" moment frustrating or confusing. Still others may have enjoyed the wandering and found the openendedness a pleasure. Some of you may rankle at the apparent repetition, some at the complexity, and some at the incompletion. Some will have long ago stopped reading entirely. But for those of you who are still here, I wish to thank you for listening and end by pointing to several recurring themes, each paired with an ethical virtue, that offer a tangible way to deepen your practice of listening and move toward an ethics of attunement. What follows is a brief sketch of these four themes, which are here presented in no particular order: interconnection and generosity, impermanence and humility, iteration and patience, and invention and courage. Undoubtedly, other themes and interconnections will occur to you as you live into the ideas presented in this book.

Interconnection and Generosity (Nonsolidity, Relation)

"If you are a poet, you will see clearly that there is a cloud floating in this sheet of paper. Without a cloud, there will be no rain; without rain, the trees cannot grow; and without trees, we cannot make paper."[41] Religious resonance aside, the wholeness and holism described in this book are not a solid, immovable foundation, nor a totality or unification of everything that is. Neither are they a deism that makes a god out of oneness, nor a renunciation of the individual, of diversity, or of plurality. They are not the subsumption of everything under "one," or "God," or "the self," or anything else. Nor is holism the set of all sets—a vast, encompassing oneness that contains everything within itself. Rather, holism illuminates how everything is connected to everything else, and reveals how there are scales of "oneness" at various scales and levels of being, and it reminds us that while we may be aware of some of these interconnections, many, *many* others are hidden.

For example, it might seem improbable to hear that rainforests depend on deserts for their fertility, and yet it was recently discovered that dust particles from the Sahara Desert in Africa are essential to the growth of Amazon rainforests—that each year 40 million tons of mineral-rich dust makes its way across the Atlantic Ocean to the Amazon, where it provides essential nutrients without which the rainforests could not grow.[42] And as described in previous chapters, we are unaware of the many forms of interdependency and interconnection that manifest themselves in our everyday human interactions, from the synchronic entrainment that interanimates our physical bodies while we talk with one another, to the polyphonic dialogicality that reverberates with every word we speak and hear. And yet, as the wisdom of the Upanishads notes,

> As bees suck nectar from many a flower
> And make their honey one, so that no drop
> Can say, "I am from this flower or that,"
> All creatures, though one, know not they are that One.[43]

Interconnection gives rise to generosity because in recognizing that we are each irretrievably tied to everyone else, we are also, in some way, responsible. Evil, according to Reb Tenzin, "is ignoring our interdependence with all beings. . . . Believing in a separate self and suffering are linked."[44] Thus, to recognize interconnection and responsibility is to ask the question, How many beings have given their lives for mine? How many people? How many chickens? How many cows? How much forest, water, earth? How many fields plowed under in the forty-four thousand or so meals I've had in my life, along the tens of thousands of miles of roads I've driven, in the trees destroyed to make wood for my house, the grubs in the garden mowed over? Zen teacher Thich Nhat Hanh describes the practice of looking deeply as a way to reveal the interdependency of all beings on the planet. "When you eat a piece of bread, you may choose to be aware that our farmers, in growing the wheat, use chemical poisons a little too much. Eating the bread, we are somehow co-responsible for the destruction of our ecology. When we eat a piece of meat or drink alcohol, we can produce awareness that 40,000 children die each day in the third world from hunger and that in order to produce a piece of meat or a bottle of liquor, we have to use a lot of grain."[45] As we discussed in chapter 7, both our inability to tolerate alterity and the facile ease with which we tolerate the suffering of *others* derive, at least in part, from the same source: from our illusions of independence and our inability to see our interconnections with all beings. When we fail to see these interconnections, we fail to listen. When we fail to listen, we fail to respond. We turn away.

Thus, even though we may be blind to the specifics, our awareness of the invisible inevitability of interconnection can nurture a kind of practical generosity that acknowledges the unknown (and perhaps unknowable) while also attesting to the validity of other points of view engendered by other circumstances and other intentions. As we discussed in chapter 2, when we acknowledge interconnection in our listening, we are practicing a kind of generosity concealed by the atomism of mechanical perspectives, such as the reductive GDP formula of economic well-being discussed in chapter 1, the atomistic Shannon and Weaver mathematical model of communication discussed in chapter 5, and the mathematical formula of Chomsky's predicate calculus and transformational grammar discussed in chapter 4, each of which fails to acknowledge interconnection. But it undoubtedly bears repeating that the generosity elicited by interconnection of course extends to the atomistic approaches to scholarship in communication, linguistics, and semiotics which have so greatly contributed to our understanding of many communication phenomena and processes, and in so doing, have helped a great many people deal with communication challenges involving speaking, learning, listening, reading, and thinking. But as an exclusive lens for inquiry, atomistic and mechanistic approaches have done a disservice to our human inheritance, limiting our awareness of interconnectivity and, as a result, hampering our ability to fulfill our potential as generous and flexible ethical beings.

Iteration and Patience (Repetition, Vibration, Oscillation)

You say I am repeating
Something I have said before. I shall say it again,
Shall I say it again? . . .

. . . .

In order to arrive at what you do not know
You must go by a way which is the way of ignorance.

—T. S. ELIOT, *"East Coker"*

Although many religious traditions are steeped in repetition—whether it be the familiar homilies recited in a house of worship time and again, or the cycles of canonical scripture that repeat themselves yearly, or the sutras and sermons that enact similar ideas in the garb of multiple scenarios—for the most part, secular life is frankly intolerant of repetition. "You told me that already," we complain impatiently to a tired spouse. "I've heard this all before."

So entranced by the supposedly forward motion of "progress," so anxious for the next dose of novelty and distraction, we forget that, from a certain point of view, repetition is all we have—an endless cycle of pulsation and oscillation, heart contracting and expanding, lungs breathing in and then out, gently falling asleep and awakening again. This oscillating repetition reveals itself in patterns of self-similarity at all levels of life—from the atomic to the galactic and from the cellular to the social—and it is within these often invisibly repetitive patterns that we (mostly impatiently) dwell. We rarely appreciate, let alone recognize the beauty of, things familiar to us—as George Eliot so beautifully describes it, "these well-remembered bird-notes, this sky, with its fitful brightness, these furrowed and grassy fields."[46]

Our lives may not unfold exactly like Bill Murray's in the film *Groundhog Day*, repeating each day identically over and over again, but from a certain far distance the repetition seems uncannily close. Poetry and fiction can offer a glimpse of the underlying cycles of repetition and teach the patience required to listen to how "from some vast superhuman distance, the people in [Joyce's novel] 'Ulysses' *are* just like the people in Homer. They are tracing the same patterns, walking through the same roles, struggling to work out the same sets of relations: husband and wife, father and mother, son and daughter—who will become, in their time, husbands and wives, fathers and mothers."[47] Repetition can teach patience in the same way interconnection engenders generosity. Repetition calls for the patience to sit listening in the lap of our ignorance, willing ourselves not to rush further ahead but to deepen into the present without falling into the intoxicating habitual trance of the well-loved and familiar already known. "Repetition thus opens potentialities that went unnoticed, were aborted, or were repressed in the past."[48] In fact, repetition invites the shadowy specter of the unknown, and it requires a patient surrender and capitulation to our own ignorance. "Repetition does not abandon itself to that which is past, nor does it aim at progress."[49] It is, in short, openness without hope.

Invention and Courage (Creation, Generation, Emergence, Quickening)

As we discussed in chapter 4, the seemingly infinite generativity of language and communication gives us ample opportunities for invention and transformation. But usually such limitless invention is conceived from the point of view of speaking. Might we not take an infinitely inventive approach to listening as well? Without the courage *to listen* with courage and invention, we are tempted to succumb to Corradi Fiumara's undertow that drags us toward benumbment and the torpor of indifference. But when we find the courage to listen with and to alterity and with the nonsemiotic, musical dimensions of language, we may engage with an improvisational communicative dance that involves not re-presentation but re-enactment, wherein "by continuous accretions like this, the listener evolves into the composer; in every age, the generations take in a new word, a new figure in a rhetoric that remains recognizable, and thereby comprehensible, through continuity."[50] To play in the creative generativity of *listening to and with language* requires a kind of courage to move outside the familiar and already known into a dance with the rhythmic oscillations of polychronicity, polymodality, and polyphony, encountering contradictions, paradoxes, and more.

This is where akroatic thinking links to the ideas about harmonic vibration and resonance introduced in chapter 2. By conceptualizing communication holistically, we can deepen our ordinary understandings and practices of listening and think in new ways. The idea is to help us move beyond the transmission model and develop alternative ways of listening, thinking, and being with communication. By thinking akroatically, we may bring the musical dimensions of communication processes into awareness, moving outside the well-worn pathways of linear causality and certainty, inventing new metaphors, models, and understandings as we go. As Brower notes,

> Music transports us to a world in which the logic of everyday space, time and movement gives way to impossible possibilities, leading us into contradiction no matter which way we turn—pathways which are vertical yet circular, locations which are the same yet different, near yet far, above yet below. Far from constituting flaws in the logic of an otherwise perfect system, such paradoxes help to make music meaningful for us, a source of never-ending mystery and delight.[51]

Consider, for example, the kind of improvisational and courageous listening that would have been required for Plato to really undertake *Finnegans Wake*. What kind of dialogue would the Socrates of the *Phaedrus* have had with Joyce's sleeping dreamer known alternately as Haroun Childeric Eggeberth, Here Comes Everybody, and H. C. Earwicker? Perhaps it might sound something like this:[52]

SOCRATES: Well then, my friend H.C.E., it seems there is every reason for us not to yield to slumber in the noontide but to pursue our talk about the nature of good and bad speaking and writing.

H.C.E.: What has gone? How it ends?

SOCRATES: Does not a good and successful discourse presuppose a knowledge in the mind of the speaker of the truth about his subject?

H.C.E.: It will remember itself from every sides, with all gestures, in each our word.

SOCRATES: First you must know the truth about the subject that you speak or write about.

H.C.E.: Begin to forget it.

SOCRATES: Wait a moment. Suppose I continued to urge upon you in all seriousness, with a studied encomium of a donkey, that it was what I called it, a horse.

H.C.E. Forget, remember! Forget!

SOCRATES: Well now, when people hold beliefs contrary to fact, and are misled, it is plain that the error has crept into their minds.

H.C.E. He receives through a portal vein the dialytically separated elements of precedent decomposition for the verypetpurpose of subsequent recombination so that the heroticisms, catastrophes and eccentricites transmitted by the ancient legacy of the past can be pits hen to paper and there's scribings scrawled on eggs.

SOCRATES: No, no! You don't seem to get anywhere near what we are looking for; you go about it like a man swimming on his back, in
reverse, and start from the end instead of the beginning. Or am
I quite wrong, dear H.C.E.?

As should be clear from this textual pastiche, Plato would likely find little
to value in H.C.E.'s bewildering injunction to "forget, remember, forget."
Why? Because for Plato, knowledge and truth are always already there, fixed
and unchangeable, and discourse is merely "a means of reminding those who
know the truth."[53] But in expecting, as Plato does, for the truth to already be
known prior to speech, we are silenced. For what we do not know we can only
invent and create in dialogue—by listening others to speech. Thus, invention
requires the courage to listen for the not-already-known, and in so doing,
reveal our own particular vulnerability and weakness. Corradi Fiumara
describes the epic courage needed for transformational listening: "In our concern for listening a demand for change is made upon us. . . . Unless we are
prepared to become in some way different from what we are, listening cannot
be understood properly."[54]

Impermanence and Humility (Transformation, Death, Decay, and Nonfixity)

Whether or not you accept as fact the endless cycle of birth described by the
ancient religions, you will likely accept its accuracy as a metaphor for the
countless transformations of life, from the cycles of birth and death enacted
yearly through the changing seasons to the mythical resurrection of the phoe-
nix out of the fire. As we explored in chapter 3, this ancient idea of the infinite
changeability of life and time is expressed in the Heraclitus fragment that
says one can't step in the same river twice (because the river is always changing and so are you) as well as in the Buddhist idea of impermanence, which
holds that everything is always being born and soon passing away. But as
ancient as this wisdom may be, it's not something most of us think about or
embrace as we go about our busy everyday living.

Yet there are moments, rare and beautiful, that can give access to the hidden recirculation of life that surrounds us:

In my beginning is my end. In succession
Houses rise and fall, crumble, are extended,
Are removed, destroyed, restored, or in their place

Is an open field, or a factory, or a by-pass.
Old stone to new building, old timber to new fires,
Old fires to ashes, and ashes to the earth
Which is already flesh, fur and faeces,
Bone of man and beast, cornstalk and leaf.[55]

The end is really a beginning, the beginning an end of something else. For we are, as the poets say, stardust—recirculated atomic elements like Eliot's "flesh, fur," and cultural recombinations like Joyce's "heroticisms, catastrophes and eccentricities." Accepting impermanence in our everyday interactions with others gives rise to humility that fosters listening with an awareness that "[o]ne great part of every human existence is passed in a state which cannot be rendered sensible by the use of wideawake language, cutandry grammar and goahead plot."[56] The humility of listening opens a path through the *logos*—*dia-logos*—where we poise at the cliff's edge, remembering that "all certainty is a seat belt, a way of tying us securely to the void as the flight takes off into space."[57]

Conclusion

So by now you may have reached the end of the book, though perhaps not. Perhaps you're reading this in the midst of chapter 3, and simply flipped to the last chapter to check out how it ends. My hope is that you will read the book in whatever order suits you; and that, perhaps, you will occasionally revisit sections that spoke to you, or sections you found puzzling or perhaps even annoying. My hope is that in reading this book you will have acquainted yourself with a new listening voice that will accompany you on your life's journey far after you have laid the book down. And I hope that this listening voice will tender new horizons of freedom, curiosity, and peace in your daily interactions with others. I hope you will share these ideas, and in so doing transform them into new ways of listening, thinking, being; and I hope that you will never forget that you are a process, and will always be a process in process.

At the same time, I will hold these hopes lightly, with an open palm. The Tibetan Buddhist tradition has a famous teaching from the tenth century C.E. which says, "Abandon any hope of fruition."[58] At first this teaching might seem counterintuitive—isn't hope important? How can we make anything better without hope? But the teaching reminds us of how hope distracts us from the present moment, drawing us toward a fictional future that has not yet become. Moreover, hope can take the form of aggression toward the present, sowing seeds of perpetual dissatisfaction, becoming something like an addictive drug that dulls our being in deference to an *otherwise* that does not exist. And yet, and yet . . . were I to give up hope, who and what would all these efforts be for? What would be the point of doing anything were it not for hope? After all, one of the daily practices of Buddhism is a prayer that begins, "May all beings be happy and free of suffering." Is that prayer, or any prayer for that matter, not a hope? So the idea of abandoning hope is complicated—it involves a fine balance between intention and detachment. Because the alternative to hope is fear, and when "[t]orn between hope and fear, your mind is never at peace."[59] So I temper my hopes by remembering that hope can be a false idol, a kind of worship of a diachronic future being-state-of-affairs that *is* not. So I doubt and I hope at one and the same time—because in some perhaps small way doubt makes hope possible, creating an opening for possibility without conviction and impossibility without certainty.

NOTES

Introduction

1. Moore, *Bowling for Columbine.*
2. The word *akroasis* (ακρόασις) is Greek for "hearing." Akroatic thinking, that is to say, "listening thinking," will be the subject of all that follows.
3. Kayser, *Akróasis,* 25.
4. Joyce, *Finnegans Wake,* 3; Eliot, "Little Gidding," in *Four Quartets,* 59.

Chapter 1

1. Gadamer, *Truth and Method,* 185.
2. Corradi Fiumara, *Other Side of Language,* 90.
3. Ibid., 122.
4. Carey, *Communication as Culture;* Heidegger, *Poetry, Language, Thought.*
5. Stewart, "Speech and Human Being."
6. Carey, *Communication as Culture,* 20.
7. Shotter, *Conversational Realities.*
8. Gadamer, *Truth and Method,* 443.
9. Gleick, "Wikipedia's Women Problem."
10. Bohm, *Causality and Chance in Modern Physics,* 63.
11. Kuhn, *Structure of Scientific Revolutions,* 120.
12. Ibid., 59.
13. Bohm, *Causality and Chance in Modern Physics,* 78–79.
14. Heisenberg, *Physics and Philosophy,* 50.
15. Bohm, *Wholeness and the Implicate Order,* 9.
16. Heisenberg, *Physics and Philosophy,* 53.
17. Ibid., 129.
18. Bohm, *Wholeness and the Implicate Order,* 23–25.
19. Leonard, *Silent Pulse,* 32–33
20. Eames and Eames, *Powers of Ten.*
21. Whitman, "I Sing the Body Electric," in *Essential Whitman,* 88.
22. Pribram built his theories on insights from his lab work in the 1930s as well as on work by Lashley in 1942 and by Gabor in 1946, as well as, of course, by Bohm (Pribram, "Holography," "Holonomy, and Brain Function" and "Brain and Mathematics").
23. A truly lucid explanation of this is provided in Talbot, *Holographic Universe.*
24. Bohm and Weber, "Enfolding-Unfolding Universe," 45.
25. Talbot, *Holographic Universe,* 42–43.
26. Gleick, *Chaos,* 86.
27. Ibid., 98.
28. I am thinking here in particular of scholars such as Beall, Bodie, Brownell, Coakley, Fitch-Hauser, Imhof, Janusik, Purdy, and Wolvin, among others, who have produced impor-

tant scholarship that focuses on attributes of listening such as attitudes, assessment, behaviors, cognitions, competence, comprehension, effectiveness, memory, processing, skills, and so forth.

29. Bohm, *Causality and Chance,* 16.

30. Briggs, *Fractals,* 133.

31. Costanza et al., *Beyond GDP,* 7.

32. Ibid., 9.

33. Krause, "Bio-acoustics," 1.

34. Ibid.

35. Kayser, *Akróasis,* 128.

36. Lindenlauf, Review of Wille, *Akroasis,* 1.

Chapter 2

1. "Each hair cell is maximally sensitive to a particular frequency of sound." Roberts, Howard, and Hudspeth, "Hair Cells," 77.

2. Glennie, *Good Vibrations,* 103.

3. Leonard, *Silent Pulse,* 47.

4. Bergson, *Matter and Memory,* 276.

5. Kelly, *What Technology Wants,* 111.

6. B. A. Morelli, "ISU Gets $500,000 Grant to Improve Computer Security by Studying 'Keyboarding Signatures,'" *Ames Patch,* June 12, 2012, http://ames.patch.com/articles/isu-gets-500-000-grant-to-improve-computer-security-by-studying-keyboarding-signatures.

7. Since wavelength is inversely proportional to frequency, it is not usually given explicitly. That is, the fatter the wave, the fewer waves will pulse per second.

8. For complex reasons related to the physics of sound, some wind and brass instruments, such as trumpets, trombones, clarinets, and saxophones, tune to different pitches. We won't delve into that here, but suffice it to say that depending on the size of the instrument, a C on a clarinet, trumpet, or sax will sound the same as a Bb (or Eb) in concert pitch.

9. Brower, "Paradoxes of Pitch Space," 97.

10. Helmholtz, *On the Sensations of Tone,* 173.

11. Deutsch, Henthorn, and Dolson, "Absolute Pitch," 339–40.

12. Kayser, *Akróasis,* 137.

13. Stakhov, "Mathematics of Harmony"; Glazewski, *Music of Crystals.*

14. Oliveros, "Improvisation in the Sonosphere," 481.

15. Seifer reports that Tesla also conducted similar experiments in the presence of witnesses in his laboratory in 1896 (Seifer, *Wizard*). And O'Neill reports other resonance experiments involving witnesses (including police) at Tesla's Houston St. lab in New York City around the same time (O'Neill, *Prodigal Genius*).

16. Crowell, *Light and Matter,* 464.

17. Emily Biuso, "Sound Cannon," *New York Times,* December 13, 2009, http://query.nytimes.com/gst/fullpage.html?res=9C05E6DC1E39F930 A25751C1A96F9 C8B63; Arifa Kazimova and Daisy Sindelar, "This Pain-Inducing Acoustic Device Acoustic Device Used to Control Crowds in Azerbaijan Might Be U.S.-Made," *Atlantic,* March 14, 2013; and Robert Johnson and Linette Lopez, "The Manufacturer of This Sonic Weapon Explains to Us How It's Not Really a Weapon at All," *Business Insider,* November 15, 2011.

18. The Lithotriptor sends out a wide-spectrum-frequency sound wave that can affect the various substances that make up a kidney "stone" without damaging surrounding other tissue. But scientists don't really know how the shock wave breaks the stones. It may be resonance and it may not. See Cleveland and McAteer, "Physics of Shock Wave Lithotripsy."

19. Kish, "FlashSonar," 15.

20. Kant, *Critique of Pure Reason,* 193–94. For clarity, I have slightly rephrased this quote.

21. James, *Principles of Psychology,* 1:462.

22. Rosenfield and Ziff, "How the Mind Works."

23. Rosenfield, "Video Ergo Sum," 80.

24. There is an ongoing and lively debate about the question of perceptual and linguistic "universals" that are biologically inherent. For more information, see Claidière, Jraissati, and Chevallier, "Colour Sorting Task"; and Dedrick, "Color."

25. In English the eleven colors are black, white, red, yellow, green, blue, brown, purple, pink, orange, and gray.

26. Saarela and Hari, "Listening to Humans." Notice how the electronics metaphor (circuitry) is used to describe the brain. We will look further into the role of metaphors in listening in chapter 5.

27. U.S. Census Bureau, 1790 Overview, http://www.census.gov/history/www/through_the_decades/overview/1790.html; 1930 Overview, http://www.census.gov/history/www/through_the_decades/overview/1930.html; History, 1890, http://www.census.gov/history/www/through_the_decades/index_of_questions/1890_1.html; 2000 Overview, http://www.census.gov/history/www/through_the_decades/overview/2000.html

28. In the only instance of racializing religion, immigrants from South Asia were combined under the "Hindoo" category. Hochschild and Powell, "Racial Reorganization and the U.S. Census," 60.

29. Brewer and Palmer, "Eyewitness Identification Tests," 82.

30. Memon, Mastroberardino, and Fraser, "Münsterberg's Legacy."

31. Simons and Chabris, "Gorillas in Our Midst."

32. Ibid., 1065.

33. Englehardt, "Problems with Eyewitness Testimony," 27.

34. Loftus and Palmer, "Reconstruction of Automobile Destruction."

35. Online Etymology Dictionary, s.v. "obey."

36. Doyle, "Scandal in Bohemia," 26.

37. Rimmer, "Listening to the Monkey," 264.

38. McClary, *Feminine Endings.*

39. Cage, "Reflections of a Progressive Composer," 89.

40. Schafer, *Tuning of the World,* 272.

41. Ihde, *Listening and Voice,* 49.

42. Oliveros, *Deep Listening.*

43. Schaeffer, *In Search of a Concrete Music.*

44. Ibid., 116.

45. Ibid., 117.

46. Ibid., 121.

47. Stevens, "The Snow Man," in *Harmonium,* 16.

48. Thoreau, *Journal,* February 9, 1839.

49. Nancy, *Listening.*

Chapter 3

1. Flaubert, *Madame Bovary,* 177.

2. There is an interesting dispute about the origin of the grammarian school and Pāṇini's role as either progenitor or inheritor. Some scholars have argued that the study of grammar dates back to the eighth century B.C.E., while others place the date closer to the fifth or sixth century. It is indisputable, however, that Pāṇini's text *Ashtadhyayi* references close to a dozen

grammarians who preceded him and whose authority he cites. This suggests that the Vedic study of language may be even older than the earliest date considered.

3. Joshi, "Veda as Word," 14.

4. Beck, *Sonic Theology*.

5. "Speech," in Doniger, *Rig Veda*, 63.

6. "The Riddle of the Sacrifice," in Doniger, *Rig Veda*, 77.

7. *Mahābhāṣya of Patañjali*, 20.

8. Radhakrishnan, *Indian Philosophy*, 138.

9. Cohen, *Text and Authority*.

10. *Kena Upanishad*, in *Upanishads*, 70.

11. Doniger, *Hindus*.

12. *Chandogya Upanishad*, in *Upanishads*, 182.

13. *Isha Upanishad*, in *Upanishads*, 208.

14. Joshi, "Veda as Word," 15.

15. Matilal, *Word and the World*.

16. Bloomfield, *Language*, 11. Similarly, nineteenth-century scholar Max Müller notes that the Indian science of grammar is the only known system in no way influenced by the Greeks. Müller, *Lectures on the Science of Language*, 116.

17. Itkonen, *Universal History of Linguistics*, 68–69.

18. Ibid., 12–13.

19. According to Matilal, "Yaska's contribution lay in singling out two main (ontological) categories, a process or an action and an entity or a being or a thing." Matilal, *Word and the World*, 19.

20. Matilal, "Error and Truth," 217.

21. Ibid., 218.

22. A syllogism is a model of formal logic wherein two categorical assertions (called premises) are followed by a logical consequent (the conclusion) that has been deduced from those assertions. The most famous example: All men are mortal. Socrates is a man. Therefore Socrates is mortal.

23. Reyna, *Introduction to Indian Philosophy*, 127.

24. Murti, *Studies in Indian Thought*, 136.

25. Matilal, "Śabdabodha and the Problem of Knowledge-Representation," 107.

26. Reyna, *Introduction to Indian Philosophy*, 130.

27. Matilal, "Śabdabodha and the Problem of Knowledge-Representation," 109.

28. Deshpande, "Language and Testimony," 21.

29. MN 72, *Aggivacchagotta Sutta*, in *Middle Length Discourses*, 591.

30. *Dhammapada*, 29.

31. The Pali canon is the earliest existing collection of texts that purportedly transcribe the Buddha's actual teachings. Pali is an ancient language related to classical Sanskrit, and the canonic texts are said to date to around 100 B.C.E.

32. DN 22, *Mahasatipatthana Sutta*, in *Long Discourses*, 340.

33. DN 9, *Potthapada Sutta*, in *Long Discourses*, 162–63.

34. Mair, *Introduction and Notes*.

35. "Zhuangzi," 213.

36. Mair, "Introduction and Notes," xxiv, xxvii.

37. Waterfield, *First Philosophers*, xxxiii.

38. As quoted by the sixth-century C.E. scholar Simplicius, in Barnes, *Early Greek Philosophy*, 82–83.

39. Ibid., 78.

40. Diogenes Laertius, *Lives of Eminent Philosophers* 8.4, "Archytas (Fourth Century B.C.)."

41. Plato, *Republic*, 678.

42. Aristotle, *Prior Analytics*, 66.

43. Aristotle, *Metaphysics*, 749.

44. McEvilley, *Shape of Ancient Thought*.

45. Heidegger, *Early Greek Thinking*, 60.

46. Warren, *Presocratics*. Note, however, that others, such as Barnes, translate *logos* as "account." Barnes, *Early Greek Philosophy*, 50. We will discuss Heidegger's translation of this fragment toward the end of the chapter.

47. Waterfield, *First Philosophers*, 32n2.

48. Corradi Fiumara, *Other Side of Language*, 199.

49. But as we discussed in chapter 1, the principle of noncontradiction has been challenged not just by some strands of ancient Eastern philosophy, but also by twentieth-century findings in quantum physics.

50. Plato, *Theaetetus*, 914.

51. Plato, *Sophist*, 1016–17.

52. Ibid., 977.

53. Johnstone, "Sophistical Wisdom," 275.

54. Plato, *Cratylus*, 422.

55. Ibid., 426.

56. Ibid., 444.

57. Ibid., 473.

58. Ibid., 474.

59. Whitehead, *Process and Reality*, 39.

60. Bronkhorst, "Peacock's Egg," 476.

61. Bhartṛhari, *Vākyapadīya*, 1.

62. Matilal, *Word and the World*, 39.

63. Murti, "Some Comments," 321.

64. Matilal, *Word and the World* , 77. See also Deshpande, "Language and Testimony."

65. Bhartṛhari, *Vākyapadīya*, 10.

66. Beck, *Sonic Theology*, 53.

67. Deshpande, "Language and Testimony," 25.

68. Bronkhorst, for example, frames the Indian history of epistemology in terms of the Greeks. "We know that in ancient Greece some thinkers, the Eleatics, did not hesitate to reject perceived reality on the basis—not of tradition, revelation, or special insight—but of mere argument. The early Indian thinkers, too, proceeded on the basis of their newly acquired confidence in the power of human reason." Bronkhorst, "Peacock's Egg," 477.

69. Johnson, "Life of Cowley" and "Preface."

70. Lewis, *God's Crucible*.

71. Descartes, *Discourse on Method and The Meditations*, 54–55.

72. Kant, *Critique of Pure Reason*, 173. To Kant, sensibility (or "sensuous intuition") is the phenomena that appear in the empirical world, and our intuition is the application of the concepts to these phenomena. Because they do not arise from experience, Kant calls the concepts transcendental, and he says that "a very different certificate of birth will be required from that of mere descent from experience." Ibid., 221.

73. Ibid., 193–94.

74. Ibid., 230.

75. Ibid., 273.

76. Shastri, *Concise History*.

77. Müller, *Lectures on the Science of Language*,164. See also Lehmann, *Reader*, and Macfie, *Eastern Influences*.

78. Very few people had access to Sanskrit manuscripts at this time, and Franz Bopp and other European scholars only first learned of these texts in translation. Master describes how "Jones's work excited great interest in Germany particularly. His translation of Sakuntala was rendered into German in 1791 by Georg Forster and was read with enthusiasm by Goethe and by Herder, the two great protagonists of the national romantic school. A German translation of Jones's translation of Manu's Code appeared in 1797, and his occasional papers were also translated into German in 1795–7" (Master, "Influence of Sir William Jones," 803). According to Master, "The first translation of any part of a Sanskrit work into a European language appears to have been made at second hand by the Dutch preacher Abraham Roger, who published in 1651 *Open-Deuretot het verborgen Heydendom*, containing some proverbs of Bhartrhari, translated into Portuguese for him by a Brahman, and observations on the ancient Brahmanical literature. This book appeared in a German translation in Nuremberg in 1663" (ibid., 798). According to Master, Herder included the Bhartrhari proverbs from Roger's version in 1778. Wilhelm also claims that Goethe, Heine, Novalis, Hegel, and Schopenhauer were introduced to Indian literature through Herder (Wilhelm, "German Response to Indian Culture").

Further, because of the relationship between colonialism and Indology, most of the Sanskrit manuscripts were in England (with some access in France), and Bopp (like other German scholars) had to travel abroad to learn Sanskrit. In 1812 Bopp began his five-year study in Paris with his tutor de Chezy, who employed various translations as teaching material for his pupils. According to Master, "Antoine de Chezy, who taught F. von Schlegel Persian in 1803, was enabled by this catalogue to pick out what he needed for study from these manuscripts, which, as he tells us in an unpublished letter, he had always longed to understand. He commenced his study in 1806, using the translations of Wilkins and Jones as dictionaries, and later Carey and Marshman's translations, which were brought to him by George Archdall. With the further help of Wilkins's grammar (1808) he taught Bopp, Humboldt, August von Schlegel" (Master, "Influence of Sir William Jones," 803).

Lastly, translations were also important for standardizing European scripts for transliterations of Devanagari characters. Masters writes, "It is perhaps not too much to say that comparative studies would have been impossible without a scientific system of transliteration into Roman characters of the various languages involved" (ibid., 805).

79. Müller, *Lectures on the Science of Language*, 168.

80. These connections are well established. First, Colebrook was the first to translate Pāṇini's grammar into English and published the preface to his translation in *Asiatic Researches* in 1801 (Colebrook, "On the Sanskrit and Prakrit Languages"). Second, Bopp cites Pāṇini extensively in all three volumes of his comparative grammar, the first part published in 1833 (Bopp, *Comparative Grammar*). Third, contemporary specialists conclude that "[i]t seems safe to conclude that Bopp's view on the structure of the Indo-European languages was to at least some extent influenced by Pāṇini and his school" (Bronkhorst, "Pāṇini's View of Meaning," 460).

81. Pollock, "Future Philology?," 939.

82. Peile, *Philology*, 11.

83. It is important to note that Humboldt's perspective does not consider all thought to be linguistic thought, but in the case of verbal thinking, thought and language are approached as one.

84. Humboldt, *Humanist Without Portfolio*, 236.

85. Humboldt, *On Language*, 3.

86. Humboldt, *Humanist Without Portfolio*, 246.

87. Humboldt, *On Language*, 63.

Chapter 4

1. Saussure, *Course in General Linguistics*, 6.

2. Ibid., 14.

3. Ibid., 18.

4. In German *Sprache* means both "speech" and "language."

5. Some of the claims of the Chomsky school have been questioned by a number of linguists. However, it is noteworthy that Chomsky's atomistic approach to linguistics has been adopted by many cognitive scientists. For a fascinating account of why this is so, see Harris, *Linguistics Wars*.

6. Chomsky, *Syntactic Structures*.

7. Carroll, *Through the Looking Glass*, 182–83.

8. Ibid., 240.

9. Ibid., 183.

10. Heidegger, *Being and Time*, 88–89.

11. The fact of Heidegger's participation in and endorsement of Nazism and his subsequent silence on the subject throughout his lifetime casts a long shadow over his work. Some scholars attribute his Nazism to a reprehensible moral and personal failing but nevertheless appreciate the enormous value of his work. Other scholars, finding seeds of fascism in his scholarship, entirely reject his vast corpus. Either way, as Michael Hyde and others note, "it is not safe to love Heidegger unless you also hate him." Caputo, *Against Ethics*, 227.

12. Heidegger, *Discourse on Thinking*, 53.

13. Heidegger, "Letter on Humanism," 221.

14. Bohm, *Wholeness and the Implicate Order*, 62.

15. Buber, *I and Thou*, 7.

16. Krishnamurti, *Freedom from the Known*, 91–92.

17. Heidegger, "Letter on Humanism," 217.

18. Merleau-Ponty, *Phenomenology of Perception*, 211.

19. Ibid., 221.

20. Ibid., 229.

21. Merleau-Ponty, *Consciousness and the Acquisition of Language*, 92.

22. "The distinction between automatic, habitual control and attentional, supervisory control is an important one, which can also be linked to extensive evidence from social psychology." Baddeley, "Working Memory," 835. See also Baddeley, *Working Memory*, and Norman and Shallice, "Attention to Action."

23. James, *Psychology*, 6.

24. Baddeley, *Working Memory*, 179.

25. Aside from the central executive, the other subsystems are considered more controversial. But insofar as the relationship between thought and language is concerned, Baddeley contends that new linguistic learning of vocabulary depends on the phonological loop and that auditory perceptions can be also be encoded in the visual-spatial sketchpad.

26. Baddeley, *Working Memory*, 236.

27. Englehardt, "Problems with Eyewitness Testimony," 27.

28. Pasupathi, Stallworth, and Murdoch, "How What We Tell."

29. Prideaux, "Comparison," 17–18.

30. Bergson, *Matter and Memory*, 24.

31. Ibid., 194.

32. Edelman and Tononi, *Universe of Consciousness*.

33. James, *Psychology*, 39.

34. Bhartṛhari, *Vākyapadīya*, 29.

35. Heidegger, *Being and Time,* 204.

36. Theodorou, "Bhartṛhari," 3.

37. Sapir, "Status of Linguistics," 162.

38. Lakoff, *Women, Fire, and Dangerous Things,* 92–93.

39. Gould, *Panda's Thumb,* 206.

40. James, *Psychology,* 180.

41. Lakoff and Johnson, *Metaphors We Live By,* 156.

42. Ibid., 14.

43. Ibid., 156.

44. Lakoff and Johnson, *Philosophy in the Flesh.*

45. Brower, "Paradoxes of Pitch Space," 66.

46. Ibid., 70.

47. Fauconnier and Turner, *Way We Think,* 274.

48. Ibid., 221.

49. This is the title of Austin's groundbreaking lectures on speech act theory. Austin, *How to Do Things with Words.*

50. Heidegger, *Discourse on Thinking.*

51. Gurevitch, "Power of Not Understanding," 165.

52. Merton, *Thoughts on the East,* 38.

53. "Zhuangzi," 226.

54. Ibid., 223.

55. Ibid.

56. Hanh, *Zen Keys,* 10.

57. Merton, *Thoughts on the East,* 32.

58. Brach, *Radical Acceptance,* 74–75.

59. Theodorou, "Bhartṛhari," 5.

60. Bhartṛhari, *Vākyapadīya,* 18.

61. Heidegger, *Poetry, Language, Thought,* 4.

62. Barnes, *Early Greek Philosophy,* 50.

63. Heidegger, *Early Greek Thinking,* 66.

64. Corradi Fiumara, *Other Side of Language,* 125.

65. Ibid., 90.

66. Ibid., 123.

67. Levin, *The Listening Self.*

68. Heidegger, *Early Greek Thinking,* 66.

69. Heidegger, *Poetry, Language, Thought,* 206.

70. Heidegger, *Early Greek Thinking,* 64–65.

71. Woolf, *To the Lighthouse,* 141.

72. Ibid., 159.

73. Oliver, "Flare," in *The Leaf and the Cloud,* 5.

74. Woolf, *To the Lighthouse,* 165–67.

Chapter 5

1. For those many readers who are too young to remember, this was the title of a very popular (and instantly annoying) children's song featured in the 1964 World's Fair and later incorporated into a Disney ride.

2. Anzaldua, "How to Tame a Wild Tongue," 157.

3. I was repeatedly told that it is widely held that many beggar children in India are employed by gangs that use/abuse the children for money. Most Indians and foreigners who

live in India give money to NGOs instead of to the children directly. Some give food when they have it.

4. Chomsky, *Rules and Representations,* 230.

5. Chomsky, "Explaining Language Use," 215.

6. Ibid.

7. Heidegger, *Being and Time,* 205.

8. *Merriam-Webster's Collegiate Dictionary,* definitions 1, 2a, 3a.

9. Reddy, "Conduit Metaphor," 290.

10. Shannon, "Mathematical Theory of Communication."

11. Saussure, *Course in General Linguistics,* 11.

12. Ibid., 12. As a Sanskrit scholar, Saussure worked in the area of Indo-European philology and wrote his dissertation on the genitive case in Sanskrit. Nevertheless, his work owes an often underappreciated debt to the Indian grammarian tradition. But as with most of the Euro-American linguistic tradition, this debt is rarely acknowledged. Thus, on the first page of the first chapter, "A Glance at the History of Linguistics," Saussure begins with the Greeks and fails to mention the Indian grammarians at all. "First, something called 'grammar' was studied. This study, initiated by the Greeks and continued mainly by the French, was based on logic." A few pages later, he writes, "Linguistics proper, which puts comparative studies in their proper place, owes its origin to the study of the Romance and Germanic languages." Ibid., 4–5.

13. Freire, *Pedagogy of the Oppressed,* 59.

14. Ibid., 61.

15. Carey, *Communication as Culture,* 18.

16. Ibid., 23.

17. Ibid., 26.

18. Gadamer, *Truth and Method,* 433.

19. Humboldt, *On Language,* 21.

20. Stewart, "Symbol Model vs. Language," 4,

21. Bash, *True Nature.*

22. Shotter, "Before Theory and After Representationalism," 108.

23. Humboldt, *Humanist Without Portfolio,* 236.

24. Roberts and Bavelas, "Communicative Dictionary," 142.

25. Ibid., 146.

26. Nagler, "Notes on Sacred Song," 175.

27. Humboldt, *Humanist Without Portfolio,* 246.

28. Gadamer, *Truth and Method,* 458

29. Shotter, "Before Theory," 106.

30. Humboldt, *On Language,* 8.

31. Bakhtin, *Problems of Dostoevsky's Poetics,* 167.

32. Bakhtin, *Dialogic Imagination,* 271.

33. Baxter, "Problematizing the Problem," 123.

34. Taylor, "What Is 'Organizational Communication'?," 26.

35. Bakhtin, *Dialogic Imagination,* 279.

36. Dance, "Hearing Voices," 199.

37. Vygotsky, *Thought and Language,* 230.

38. Ibid., 256.

39. Voloshinov, "Construction of the Utterance," 118.

40. Voloshinov, "Discourse in Life and Discourse in Poetry," 16.

41. Voloshinov, "Construction of the Utterance," 114.

42. Pasupathi, Stallworth, and Murdoch, "How What We Tell," 17.

43. Voloshinov, "Word and Its Social Function," 143.

44. Vocate, *Theory of A. R. Luria*, 18.

45. Bergson, *Matter and Memory*, 138–39.

46. Vygotsky, *Thought and Language*, 249.

47. Pasupathi, Stallworth, and Murdoch, "How What We Tell," 15.

48. Vygotsky, *Thought and Language*, 249.

49. Ibid., 250.

50. Theodoru, "Bhartrihari," 5.

51. Humboldt, *On Language*, 26.

52. From what I have seen, there is no evidence that Luria drew on Bhartṛhari's work for his own, though it is of course possible. Furthermore, as described in chapter 2, the European line of thinking that led from Humboldt forward was greatly influenced by the Indian grammarians.

53. Vygotsky, *Thought and Language*, 249.

54. Luria, *Language and Cognition*, 158.

55. According to Vocate, "Luria postulated that there are only 40–50 main types such as finality, inception, causation, function, operation, and so on. . . . Luria's semantic set . . . ties motive to subjective meaning and to word meaning in a gestalt of total meaning." Vocate, "Self-Talk and Inner Speech," 22.

56. Pillai, Translator's Note, 157.

57. Bhartṛhari, *Vākyapadīya*, 11.

58. Vocate, *Theory of A. R. Luria*, 122.

59. Coward, *Sphoṭa Theory of Language*, 129.

60. Ibid.

61. Pillai, Translator's Note, 153.

62. Vygotsky, *Thought and Language*, 251.

63. Pillai, Translator's Note, 157.

64. Luria, *Language and Cognition*, 150.

65. Bhartṛhari, *Vākyapadīya*, 10.

66. Vocate, "Self-Talk and Inner Speech," 22.

67. Luria, *Language and Cognition*, 158.

68. Pillai, Translator's Note, 157.

69. Bhartṛhari, *Vākyapadīya*, 10.

70. Vygotsky, *Thought and Language*, 251.

71. Bergson, *Matter and Memory*, 238.

72. Yakubinsky, "On Dialogic Speech," 251.

73. Roberts and Bavelas, "Communicative Dictionary," 138.

74. DeSouza, DaSilveira, and Gomes, "Verbalized Inner Speech," 156.

75. Ong, *Orality and Literacy*, 32.

76. Voloshinov, "Discourse in Life and Discourse in Poetry," 11.

77. Merleau-Ponty, *Phenomenology of Perception*, 413.

78. Buber, *I and Thou*, 11.

79. Buber, *Between Man and Man*, 20.

80. Buber, *Knowledge of Man*, 105.

81. See, for example, Bertau, "Developmental Origins"; Gratier and Bertau, "Polyphony"; Trevarthen, "Infant's Voice Grows."

82. Powers and Trevarthen, "Voices of Shared Emotion and Meaning," 209.

83. Ibid.

84. Trevarthen, "Infant's Voice Grows," 11.

85. Fuchs and De Jaegher, "Enactive Intersubjectivity," 476.

86. Roberts and Bavelas, "Communicative Dictionary."

87. Fuchs and De Jaegher, "Enactive Intersubjectivity," 477.
88. Ibid., 476–77.
89. Kaplan, "Life of Dialogue," 40.
90. Heidegger, *Discourse on Thinking*, 53.
91. Arendt, *Human Condition*, 190.
92. Jakubinskij, "On Verbal Dialogue," 333.
93. Lichtheim, *Ancient Egyptian Literature*, 74.
94. *Tanakh*, 1291.
95. See Lichtheim, "Ancient Egyptian Literature," and Loprieno, Foreword. Loprieno describes how in the 1970s Lichtheim revolutionized the field of Near Eastern studies by "placing Egypt within a literary tradition shared with the world of Western Asia, echoes of which, mediated by the Bible, were eventually inherited by Western Civilization" (xxv).
96. Bergson, *Matter and Memory*, 70.

Chapter 6

1. Joyce, *Finnegans Wake*, 6.
2. Ibid., 3.
3. Sinclair, *I, Candidate for Governor*, 109.
4. Derrida traces this ambivalence in the term *pharmakos* to interrogate the question of writing in Plato's *Phaedrus* and explore the background "oppositions between between conscious and unconscious, freedom and constraint, voluntary and involuntary, speech and language." Derrida, *Dissemination*, 132.
5. Brodrick, *Sixth Lamentation*, 152.
6. Ibid., 370.
7. Eliot, "East Coker," in *Four Quartets*, 29.
8. Gurevitch, "Other Side of Dialogue," 1189.
9. Gurevitch, "Power of Not Understanding," 165.
10. Eliot, "East Coker," 31.
11. Ihde, *Listening and Voice*, 55.
12. McLuhan, *Gutenberg Galaxy*; Ong, *Orality and Literacy*.
13. Ong, *Ramus*, 291.
14. Bergson, *Time and Free Will*, 100.
15. Ibid.
16. Plato, *Theaetetus*, 172.
17. Sherover, *Are We in Time*, 8–9.
18. Kant, *Basic Writings*, 45.
19. Ibid., 49.
20. Sherover, *Are We in Time*, 50.
21. Ibid., 45–46.
22. Bergson, *Matter and Memory*, 319.
23. Bergson, *Time and Free Will*, 122.
24. Saussure, *Course in General Linguistics*, 232, 18–19.
25. Ibid., 77.
26. Ibid., 87.
27. Ibid., 83.
28. Ibid., 91.
29. Balslev, *Study of Time*.
30. Lao Tzu, *Hua Hu Ching*, 16.

31. Heidegger, *Early Greek Thinking,* 34.

32. Husserl, *Phenomenology of Internal Time-Consciousness,* 31.

33. Just recently, for example, Web-based computer programs around the world were paralyzed because they could not accommodate the "leap second" that had been added to the world atomic clock to compensate for the disjunction between clock time and its measurement. Cade Metz, " 'Leap Second' Bug Wreaks Havoc Across Web," *Wired,* July 1, 2012, http://www.wired.com/wiredenterprise/2012/07/leap-second-bug-wreaks-havoc-with-java-linux/.

34. Levin, *Listening Self,* 262.

35. Gebser, *Ever-Present Origin.*

36. Ibid., 537.

37. Holmes, *Life of Mozart,* 267–68.

38. Jenny, *Cymatics,* 210.

39. Ibid., 286.

40. Volk, "From Vibration to Manifestation," 3.

41. Sinha et al., "When Time Is Not Space."

42. Ibid., 137.

43. Ibid., 158.

44. Humboldt, *On Language,* 21.

45. Bakhtin, *Speech Genres,* 121; Voloshinov, *Marxism and the Philosophy of Language,* 86.

46. Bakhtin, *Speech Genres,* 68; Bergson, *Time and Free Will,* 44.

47. Merleau-Ponty, *Phenomenology of Perception,* 180.

48. Shotter, "Before Theory and After Representationalism," 124.

49. Merleau-Ponty, *Phenomenology of Perception,* 354.

50. Fuchs and De Jaegher, "Enactive Intersubjectivity," 465.

51. Clark, "Time and Mind," 361.

52. Condon, "Analysis of Behavioral Organization," 305–6.

53. Ibid., 306.

54. Fuchs and De Jaegher, "Enactive Intersubjectivity," 476.

55. Saarela and Hari, "Listening to Humans."

56. Ramseyer and Tschacher, "Synchrony in Dyadic Psychotherapy Sessions."

57. Condon, "Analysis of Behavioral Organization," 311.

58. McNeill, *Hand and Mind,* 245.

59. Francaviglia and Servidio, "Gesture as a Cognitive Support."

60. Lindblom and Ziemke, "Interacting Socially," 58, 57.

61. Pasupathi, Stallworth, and Murdoch, "How What We Tell," 17.

62. Bavelas, Coates, and Johnson. "Listeners as Co-narrators," 945.

63. Jakubinskij, "On Verbal Dialogue," 326.

64. Humboldt, *On Language,* 57.

65. Bergson, *Time and Free Will,* 44.

66. Condon, "Analysis of Behavioral Organization," 307.

67. Ibid., 310.

68. Loehr, "Aspects of Rhythm," 201, 209. See also Cummins, "Rhythm as Entrainment."

69. Bertau, "Developmental Origins," 39.

70. Bhartṛhari, *Vākyapadīya,* 10.

71. Ibid., 18.

72. Ibid., 23.

73. Bergson, *Time and Free Will,* 131, 160.

74. Bergson, *Matter and Memory,* 274–75.

75. Bergson, *Time and Free Will,* 129.

76. Benveniste, "Latin Tempus."

77. Bertau, "Exploring Voice," 62.

78. Joyce, *Finnegans Wake,* 158.

79. Gratier and Bertau, "Polyphony," 111.

80. Powers and Trevarthen, "Voices of Shared Emotion and Meaning," 232.

81. Erickson, "Musicality in Talk and Listening," 461.

82. Joyce, *Finnegans Wake,* 16.

83. Whitman, "Song of Myself," in *Essential Whitman,* 77.

84. Woolf, *To the Lighthouse,* 160–61.

85. Whitman, "Song of Myself," 38.

Chapter 7

1. All citations from the book of Job are to the Jerusalem Bible.

2. Voigt, "Quickening," 217.

3. Woolf, *Mrs. Dalloway,* 32–33.

4. Plato, *Phaedrus,* 520; Yamada, *Gateless Gate,* 177."

5. Schrag, *Communicative Praxis,* 204.

6. Hyde, *Life-Giving Gift of Acknowledgment,* 45.

7. Hurtado, *Color of Privilege,* 135.

8. Sontag, *Regarding the Pain of Others,* 113.

9. Simpkinson, "What I Would Say."

10. Nussbaum, *Upheavals of Thought.*

11. MN 141, *Saccavibhanga Sutta,* in *Middle Length Discourses,* 1098.

12. Noddings, *Caring,* 30.

13. Ibid., 33.

14. Arendt, *Essays in Understanding,* 323.

15. Adorno, *Negative Dialectics;* Bauman, *Postmodern Ethics.*

16. Cornell, "Ethical Message," 170, quoting Adorno, *Negative Dialectics,* 172.

17. Cornell, "Ethical Message," 171.

18. Levin, *Listening Self,* 101–2.

19. Bauman, *Postmodern Ethics,* 247.

20. Nussbaum, *Upheavals of Thought,* 321.

21. Hanh, *Being Peace,* 42–43.

22. Levinas, *Totality and Infinity,* 50–51.

23. Jensen, *Culture of Make Believe,* 76.

24. Husband, "Between Listening and Understanding," 443.

25. Levinas, *Otherwise than Being,* 124–25.

26. Noddings, *Caring,* 34.

27. Carter and Erlmann, "Ambiguous Traces," 50.

28. Schopenhauer, *On the Basis of Morality,* 104.

29. Egelko, "Texas Cheerleader Suing—Didn't Root for Attacker," *San Francisco Chronicle,* November 5, 2010.

30. Gurevitch, "Other Side of Dialogue," 1188.

31. Gurevitch, "Power of Not Understanding," 163.

32. See, for example, Brady, *Wisdom of Listening;* Kuusisto, *Eavesdropping;* Levin, *Listening Self;* Lindahl, *Sacred Art of Listening;* Merker, *Listening;* Shafir, *Zen of Listening.*

33. Corradi Fiumara, *Other Side of Language,* 163.

34. Levinas, *Alterity and Transcendence,* 87.

35. Anderson, "Wondrous Practice of All Buddhas."

36. Glassman, *Bearing Witness*, 16.

37. Corradi Fiumara, *Other Side of Language*, 163.

38. Ibid., 164.

39. Wood, "Voice of Ethics."

40. "Others will determine, perhaps, whether Buber would recognize himself in this [Levinas's] interpretation." Derrida, "Violence and Metaphysics," 314n37.

41. For more biographical information, see Friedman, *Martin Buber's Life and Work;* and Malka, *Emmanuel Levinas.*

42. Buber, *I and Thou*, 18. A brief note on translations: although only Walter Kaufmann's translation of *I and Thou* remains in print, I generally prefer Smith. For example, Smith's use of "Thou" conveys a sense of the other's distance and alterity in a manner less apparent in Kaufmann's "You." Similarly, I find phrases like Smith's "All real living is meeting" preferable to Kaufmann's "All actual life is encounter" because the gerund "living" is more evocative and participatory than the nominalized concretization as "life." Also, to my ear, the noun form "meeting" conveys more activity and engagement than "encounter" in contemporary American English.

43. Levinas, *Totality and Infinity*, 201.

44. Levinas, "Ethics as First Philosophy," 85.

45. Levinas, *Totality and Infinity*, 196.

46. Levinas, "Martin Buber, Gabriel Marcel," 317.

47. Buber, *I and Thou*, 108–9.

48. Levinas, *Otherwise than Being*, ix.

49. Levinas, *Is It Righteous to Be*, 133.

50. Buber, *Between Man and Man*, 22.

51. Ibid., 6.

52. Buber, *Knowledge of Man*, 59.

53. Ihde, *Listening and Voice*, 55.

54. Rée, *I See a Voice*, 52.

55. McLuhan, *Gutenberg Galaxy*, 106, 298.

56. Ong, *Ramus*, 291.

57. A brief note on the difference between sound and light may be helpful here. Light is an electromagnetic wave phenomenon that travels through air but is impeded by matter— i.e., light waves don't shine through the body. Sound, in contrast, is a mechanical wave phenomenon that can travel through multiple media (solids, liquids, gases), actually vibrating the material it travels through—i.e., the flesh and bones of the body.

58. Levinas, "Other in Proust," 164.

59. Levinas, *Totality and Infinity*, 99.

60. Levinas, "Transcendence of Words," 149.

61. Ibid., 147.

62. Why this might be so is beyond the scope of this chapter, though several possibilities suggest themselves. Perhaps it stems from the problems of union and fusion implied by sound and voice, which muted, for Levinas, their conceptual value. Or perhaps his debate with Buber interfered with bringing voice to face. Or perhaps it had to do with the "terror" and "horror" Levinas associates with the voice of silence in the *il y a*. But for whatever reason, Levinas eventually chose a unimodal face without voice, the result has been an almost total neglect of listening.

63. Ong, *Orality and Literacy*, 32.

64. Gadamer, *Truth and Method*, 462.

65. Girodet, *Dictionnaire Bordas*, 281.

66. Ibid., 261.

67. Nancy, *Listening*, 6.

68. According to Ciocan and Hansel, Levinas tends to employ *entendre* (hearing) far more often than *écouter* (listening). What this suggests to me is that, in keeping with the argument of this chapter, Levinas didn't think much (that is to say, neither substantively nor, perhaps, appreciatively) of the place of listening in his ethics. Ciocan and Hansel, *Levinas Concordance*.

69. Levinas, *Time and the Other*, 170.

70. Similarly, the French *vocation* has two primary senses: a penchant or *appel* (call) and a destiny, role, or mission. Boussinot, *Dictionnaire Bordas*, 921.

71. Merton, *Thoughts in Solitude*, 101.

72. Beck, *Sonic Theology*, 251.

73. Corradi Fiumara, *Other Side of Language*, 144.

74. Laub, "Bearing Witness," 57.

75. Corradi Fiumara, *Other Side of Language*, 144.

76. Ibid., 160–61.

77. Morton, *Journey Is Home*, 128.

78. Levinas, *Totality and Infinity*, 215, 213.

79. Buber, *Between Man and Man*, 39.

80. Morton, *Journey Is Home*, 206.

81. LaPolla, Kratochvíl, and Coupe, "On Transitivity."

82. According to the *Oxford English Dictionary*, an archaic transitive form of the verb "listen" existed until the early nineteenth century.

83. Morton, *Journey Is Home*, 209.

84. Friedman in Buber, *Between Man and Man*, xvii.

85. Corradi Fiumara, *Other Side of Language*, 125.

86. As legend has it, the ancient dictator Dionysus took advantage of the extraordinary acoustics of an S-shaped cave to spy on his enemies. In time, the cave came to be called "The ear of Dionysius."

Chapter 8

1. Corradi Fiumara, *Other Side of Language*, 84.

2. Ibid., 86.

3. Kohut, *Self Psychology and the Humanities*, 82.

4. Purdy, "Listening, Culture," 57.

5. Heidegger, *Being and Time*, 172.

6. Etymologically, from *akroasis* comes "acroamatic" ("privately communicated by oral teaching to chosen disciples only; esoteric, secret," OED) and "acroama" ("derives originally Ancient Greek Philos. Oral teaching heard only by initiated disciples; esoteric doctrines," OED).

7. White, *Kaironomia*.

8. "The Creation of the Sacrifice," in Doniger, *Rig Veda*, 33.

9. Sipiora, "Introduction," 1.

10. Kinneavy, "*Kairos*," 80.

11. Poulakos, "Toward a Sophistic Definition," 40–41.

12. Heath, "Theon and the History."

13. Pernot, *Rhetoric in Antiquity*, 146.

14. Ibid., 138.

15. Swearingen, "Song to Speech."

16. *Isocrates I,* 164.

17. Kayser, *Akróasis,* 95.

18. Ibid., 30–31.

19. Hill, "Changing Times," 216.

20. Patchett, *Patron Saint of Liars,* 353.

21. *Isocrates I,* 64.

22. See, for example, White, *Kaironomia;* Carter, "*Stasis* and *Kairos*"; and Sipiora, "Introduction."

23. Pernot, *Rhetoric in Antiquity,* 13.

24. Ibid., 13.

25. Sullivan, "*Kairos* and the Rhetoric of Belief."

26. Helsley, "*Kairos,*" 371.

27. Carter, "*Stasis* and *Kairos,*" 105.

28. Helsley, "*Kairos,*" 371.

29. Harker, "Ethics of Argument," 94.

30. Bitzer, "Rhetorical Situation," 2.

31. Sipiora, "Introduction," 17.

32. Kinneavy and Eskin, "*Kairos* in Aristotle's Rhetoric."

33. Harker, "Ethics of Argument."

34. Bertau, "Reflections on *Kairos*"; Hawhee, *Bodily Arts.*

35. Sullivan, "*Kairos* and the Rhetoric of Belief."

36. Hawhee, *Bodily Arts,* 71.

37. Steiner, *Inner Nature of Music,* 68.

38. Levinas, *Time and the Other,* 33.

39. Ibid., 39.

40. Heidegger, *Concept of Time,* 49.

41. Hanh, *Peace Is Every Step,* 93.

42. Koren et al., "Bodélé Depression."

43. *Chandogya Upanishad,* in *Upanishads,* 184.

44. Anderson, "Wondrous Practice of All Buddhas."

45. Hanh, *Being Peace,* 65.

46. Eliot, *Mill on the Floss,* 42.

47. Menand, "Silence, Exile, Punning," 74.

48. Ricoeur, *Time and Narrative,* 76.

49. Heidegger, *Being and Time,* 438.

50. Schaeffer, *In Search of a Concrete Music,* 119–20.

51. Brower, "Paradoxes of Pitch Space," 95.

52. This is a mostly faithful playful recombination of Plato and Joyce from *Phaedrus* and *Finnegans Wake.*

53. Plato, *Phaedrus,* 505.

54. Corradi Fiumara, *Other Side of Language,* 165.

55. Eliot, "East Coker," 23.

56. James Joyce, letter to Harriet Shaw Weaver, November 24, 1926, in Joyce, *Selected Letters.*

57. Jabès, *Book of Questions,* 19.

58. Kongtrul, *Great Path of Awakening,* 83.

59. Khyentse, *Hundred Verses,* 101.

BIBLIOGRAPHY

Adorno, Theodor W. *Negative Dialectics.* New York: Continuum, 1973.

Anderson, Reb Tenzin. "The Wondrous Practice of All Buddhas." Dharma Talk presented at the Clouds in Water Zen Center Retreat, St. Paul, Minn., May 2005.

Allen, Woody (director). *Annie Hall.* VHS. Los Angeles: MGM/UA Home Video, 1977.

Anzaldua, Gloria. "Haciendo Caras, Una Entrada." In *Making Face, Making Soul: Haciendo Caras,* xv–xxvii. San Francisco: Aunt Lute Foundation, 1990.

———. "How to Tame a Wild Tongue." In *Encountering Cultures,* edited by Richard Holeton, 152–62. Englewood Cliffs, N.J.: Prentice-Hall, 1995.

Arendt, Hannah. *Essays in Understanding, 1930–54: Formation, Exile, and Totalitarianism.* Edited by Jerome Kohn. New York: Schocken Books, 1994.

———. *The Human Condition.* Chicago: University of Chicago Press, 1998.

Aristotle. *Metaphysics.* In *The Basic Works of Aristotle,* edited by Richard McKeon, translated by W. D. Ross. New York: Modern Library, 2001.

———. *Physics.* In *Basic Works of Aristotle,* 214–394.

———. *Prior Analytics.* In *Basic Works of Aristotle,* 65–109.

Austin, John L. *How to Do Things with Words.* The Henry James Lectures Delivered at Harvard University in 1955. Oxford: Oxford University Press, 1962.

Baddeley, Alan. *Working Memory, Thought, and Action.* Oxford: Oxford University Press, 2007.

———. "Working Memory: Looking Back and Looking Forward." *Nature Reviews Neuroscience* 4, no. 10 (2003): 829–39.

Bakhtin, Mikhail M. *The Dialogic Imagination: Four Essays.* Edited by Michael Holquist. Translated by Caryl Emerson and Michael Holquist. Austin: University of Texas Press, 1981.

———. *Problems of Dostoevsky's Poetics.* Translated by R. W. Rotsel. Ann Arbor, Mich.: Ardis, 1973.

———. *Speech Genres and Other Late Essays.* Edited by Caryl Emerson and Michael Holquist. Translated by Vern McGee. Austin: University of Texas Press, 1986.

Bakhtin School Papers. Edited by Ann Shukman. Oxford: RPT, 1983.

Balslev, Anindita Niyogi. *A Study of Time in Indian Philosophy.* Delhi: Motilal Banarsidass, 2009.

Barnes, Jonathan, ed. *Early Greek Philosophy.* New York: Penguin Books, 1987.

Bash, Barbara. "Disappearing Words." *True Nature: A Visual Blog.* May 4, 2009. http://barbarabash.blogspot.com/2009/05/disappearing-words.html.

Batchelor, Stephen. *The Awakening of the West: The Encounter of Buddhism and Western Culture.* Berkeley: Parallax Press, 1994.

Bauman, Zygmunt. *Postmodern Ethics.* Malden, Mass.: Basil Blackwell, 1993.

Bavelas, Janet B., Linda Coates, and Trudy Johnson. "Listeners as Co-narrators." *Journal of Personality and Social Psychology* 79, no. 6 (2000): 941–52.

———. "Listener Responses as a Collaborative Process: The Role of Gaze." *Journal of Communication* 52, no. 3 (2002): 566–80.

Baxter, L. "Problematizing the Problem in Communication: A Dialogic Perspective." *Communication Monographs* 74, no. 1 (2007): 118–24.

Beck, Guy L. *Sonic Theology: Hinduism and Sacred Sound.* Studies in Comparative Religion. Columbia: University of South Carolina Press, 1993.

Benveniste, Émile. "Latin Tempus." In *Mélanges de philologie, de littérature et d'histoire anciennes offerts à Alfred Ernout,* 11–16. Paris: C. Klincksieck, 1940.

Bergson, Henri. *Matter and Memory.* Translated by Nancy M. Paul and W. Scott Palmer. London: George Allen and Unwin, 1911.

———. *Time and Free Will: An Essay on the Immediate Data of Consciousness.* 3rd ed. Translated by F. L. Pogson. Mineola, N.Y.: Dover, 2001.

Bertau, Marie-Cécile. "Developmental Origins of the Dialogical Self: Some Significant Moments." In *The Dialogical Self in Psychotherapy,* edited by H. J. M. Hermans and Giancarlo Dimaggio, 29–42. New York: Brunner-Routledge, 2004.

———. "Exploring Voice: A Psycholinguist's Inquiry into the Dynamic Materiality of Language." In Bertau, Gonçalves, and Raggatt, *Dialogic Formations,* 41–68.

———. "Reflections on *Kairos.*" In *Astonishment and Evocation: Festschrift for Stephen Tyler's 75th Birthday, 8 May 2007,* edited by Ivo Strecker and Markus Verne, vol. 2, 88–93. Pre-publication manuscript, 2006.

———. "Voice: A Pathway to Consciousness as 'Social Contact to Oneself.'" *Integrative Psychological Behavior* 42 (2008): 92–113.

———. "Voices of Others unto the Self, Voices of Others in the Self: Polyphony as Means and Resource for Constructing and Reconstructing Social Reality." In *"After You!": Dialogical Ethics and the Pastoral Counselling Process,* edited by Axel Liègeois, Roger Burggraeve, Marina Riemslagh, and Jozef Corveleyn, 37–66. Leuven: Peeters, 2013.

Bertau, Marie-Cécile, Miguel Gonçalves, and P. T. F. Raggatt, eds. *Dialogic Formations: Investigations into the Origins and the Development of the Dialogical Self.* Charlotte, N.C.: Information Age, 2011.

Bhartṛhari. *The Vākyapadīya: Critical Text of Cantos I and II.* Translated by K. Raghavan Pillai. Delhi: Motilal Banarsidass, 1971.

Bitzer, Lloyd F. "The Rhetorical Situation." *Philosophy and Rhetoric* 1, no. 1 (1968): 1–14.

Bloomfield, Leonard. *Language.* New York: Henry Holt, 1933.

Bohm, David. *Causality and Chance in Modern Physics.* Princeton: D. Van Nostrand, 1957.

———. *Thought as a System.* New York: Routledge, 1994.

———. *Wholeness and the Implicate Order.* New York: Ark Paperbacks, 1983.

Bohm, David, and Lee Nichol. *On Dialogue.* London: Routledge, 1996.

Bohm, David, and Renee Weber. "The Enfolding-Unfolding Universe: A Conversation with David Bohm." In *The Holographic Paradigm and Other Paradoxes: Exploring the Leading Edge of Science,* edited by Ken Wilber, 44–104. Boston: Shambhala, 1985.

Bolduc, Michelle K., and David A. Frank. "Chaim Perelman and Lucie Olbrechts-Tyteca's 'On Temporality as a Characteristic of Argumentation': Commentary and Translation." *Philosophy and Rhetoric* 43, no. 4 (2010): 308–36.

Bopp, Franz. *A Comparative Grammar of the Sanskrit, Zend, Greek, Latin, Lithuanian, Gothic, German, and Sclavonic Languages.* 4th ed. London: Williams and Norgate, 1885.

Boussinot, Roger. *Dictionnaire Bordas des synonymes, analogies, antonymes.* 2nd ed. Paris: Bordas, 1994.

Brach, Tara. *Radical Acceptance: Embracing Your Life with the Heart of a Buddha.* New York: Bantam Books, 2003.

Brady, Mark, ed. *The Wisdom of Listening.* Boston: Wisdom, 2003.

Brewer, Neil, and Matthew A. Palmer. "Eyewitness Identification Tests." *Legal and Criminological Psychology* 15 (2010): 77–96.

Briggs, John. *Fractals: The Patterns of Chaos.* New York: Simon and Schuster, 1992.

Brinck, Ingar. "Intersubjectivity and Intentional Communication." In *The Shared Mind: Perspectives on Intersubjectivity,* edited by Jordon Zlatev, 115–40. Amsterdam: John Benjamins, 2008.

Brodrick, William. *The Sixth Lamentation*. New York: Penguin Books, 2003.

Bronkhorst, Johannes. "Bhattoji Diksita on Sphota." *Journal of Indian Philosophy* 33 (2005): 3–41.

———. "Pāṇini's View of Meaning and Its Western Counterpart." In *Current Advances in Semantic Theory*, edited by Maxim I. Stamenov, 455–64. Amsterdam: John Benjamins, 1992.

———. "The Peacock's Egg: Bhartrhari on Language and Reality." *Philosophy East and West* 51, no. 4 (2001): 474–91.

Brower, Candace. "Paradoxes of Pitch Space." *Music Analysis* 27, no. 1 (2008): 51–106.

Buber, Martin. *Between Man and Man*. Translated by Ronald Gregor Smith. New York: Macmillan, 1975.

———. *I and Thou*. 2nd ed. Translated by Ronald Gregor Smith. New York: Scribner, 1958.

———. *The Knowledge of Man: Selected Essays*. Translated by Maurice Freedman and Ronald Gregor Smith. New York: Humanity Books, 1998.

Cage, John. "Reflections of a Progressive Composer on a Damaged Society." *October* 82 (Autumn 1997): 77–93.

Caputo, John D. *Against Ethics: Contributions to a Poetics of Obligation with Constant Reference to Deconstruction*. Studies in Continental Thought. Bloomington: Indiana University Press, 1993.

———. *More Radical Hermeneutics: On Not Knowing Who We Are*. Bloomington: Indiana University Press, 2000.

Carbaugh, Donal. "'Just Listen': 'Listening' and Landscape Among the Blackfeet." *Western Journal of Communication* 63, no. 3 (1999): 250–70.

Carey, James. *Communication as Culture: Essays on Media and Society*. Boston: Unwin Hyman, 1989.

Carroll, Lewis. *Through the Looking Glass*. In *The Best of Lewis Carroll*, 163–294. New York: Castle Books, 2011.

Carter, Michael. "*Stasis* and *Kairos*: Principles of Social Construction in Classical Rhetoric." *Rhetoric Review* 7, no. 1 (1988): 97–112.

Carter, Paul, and Veit Erlmann. "Ambiguous Traces, Mishearing, and Auditory Space." In *Hearing Cultures: Essays on Sound, Listening, and Modernity*, edited by Veit Erlmann, 43–63. New York: Berg, 2004.

Childs, Becky, and Christine Mallinson. "The Significance of Lexical Items in the Construction of Ethnolinguistic Identity: A Case Study of Adolescent Spoken and Online Language." *American Speech* 81, no. 1 (2006): 3–29.

Chomsky, Noam. "Explaining Language Use." *Philosophical Topics* 20, no. 1 (1992): 205–31.

———. *Syntactic Structures*. New York: Mouton de Gruyter, 2002.

Chuang-Tzu. *Chuang-Tzu: A New Selected Translation with an Exposition of the Philosophy of Kuo Hsiang*. Translated by Youlan Feng. 2nd ed. New York: Paragon, 1964.

Ciocan, Cristian, and Georges Hansel. *Levinas Concordance*. Dordrecht: Springer, 2005.

Claidière, Nicolas, Yasmina Jraissati, and Coralie Chevallier. "A Colour Sorting Task Reveals the Limits of the Universalist/Relativist Dichotomy: Colour Categories Can Be Both Language Speci?c and Perceptual." *Journal of Cognition and Culture* 8, no. 3 (2008): 211–33.

Clark, Andy. "Beyond the Flesh: Some Lessons from a Mole Cricket." *Artificial Life* 11, nos. 1–2 (2005): 233–44.

———. "Time and Mind." *Journal of Philosophy* 95, no. 7 (1998): 354–76.

Clark, Eve V. "Young Children's Uptake of New Words in Conversation." *Language in Society* 36, no. 2 (2007): 157–82.

Cleveland, Robin O., and James A. McAteer. "The Physics of Shock Wave Lithotripsy." In *Smith's Textbook of Endourology*, edited by Arthur D. Smith, Gopal Badlani, and Louis Kavoussi, 529–98. Hoboken, N.J.: Wiley-Blackwell, 2011.

Cohen, Signe. *Text and Authority in the Older Upaniṣads.* Brill's Indological Library 30 Leiden: Brill, 2008.

Colebrooke, H. T. "On the Sanskrit and Prakrit Languages." 1801. In *Miscellaneous Essays, by H. T. Colebrooke, with Life of the Author, by His Son, Sir T. E. Colebrooke,* vol. 1. New ed. London: Trubner, 1873.

Condon, William S. "An Analysis of Behavioral Organization." *Sign Language Studies* 13 (1976): 285–318.

Cornell, Drucilla. "The Ethical Message of Negative Dialectics." In *American Continental Philosophy,* edited by Walter Brogan and James Risser, 147–78. Bloomington: Indiana University Press, 2000.

Corradi Fiumara, Gemma. *The Other Side of Language: A Philosophy of Listening.* New York: Routledge, 1990.

Costanza, Robert, Maureen Hart, Stephen Posner, and John Talberth. *Beyond GDP: The Need for New Measures of Progress.* The Pardee Papers 4. Boston: Boston University, 2009.

Coward, Harold G. *The Sphoṭa Theory of Language: A Philosophical Analysis.* Dehli: Motilal Banarsidass, 1980.

Crowell, Benjamin. *Light and Matter.* http://www.lightandmatter.com/html_books/lm/choo/choo.html.

Cummins, Fred. "Rhythm as Entrainment: The Case of Synchronous Speech." *Journal of Phonetics* 37 (2009): 16–28.

Dance, Frank E. X. "Hearing Voices." In Vocate, *Intrapersonal Communication,* 195–210.

Dedrick, Don. "Color, Color Terms, Categorization, Cognition, Culture: An Afterword." *Journal of Cognition and Culture* 5, nos. 3–4 (2005): 487–95.

Derrida, Jacques. *Dissemination.* London: Continuum, 1981.

———. "Violence and Metaphysics." In *Writing and Difference,* translated by Alan Bass, 79–153. Chicago: University of Chicago Press, 1978.

Descartes, René. *Discourse on Method and the Meditations.* Translated by F. E. Sutcliffe. New York: Penguin Books, 1968.

Deshpande, Madhav. "Language and Testimony in Classical Indian Philosophy." *Stanford Encyclopedia of Philosophy,* edited by Edward N. Zalta (Spring 2011). http://plato.stanford.edu/archives/spr2011/entries/language-india /.

DeSouza, Mariane L., Amanda DaSilveira, and William B. Gomes. "Verbalized Inner Speech and the Expressiveness of Self-Consciousness." *Qualitative Research in Psychology* 5 (2008): 154–70.

Deutsch, Diana, Trevor Henthorn, and Mark Dolson. "Absolute Pitch, Speech, and Tone Language: Some Experiments and a Proposed Framework." *Music Perception* 21, no. 3 (2004): 339–56.

The Dhammapada. Edited by Anne Bancroft. Element Classics of World Spirituality. Rockport, Mass.: Element, 1997.

Diogenes Laertius. *Lives of Eminent Philosophers.* Translated by Robert Drew Hicks. London: W. Heinemann, 1925. http://www.perseus.tufts.edu/hopper/text?doc=Perseus%3Atext%3A1999.01.0258%3Abook%3D8%3Achapter%3D4.

Doniger, Wendy, ed. *The Rig Veda: An Anthology.* New York: Penguin Classics, 1981.

———. *The Hindus: An Alternative History.* New York: Penguin Press, 2009.

———. "The Uses and Misuses of Polytheism and Monotheism in Hinduism." The University of Chicago Divinity School, 2010. divinity.uchicago.edu/martycenter/publications/webforum/012010/mo notheism for religion and culture-titlecorr.pdf.

Doyle, Sir Arthur Conan. "A Scandal in Bohemia." Ebook (November 2008).

Eames, Charles, and Ray Eames (directors). *Powers of Ten.* VHS. [Santa Monica, Cal.]: Pyramid Films, 1977.

Eckert, Penelope. *The Social Order of Belton High.* New York: Basil Blackwell, 2000.

Edelman, Gerald M., and Giulio Tononi. *A Universe of Consciousness: How Matter Becomes Imagination.* New York: Basic Books, 2000.

Eliot, George. *The Mill On the Floss.* New York: Signet Classics, 2002.

Eliot, T. S. *Four Quartets.* New York: Harcourt, Brace, 1943.

Ellison, Ralph. *Invisible Man.* New York: Vintage International, 1995.

Engelhardt, Laura. "The Problems with Eyewitness Testimony: Commentary on a Talk by George Fisher and Barbara Tversky." *Stanford Journal of Legal Studies* 1, no. 1 (1999): 25–29

Erickson, Frederick. "Musicality in Talk and Listening: A Key Element in Classroom Discourse as an Environment for Learning." In Malloch and Trevarthen, *Communicative Musicality,* 449–63.

Fauconnier, Gilles, and Mark Turner. *The Way We Think: Conceptual Blending and the Mind's Hidden Complexity.* New York: Basic Books, 2002.

Fishbane, Michael. *Sacred Attunement.* Chicago: University of Chicago Press, 2008.

Flaubert, Gustave. *Madame Bovary.* Translated by Geoffrey Wall. New York: Penguin Books, 2003.

Francaviglia, Mauro, and Rocco Servidio. "Gesture as a Cognitive Support to Solve Mathematical Problems." *Psychology* 2, no. 2 (2011): 91–97.

Freire, Paulo. *Pedagogy of the Oppressed.* Translated by Myra Bergman Ramos. New York: Seabury Press, 1968.

Friedman, Martin. *Martin Buber's Life and Work.* 3 vols. New York: Dutton, 1981–83.

Fuchs, Thomas, and Hanne De Jaegher. "Enactive Intersubjectivity: Participatory Sense-Making and Mutual Incorporation." *Phenomenology and the Cognitive Sciences* 8 (2009): 465–86.

Gadamer, Hans Georg. *Truth and Method.* 2nd rev. ed. New York: Continuum, 2003.

Gebser, Jean. *The Ever-Present Origin.* Athens: Ohio University Press, 1984.

Girodet, Jean. *Dictionnaire Bordas des pièges et difficultés de la langue Française.* Paris: Bordas, 2001.

Glassman, Bernie. *Bearing Witness: A Zen Master's Lessons in Making Peace.* New York: Bell Tower, 1998.

Glazewski, Andrzej. *The Music of Crystals, Plants, and Human Beings.* London: British Society of Dowsers, 1951.

Gleick, James. *Chaos: Making a New Science.* New York: Viking, 1987.

———. "Wikipedia's Women Problem." *NYRblog,* April 29, 2013. http://www.nybooks.com/blogs/nyrblog/2013/apr/29/wikipedia-women-problem/.

Glennie, Evelyn. *Good Vibrations.* Long Preston, North Yorkshire, England: Magna Print Books, 1990.

Gould, Stephen Jay. *The Panda's Thumb: More Reflections in Natural History.* New York: W. W. Norton, 1992.

Gratier, Maya, and Marie-Cécile Bertau. "Polyphony: A Vivid Source of Self and Symbol." In Bertau, Gonçalves, and Raggatt, *Dialogic Formations,* 85–119.

Gurevitch, Z. D. "The Other Side of Dialogue: On Making the Other Strange and the Experience of Otherness." *American Journal of Sociology* 93, no. 5 (1988): 1179–99.

———. "The Power of Not Understanding: The Meeting of Conflicting Identities." *Journal of Applied Behavioral Science* 25, no. 2 (1989): 161–73.

Hanh, Thich Nhat. *Being Peace.* Berkeley, Cal.: Parallax Press, 1987.

———. *Peace Is Every Step.* New York: Bantam Books, 1992.

———. *Zen Keys.* New York: Doubleday, 1974.

Harker, Michael. "The Ethics of Argument: Rereading *Kairos* and Making Sense in a Timely Fashion." *College Composition and Communication* 59, no. 1 (2007): 77–97.

Harris, Randy Allen. *The Linguistics Wars.* New York: Oxford University Press, 1995.

Hawhee, Debra. *Bodily Arts: Rhetoric and Athletics in Ancient Greece.* Austin: University of Texas Press, 2004.

Heath, Malcolm. "Theon and the History of the Progymnasmata." *Greek, Roman, and Byzantine Studies* 43, no. 3 (2002): 129–60.

Heidegger, Martin. *Being and Time.* Translated by John Macquarrie and Edward Robinson. Malden, Mass.: Basil Blackwell, 1962.

————. *The Concept of Time: The First Draft of "Being and Time."* Translated by Ingo Farin with Alex Skinner. New York: Continuum, 2011.

————. *Discourse on Thinking.* Translated by John M. Anderson and E. Hans Freund. New York: Harper and Row, 1966.

————. *Early Greek Thinking.* Translated by David Farrell Krell and Frank Capuzzi. New York: Harper and Row, 1984.

————. "Letter on Humanism." In *Basic Writings: From "Being and Time" (1927) to "The Task of Thinking" (1964),* 2nd ed., edited by David Farrell Krell, 213–66. San Francisco: HarperSanFrancisco, 1993.

————. *On the Way to Language.* New York: Harper and Row, 1959.

————. *On Time and Being.* Translated by Joan Stambaugh. New York: Harper Torchbooks, 1972.

————. *Poetry, Language, Thought.* Translated by Albert Hofstadter. New York: Harper and Row, 1971.

————. "What Is Metaphysics?" In *Martin Heidegger, Basic Writings,* 89–110. SanFrancisco: HarperSanFrancisco, 1993.

Heisenberg, Werner. *Physics and Philosophy.* New York: Harper and Row, 1958.

Helmholtz, Hermann von. *On the Sensations of Tone as a Physiological Basis for the Theory of Music.* 2nd English ed. New York: Dover, 1954.

Helsley, Sheri L. *"Kairos."* In *Encyclopedia of Rhetoric and Composition: Communication from Ancient Times to the Information Age,* edited by Theresa Enos, 371. New York: Routledge, 2010.

Hill, Carolyn Eriksen. "Changing Times in Composition Classes: *Kairos,* Resonance, and the Pythagorean Connection." In Sipiora and Baumlin, *Rhetoric and Kairos,* 211–25.

Hochschild, Jennifer L., and Brenna Marea Powell. "Racial Reorganization and the United States Census, 1850–1930: Mulattoes, Half-Breeds, Mixed Parentage, Hindoos, and the Mexican Race." *Studies in American Political Development* 22 (2008): 59–96.

Holmes, Edward. *The Life of Mozart, Including His Correspondence.* New York: Harpers, 1845.

Humboldt, Wilhelm von. *Humanist Without Portfolio: An Anthology of the Writings of Wilhelm von Humboldt.* Translated by Marianne Cowan. Detroit: Wayne State University Press, 1963.

————. *On Language: On the Diversity of Human Language Construction and Its Influence on the Mental Development of the Human Species.* Edited by Michael Losonsky. Translated by Peter Heath. Cambridge Texts in the History of Philosophy. Cambridge: Cambridge University Press, 1999.

Hurtado, Aida. *The Color of Privilege: Three Blasphemies On Race and Feminism.* Ann Arbor: University of Michigan Press, 1996.

Husband, Charles. "Between Listening and Understanding." *Continuum* 23, no. 4 (2009): 441–43.

Husserl, Edmund. *The Phenomenology of Internal Time-Consciousness.* Edited by Martin Heidegger. Translated by James S. Churchill. Bloomington: Indiana University Press, 1964.

Hyde, Bruce. "Listening Authentically: A Heideggarian Perspective on Interpersonal Communication." In *Interpretive Approaches to Interpersonal Communication,* edited by Kathryn Carter and Mick Presnell, 179–95. Albany: State University of New York Press, 1994.

Hyde, Michael J. *The Call of Conscience: Heidegger and Levinas.* Columbia: University of South Carolina Press, 2001.

———. *The Life-Giving Gift of Acknowledgment: A Philosophical and Rhetorical Inquiry.* West Lafayette: Purdue University Press, 2006.

Ihde, Don. *Listening and Voice: A Phenomenology of Sound.* Athens: Ohio University Press, 1976.

Innis, Harold. *The Bias of Communication.* Toronto: University of Toronto Press, 1951.

Isocrates I. Translated by David Mirhady and Yun Lee Too. Austin: University of Texas Press, 2000.

Itkonen, Esa. *Universal History of Linguistics.* Amsterdam: John Benjamins, 1991.

Jabès, E. *The Book of Questions: El, or the Last Book.* Middletown: Wesleyan University Press, 1984.

Jakubinskij, Lev P. "On Verbal Dialogue." Translated by Jane E. Knox. *Dispositio: Revista Hispanica de Semiotica Literaria* 4, nos. 11–12 (1979): 321–36.

James, William. *The Principles of Psychology.* 3 vols. 3 vols. Edited by Frederick H. Burkhardt, Fredson Bowers, and Ignas K. Skrupskelis. Cambridge, Mass.: Harvard University Press, 1981.

Jaspers, Karl, and Hannah Arendt. *Anaximander, Heraclitus, Parmenides, Plotinus, Lao-Tzu, Nagarjuna.* Edited by Hannah Arendt, translated by Ralph Manheim. New York: Harcourt Brace Jovanovich, 1974.

Jenny, Hans. *Cymatics.* Newmarket, N.H.: Macromedia, 2001.

Jensen, Derrick. *The Culture of Make Believe.* White River Junction, Vt.: Chelsea Green, 2002.

The Jerusalem Bible. Edited by Alexander Jones. New York: Doubleday, 1968.

Johnson, Samuel. "Life of Cowley." In *The Lives of the Most Eminent English Poets.* 1779–81.

———. Preface to *A Dictionary of the English Language.* 1755.

Johnstone, Christopher Lyle. "Sophistical Wisdom: *Politikê Aretê* and 'Logosophia.'" *Philosophy and Rhetoric* 39, no. 4 (2006): 265–89.

Jordan, June. "Nobody Mean More to Me than You and the Future Life of Willie Jordan." *Harvard Educational Review* 58, no. 3 (1988): 363–75.

Joshi, Kireet. "Veda as Word." In *Veda as Word,* edited by Shashiprabha Kumar, 13–20. New Delhi: Special Centre for Sanskrit Studies, Jawaharlal Nehru University, 2005.

Joyce, James. *Finnegans Wake.* New York: Penguin Books, 1976.

———. *Selected Letters of James Joyce.* Edited by Richard Ellman. New York: Viking Press, 1975.

Kant, Immanuel. *Critique of Pure Reason.* Translated by Paul Guyer and Allen W. Wood. Cambridge: Cambridge University Press, 1998.

Kaplan, Abraham. "The Life of Dialogue." In *The Reach of Dialogue: Confirmation, Voice, and Community,* edited by Rob Anderson, Kenneth N. Cissna, and Ronald C. Arnett, 34–47. Cresskill, N.J.: Hampton Press, 1994.

Kayser, Hans. *Akróasis: The Theory of World Harmonics.* Translated by Robert Lilienfeld. Boston: Plowshare Press, 1970.

Kelly, Kevin. *What Technology Wants.* New York: Viking, 2010.

Khyentse, Dilgo. *The Hundred Verses of Advice of Padampa Sangye.* New Delhi: Shechen, 2008.

Kinneavy, James L. "*Kairos:* A Neglected Concept in Classical Rhetoric." In *Rhetoric and Praxis: The Contribution of Classical Rhetoric to Practical Reasoning,* edited by Jean Dietz Moss, 79–105. Washington, D.C.: Catholic University of America Press, 1986.

———. "*Kairos* in Classical and Modern Rhetorical Theory." In Sipiora and Baumlin, *Rhetoric and Kairos,* 58–76.

Kinneavy, James L., and Catherine R. Eskin. "*Kairos* in Aristotle's Rhetoric." *Written Communication* 17, no. 3 (2000): 432–44.

Kish, Daniel. "Flash Sonar Program: Helping Blind People Learn to See." World Access for the Blind. http://www.worldaccessfortheblind.org/sites/default/files/snr-pgm-rv1113.htm.

Kohut, Heinz. *Self Psychology and the Humanities: Reflections on a New Psychoanalytic Approach.* New York: W. W. Norton, 1985.

Kongtrul, Jamgon. *The Great Path of Awakening: The Classic Guide to Using the Mahayana Buddhist Slogans to Tame the Mind and Awaken the Heart.* Translated by Ken McLeod. Boston: Shambhala, 2000.

Koren, Ilan, Yoram J. Kaufman, Richard Washington, Martin C. Todd, Yinon Rudich, J. Vanderlei Martins, and Daniel Rosenfeld. "The Bodélé Depression: A Single Spot in the Sahara That Provides Most of the Mineral Dust to the Amazon Forest." *Environmental Research Letters* 1, no. 1 (2006).

Krause, Bernie. "Bio-acoustics . . . Habitat Ambience and Ecological Balance." *Whole Earth Review,* no. 57 (1987): 1–7.

Krishnamurti, Jiddu. *Freedom from the Known.* Edited by Mary Lutyens. San Francisco: Harper and Row, 1975.

———. *The Whole Movement of Life Is Learning: J. Krishnamurti's Letters to His Schools.* Bramdean, Hampshire: Krishnamurti Foundation Trust, 2006.

Kuhn, Thomas S. *The Structure of Scientific Revolutions.* 3rd ed. Chicago: University of Chicago Press, 1996.

Kuusisto, Stephen. *Eavesdropping: A Life by Ear.* New York: W. W. Norton, 2006.

Lakoff, George. *Women, Fire, and Dangerous Things: What Categories Reveal About the Mind.* Chicago: University of Chicago Press, 1987.

Lakoff, George, and Mark Johnson. *Metaphors We Live By.* 2nd ed. Chicago: University of Chicago Press, 2003.

———. *Philosophy in the Flesh: The Embodied Mind and Its Challenge to Western Thought.* New York: Basic Books, 1999.

Lao Tzu. *Hua Hu Ching: The Unknown Teachings of Lao Tzu.* Translated by Brian Walker. San Francisco: HarperCollins, 1995.

LaPolla, Randy J., František Kratochvíl, and Alexander R. Coupe. "On Transitivity." *Studies in Language* 35, no. 3 (2011): 469–92.

Laub, Dori. "Bearing Witness, or the Vicissitudes of Learning." In *Testimony: Crises of Witnessing in Literature, Psychoanalysis, and History,* by Shoshana Felman and Dori Laub, 57–74. New York: Routledge, 1992.

Lehmann, Winfred P. *A Reader in Nineteenth Century Historical Indo-European Linguistics.* Bloomington: Indiana University Press, 1967.

Leonard, George, *The Silent Pulse: A Search for the Perfect Rhythm That Exists in Each of Us.* New York: Arkana, 1978.

Levin, David Michael. *The Listening Self: Personal Growth, Social Change, and the Closure of Metaphysics.* New York: Routledge, 1989.

Levinas, Emmanuel. *Alterity and Transcendence.* Translated by Michael B. Smith. New York: Columbia University Press, 1999.

———. *Entre Nous: On Thinking-of-the-Other.* Translated by Michael B. Smith and Barbara Harshav. New York: Columbia University Press, 1998.

———. "Ethics as First Philosophy." In Levinas, *Levinas Reader,* 75–87.

———. "The I and the Totality." In Levinas, *Entre Nous,* 25–52.

———. "Is Ontology Fundamental?" In Levinas, *Entre-Nous,* 1–11.

———. *The Levinas Reader.* Edited by Seán Hand. Oxford: Basil Blackwell, 1989

———. "Martin Buber, Gabriel Marcel and Philosophy." In *Martin Buber: A Centenary Volume,* edited by Haim Gordon and Jochanan Bloch, 305–21. [New York]: Ktav, 1984.

———. "The Other in Proust." In Levinas, *Levinas Reader,* 160–65.

———. *Otherwise than Being, or, Beyond Essence.* Translated by Alphonso Lingis. Pittsburgh: Duquesne University Press, 1998.

———. *Time and the Other and Additional Essays.* Translated by Richard A. Cohen. Pittsburgh: Duquesne University Press, 1987.

———. *Totality and Infinity: An Essay on Exteriority.* Translated by Alphonso Lingis. Pittsburgh: Duquesne University Press, 1969.

———. "The Transcendence of Words: On Michel Leiris's *Biffures.*" In *Outside the Subject,* translated by Michael B. Smith, 144–50. Stanford: Stanford University Press, 1993.

Lewis, David Levering. *God's Crucible: Islam and the Making of Europe, 570–1215.* New York: W. W. Norton, 2008.

Lichtheim, Miriam. *Ancient Egyptian Literature: A Book of Readings.* Vol. 1, *The Old and Middle Kingdoms.* Berkeley: University of California Press, 2006.

Lindahl, Kay. *The Sacred Art of Listening: Forty Reflections for Cultivating a Spiritual Practice.* Woodstock, Vt.: SkyLight Paths, 2002.

Lindblom, Jessica, and Tom Ziemke. "Interacting Socially Through Embodied Action." In *Enacting Intersubjectivity: A Cognitive and Social Perspective on the Study of Interactions,* edited by Francesca Morganti, Antonella Carassa, and Guiseppe Riva. Amsterdam: IOS Press, 2008.

Lindenlauf, Astrid. Review of *Akroasis: Der akustische Sinnesbereich in der griechischen Literatur bis zum Ende der klassischen Zeit,* by Günther Wille. *Bryn Mawr Classical Review* 9, no. 31 (2005).

Lipari, Lisbeth. "Listening, Thinking, Being." *Communication Theory* 20 (2010): 348–62.

———. "Listening for the Other: Ethical Implications of the Buber-Levinas Encounter." *Communication Theory* 14, no. 2 (2004): 122–41.

———. "Listening Otherwise: The Voice of Ethics." *International Journal of Listening* 23, no. 1 (2009): 44–59.

———. "Rhetoric's Other: Levinas, Listening, and the Ethical Response." *Philosophy and Rhetoric* 45, no. 3 (2012): 227–45.

Loehr, Daniel. "Aspects of Rhythm in Gesture and Speech." *Gesture* 7, no. 2 (2007): 179–214.

Loftus, Elizabeth F., and John C. Palmer. "Reconstruction of Automobile Destruction: An Example of the Interaction Between Language and Memory." *Journal of Verbal Learning and Verbal Behavior* 13 (1974): 585–89.

The Long Discourses of the Buddha: A Translation of the Digha Nikāya. Edited by Maurice Walshe. Boston: Wisdom, 1987.

Loprieno, Antonio. Foreword to *Ancient Egyptian Literature: A Book of Readings,* vol. 1, *The Old and Middle Kingdoms,* xxiii–xxxi. Berkeley: University of California Press.

Luria, Alexander R. *Language and Cognition.* Edited by James V. Wertsch. New York: John Wiley and Sons, 1981.

Macfie, Alexander Lyon, ed. *Eastern Influences on Western Philosophy: A Reader.* Edinburgh: Edinburgh University Press, 2003.

The Mahābhāṣya of Patañjali: With Annotations. Translated by Surendranath Dasgupta. Edited by Sibajiban Bhattacharyya. New Delhi: Indian Council of Philosophical Research, 1991.

Mair, Victor H. *Introduction and Notes for a Complete Translation of the "Chuang Tzu."* Sino-Platonic Papers 48. Philadelphia: Order from Department of Oriental Studies, University of Pennsylvania, 1994.

Malka, Salomon. *Emmanuel Levinas: His Life and Legacy.* Translated by Michael Kigel and Sonja M. Embree. Pittsburgh: Duquesne University Press, 2006.

Malloch, Stephen, and Colwyn Trevarthen, eds. *Communicative Musicality: Exploring the Basis of Human Companionship.* Oxford: Oxford University Press, 2009.

Mansbridge, Jane J. *Beyond Adversary Democracy.* New York: Basic Books, 1980.

Master, Alfred. "The Influence of Sir William Jones upon Sanskrit Studies." *Bulletin of the School of Oriental and African Studies, University of London* 11, no. 4 (1946): 798–806.

Matilal, Bimal Krishna. "Error and Truth: Classical Indian Theories." *Philosophy East and West* 31, no. 2 (1981): 215–24.

———. "Śābdabodha and the Problem of Knowledge-Representation in Sanskrit." *Journal of Indian Philosophy* 16 (1988): 107–22.

———. *The Word and the World: India's Contribution to the Study of Language.* Delhi: Oxford University Press, 1990.

McEvilley, Thomas. *The Shape of Ancient Thought: Comparative Studies in Greek and Indian Philosophies.* New York: Allworth Press, 2002.

McLuhan, Marshall. *The Gutenberg Galaxy: The Making of Typographic Man.* Toronto: University of Toronto Press, 1962.

McNeill, David. *Hand and Mind: What Gestures Reveal About Thought.* Chicago: University of Chicago Press, 1992.

Memon, A., S. Mastroberardino, and J. Fraser. "Münsterberg's Legacy: What Does Eyewitness Research Tell Us About the Reliability of Eyewitness Testimony?" *Applied Cognitive Psychology* 22 (2008): 841–51.

Menand, Louis. "Silence, Exile, Punning." *New Yorker,* July 2, 2012.

Merker, Hannah. *Listening: Ways of Hearing in a Silent World.* Dallas: Southern Methodist University Press, 1999.

Merleau-Ponty, Maurice. *Consciousness and the Acquisition of Language.* Translated by Hugh J. Silverman. Evanston: Northwestern University Press, 1973.

———. *Phenomenology of Perception.* Translated by Colin Smith. New York: Routledge, 1962.

Merton, Thomas. *Thoughts in Solitude.* Boston: Shambhala, 1956.

———. *Thoughts on the East.* New York: New Directions, 1995.

The Middle Length Discourses of the Buddha: A New Translation of the Majjhima Nikāya. Translated by Bhikkhu —anamoli and Bhikkhu Bodhi. Boston: Wisdom, 1995.

Moore, Michael (director). *Bowling for Columbine.* 2002.

Mohanty, Jitendra N. *Essays on Indian Philosophy Traditional and Modern.* Edited by Purushottama Bilimoria. Delhi: Oxford University Press, 1993.

———. "Phenomenology and Existentialism Encounter with Indian Philosophy." *International Philosophical Quarterly* 12, no. 4 (1972): 484–511.

Morton, Nelle. *The Journey Is Home.* Boston: Beacon Press, 1985.

Müller, F. Max. *Lectures on the Science of Language.* From the 2nd London ed. rev. New York: Charles Scribner, 1869.

Murti, Tiruppattur Ramesehayyar Venkatachala. "Some Comments on the Philosophy of Language in the Indian Context." *Journal of Indian Philosophy* 2 (1974): 321–31.

———. *Studies in Indian Thought: Collected Papers of Prof. T. R. V. Murti.* Edited by Harold G. Coward. Dehli: Motilal Banarsidass, 1983.

Nagler, Michael N. "Notes on Sacred Song: The Chandogya Upanishad." In *Upanishads,* 73–75.

Nancy, Jean-Luc. *Listening.* Translated by Charlotte Mandell. New York: Fordham University Press, 2007.

Noddings, Nel. *Caring: A Feminine Approach to Ethics and Moral Education.* Berkeley: University of California Press, 1984.

Norman, Donald A., and Tim Shallice. "Attention to Action." In *Cognitive Neuroscience: A Reader,* edited by Michael S. Gazzaniga, 376–90. Malden, Mass: Blackwell, 2000.

Nussbaum, Martha. *Upheavals of Thought: The Intelligence of Emotions.* Cambridge: Cambridge University Press, 2001.

O'Flaherty, James C. *Unity and Language: A Study in the Philosophy of Johann Georg Hamann.* University of North Carolina Studies in the Germanic Languages and Literatures 6. Chapel Hill: University of North Carolina Press, 1952.

Oliver, Mary. *The Leaf and the Cloud.* Cambridge, Mass.: Da Capo Press, 2000.

Oliveros, Pauline. *Deep Listening: A Composer's Sound Practice.* New York: iUniverse, 2005.

———. "Improvisation in the Sonosphere." *Contemporary Music Review* 25, no. 5 (2006): 481–82.

O'Neill, John J. *Prodigal Genius: The Life of Nikola Tesla.* New York: Ives Washburn, 1944.

Ong, Walter J. *Orality and Literacy: The Technologizing of the Word.* New York: Methuen, 1982.

———. *Ramus, Method, and the Decay of Dialogue: From the Art of Discourse to the Art of Reason.* Cambridge, Mass.: Harvard University Press, 1958.

Ortega, Kenny (director). *Michael Jackson's This Is It.* Columbia Pictures, 2009.

Pāṇini. *Ashtadhyayi.* Translated by Srisa Chandra Vasu. Benares, 1897.

Pasupathi, Monisha, Lisa M. Stallworth, and Kyle Murdoch. "How What We Tell Becomes What We Know: Listener Effects on Speaker's Long-Term Memory for Events." *Discourse Processes* 26, no. 1 (1998): 1–25.

Patchett, Ann. *The Patron Saint of Liars.* Boston: Houghton Mifflin, 1992.

Peile, John. *Philology.* Literature Primers. New York: American Book Company, 1880.

Pernot, Laurent. *Rhetoric in Antiquity.* Translated by W. E. Higgins. Washington, D.C.: Catholic University of America Press, 2005.

Philips, Susan. *The Invisible Culture: Communication in Classroom and Community on the Warm Springs Indian Reservation.* New York: Longman, 1983.

Picard, Max. *The World of Silence.* Washington, D.C.: Regnery Gateway, 1988.

Pillai, K. Raghavan. Translator's note on Karika 145. In *Vākyapadīya.*

Plato. *The Collected Dialogues of Plato, Including the Letters.* Edited by Edith Hamilton and Huntington Cairns. Bollingen 71. Princeton: Princeton University Press, 1961.

———. *Cratylus.* Translated by Benjamin Jowett. In *Collected Dialogues,* 957–1017.

———. *Phaedrus.* Translated by R. Hackforth. In *Collected Dialogues,* 476–525.

———. *Republic.* Translated by Paul Shorey. In *Collected Dialogues,* 575–844.

———. *Sophist.* Translated by F. M. Cornford. In *Collected Dialogues,* 957–1017.

———. *Theaetetus.* Translated by F. M. Cornford. In *Collected Dialogues,* 845–919.

Pollock, Sheldon. "Future Philology? The Fate of a Soft Science in a Hard World." *Critical Inquiry* 35 (Summer 2009): 931–61.

Poulakos, John. "Toward a Sophistic Definition of Rhetoric." *Philosophy and Rhetoric* 16, no. 1 (1983): 35–48.

Powers, Nikki, and Colwyn Trevarthen. "Voices of Shared Emotion and Meaning: Young Infants and Their Mothers in Scotland and Japan." In Malloch and Trevarthen, *Communicative Musicality,* 209–40.

Pribram, Karl H. "Brain and Mathematics." In *Brain and Being: At the Boundary Between Science, Philosophy, Language and Arts,* edited by Gordon G. Globus, Karl H. Pribram, and Guiseppe Vitiello, 229–241. Philadelphia: John Benjamins, 2004.

———. "Holography, Holonomy and Brain Function." In *Encylopedia of Neuroscience,* edited by George Adelman and Barry H. Smith, 899–900. 2nd ed. New York: Elsevier Science, 1999.

———. "The Implicate Brain." In *Quantum Implications: Essays in Honor of David Bohm,* edited by Basil Hiley and F. David Peat, 365–71. London: Routledge and Kegan Paul, 1987.

Prideaux, Jeff. "Comparison Between Karl Pribram's 'Holographic Brain Theory' and More Conventional Models of Neuronal Computation." http://www.acsa2000.net/bcngroup/jponkp/.

Purdy, Michael. "Listening, Culture, and Structures of Consciousness." *International Journal of Listening* 14 (2001): 47–68.

Radhakrishnan, Sarvepalli. *Indian Philosophy.* Vol. 1. London: George Allen and Unwin, 1923.

Ramseyer, Fabian, and Wolfgang Tschacher. "Synchrony in Dyadic Psychotherapy Sessions." In *Simultaneity: Temporal Structures and Observer Perspectives,* edited by S. Vrobel, 329–47. Singapore: World Scientific, 2008.

Ratcliffe, Krista. "Rhetorical Listening: A Trope for Interpretive Invention and a 'Code of Cross-Cultural Conduct.'" *College Composition and Communication,* 51, no. 2 (1999): 195–224.

Reddy, Michael J. 1979. "The Conduit Metaphor: A Case of Frame Conflict in Our Language About Language." In *Metaphor and Thought,* edited by Andrew Ortony, 284–310. Cambridge, Cambridge University Press.

Rée, Jonathan. *I See a Voice: Deafness, Language and the Senses—a Philosophical History.* New York: Metropolitan Books / Henry Holt, 1999.

Reyna, Ruth. *Introduction to Indian Philosophy: A Simplified Text.* Bombay: Tata McGraw-Hill, 1971.

Ricoeur, Paul. *Time and Narrative.* Translated by Kathleen Blamey and David Pellauer. Vol. 3. Chicago: University of Chicago Press, 1988.

Riedelsheimer, Thomas (director). *Touch the Sound: A Sound Journey with Evelyn Glennie.* DVD. Shadow Distribution, 2004.

Rimmer, Mark. "Listening to the Monkey: Class, Youth, and the Formation of a Musical Habitus." *Ethnography* 11, no. 2 (2010): 255–83.

Roberts, Gillian L., and Janet Beavin Bavelas. "The Communicative Dictionary: A Collaborative Theory of Meaning." In Stewart, *Beyond the Symbol Model,* 135–60.

Roberts, W. M., J. Howard, and A. J. Hudspeth. "Hair Cells: Transduction, Tuning, and Transmission in the Inner Ear." *Annual Review of Cellular Biology* 4 (1988): 63–92.

Rosenfield, Israel. "Video Ergo Sum." *Harper's Magazine,* April 2011, 78–82.

Rosenfield, Israel, and Arnold Ziff. "How the Mind Works: Revelations." *New York Review of Books,* June 26, 2008.

Rumi, Jelaluddin. *The Illuminated Rumi.* Translated by Coleman Barks. New York: Broadway Books, 1997.

Saarela, Miiamaaria V., and Riitta Hari. "Listening to Humans Walking Together Activates the Social Brain Circuitry." *Social Neuroscience* 3, nos. 3–4 (2008): 401–9.

Sangster, Pauline, and Charles Anderson. "Investigating Norms of Listening in Classrooms." *International Journal of Listening* 23, no. 2 (2009): 121–40.

Sapir, Edward. "The Status of Linguistics as a Science." In *Selected Writings in Language, Culture and Personality,* edited by David G. Mandelbaum. Berkeley: University of California Press, 1985.

Saussure, Ferdinand. *Course in General Linguistics.* Edited by Charles Bally and Albert Sechehaye. Translated by Wade Baskin. New York: McGraw-Hill, 1959.

Schaeffer, Pierre. *In Search of a Concrete Music.* Translated by Christine North and John Dack. Berkeley: University of California Press, 2012.

Schafer, R. Murray. *The Tuning of the World: Toward a Theory of Soundscape Design.* Philadelphia: University of Pennsylvania Press, 1980.

Schopenhauer, Arthur. *On the Basis of Morality.* Providence: Berghahn Books, 1995.

Schrag, Calvin. *Communicative Praxis and the Space of Subjectivity.* Bloomington: Indiana University Press, 1986.

Seifer, Marc J. *Wizard: The Life and Times of Nikola Tesla; Biography of a Genius.* Secaucus, N.J.: Carol, 1996.

Shafir, Rebecca. *The Zen of Listening: Mindful Communication in the Age of Distraction.* Wheaton, Ill.: Quest Books, 2000.

Shannon, Claude E. "A Mathematical Theory of Communication." *Bell System Technical Journal* 27 (July 1948): 379–423, (October 1948): 623–56.

Shastri, Gaurinath. *A Concise History of Classical Sanskrit Literature.* Delhi: Motilal Banarsidass, 1974.

Sherover, Charles M. *Are We in Time? and Other Essays On Time and Temporality.* Edited by Gregory R. Johnson. Evanston: Northwestern University Press, 2003.

Shotter, John. "Before Theory and After Representationalism: Understanding Meaning 'from Within' a Dialogical Practice." In Stewart, *Beyond the Symbol Model,* 103–30.

———. *Conversational Realities: Constructing Life Through Language.* Thousand Oaks, Cal.: Sage, 1993.

Simons, Daniel J., and Christopher F. Chabris. "Gorillas in Our Midst: Sustained Inattentional Blindness for Dynamic Events." *Perception* 28, no. 9 (1999): 1059–74.

Simpkinson, Anne A. "Evil and the Enemy: What I Would Say to Osama Bin Laden." Interview with Thich Nhat Hanh. In *From the Ashes: A Spiritual Response to the Attack on America.* Washington, D.C.: Rodale, 2001.

Sinclair, Upton. *I, Candidate for Governor: And How I Got Licked.* Berkeley: University of California Press.

Sinha, Chris, Vera Da Silva Sinha, Jorg Zinken, and Wany Sampaio. "When Time Is Not Space: The Social and Linguistic Construction of Time Intervals and Temporal Event Relations in an Amazonian Culture." *Language and Cognition* 3, no. 1 (2011): 137–69.

Sipiora, Phillip. "Introduction: The Ancient Concept of *Kairos.*" In Sipiora and Baumlin, *Rhetoric and Kairos,* 1–22.

Sipiora, Phillip, and James S. Baumlin, eds. *Rhetoric and Kairos: Essays in History, Theory and Praxis.* Albany: State University of New York Press, 2002.

Sontag, Susan. *Regarding the Pain of Others.* New York: Farrar, Straus and Giroux, 2003.

Stakhov, Alexey. "The Mathematics of Harmony." *Congressus Numerantium* 193, no. 20 (2008): 1–29.

Stevens, Wallace. *Harmonium.* New York: A. A. Knopf, 1947.

Stewart, John, ed. *Beyond the Symbol Model: Reflections on the Representational Nature of Language.* Albany: State University of New York Press, 1996.

———. "Interpretive Listening: An Alternative to Empathy." *Communication Education* 32, no. 4 (1983): 379–91.

———. "Speech and Human Being: A Complement to Semiotics." *Quarterly Journal of Speech* 72 (1986): 55–73.

———. "The Symbol Model vs. Language as Constitutive Articulate Contact." In Stewart, *Beyond the Symbol Model,* 9–63.

Steiner, Rudolf. *The Inner Nature of Music and the Experience of Tone.* Spring Valley, N.Y.: Anthroposophic Press, 1983.

Struc-Oppenberg, Ursula. "Friedrich Schlegel and the History of Sanskrit Philology and Comparative Studies." *Canadian Review of Comparative Literature* 7, no. 4 (1980): 411–37.

Sullivan, Dale L. "*Kairos* and the Rhetoric of Belief." *Quarterly Journal of Speech* 78 (1992): 317–32.

Suzuki, D. T. *An Introduction to Zen Buddhism.* London: Rider, 1948.

Swearingen, C. Jan. "Song to Speech: The Origins of Early Epitaphia in Ancient Near Eastern Women's Lamentations." In *Rhetoric Before and Beyond the Greeks,* translated by Carol S. Lipson and Roberta A. Binkley, 213–25. Albany: State University of New York Press, 2004.

Talbot, Michael. *The Holographic Universe.* New York: HarperPerennial, 1991.

Tanakh: The Holy Scriptures. Philadelphia: Jewish Publication Society, 1985.

Taylor, James R. "What Is 'Organizational Communication'? Communication as a Dialogic of Text and Conversation." *Communication Review* 3, nos. 1–2 (1999): 21–63.

Theodorou, Stephanie. "Bhartrihari." In *Internet Encyclopedia of Philosophy.* http://www.iep.utm.edu/bhartrihari/.

Thoreau, Henry David. *The Journal of Henry D. Thoreau.* Edited by Bradford Torrey and Francis H. Allen. New York: Dover, 1962.

Trevarthen, Colwyn. "The Infant's Voice Grows in Intimate Dialogue: How Musicality of Expression Inspires Shared Meaning." In Bertau, Gonçalves, and Raggatt, *Dialogic Formations*, 3–40.

The Upanishads. Translated by Eknath Easwaran. Tomales, Cal.: Nilgiri Press, 1987.

Veck, Wayne. "Listening to Include." *International Journal of Inclusive Education* 13, no. 2 (2009): 141–55.

Vocate, Donna R., ed. *Intrapersonal Communication: Different Voices, Different Minds.* Hillsdale, N.J.: Lawrence Erlbaum Associates, 1994.

———. "Self-Talk and Inner Speech." In Vocate, *Intrapersonal Communication*, 3–31.

———. *The Theory of A.R. Luria: Functions of Spoken Language in the Development of Higher Mental Processes.* Hillsdale, N.J.: Lawrence Erlbaum Associates, 1987.

Voigt, Ellen Bryant. "The Quickening." *Nation,* September 11, 1976.

Volk, Jeff. "From Vibration to Manifestation." *Quester,* Autumn 2010.

Voloshinov, V. N. "The Construction of the Utterance." Translated by Noel Owen. In *Bakhtin School Papers,* 114–38.

———. "Discourse in Life and Discourse in Poetry." Translated by John Richmond. In *Bakhtin School Papers,* 5–30.

———. *Marxism and the Philosophy of Language.* Translated by Ladislav Matejka and I. R. Titunik. Cambridge, Mass.: Harvard University Press, 1986.

———. "The Word and Its Social Function." Translated by Joe Andrew. In *Bakhtin School Papers,* 139–52.

Vygotsky, Lev. *Thought and Language.* Translated by Alex Kozulin. Cambridge, Mass.: MIT Press, 1986.

Warren, James. *Presocratics.* Berkeley: University of California Press, 2007.

Waterfield, Robin. *The First Philosophers.* Oxford: Oxford University Press, 2000.

White, Eric Charles. *Kaironomia: On the Will to Invent.* Ithaca: Cornell University Press, 1987.

Whitehead, Alfred North. *Process and Reality: An Essay in Cosmology.* Edited by David Ray Griffin and Donald W. Sherburne. Corrected ed. Gifford Lectures 1927–28. New York: Free Press, 1978.

Whitman, Walt. *The Essential Whitman.* Hopewell, N.J.: Ecco Press, 1987.

Wilhelm, Friedrich. "The German Response to Indian Culture." *Journal of the American Oriental Society* 81, no. 4 (1961): 395–405.

Wood, Roy. "The Voice of Ethics: Reflections on Ethics in Communicative Action." Paper delivered at 8th National Communication Ethics Summer Conference, June 10–13, 2004, Duquesne University, Pittsburgh.

Woolf, Virginia. *The Death of the Moth and Other Essays.* New York: Harcourt, Brace, 1942.

———. *Mrs. Dalloway.* New York: Harcourt, Brace, 1953.

———. *To the Lighthouse.* New York: Harcourt, Brace, 1955.

Yakubinsky, Lev Petrovich. "On Dialogic Speech." Translated by Michael Eskin. *PMLA* 112, no. 2 (1997): 243–56.

Yamada, Kōun. *The Gateless Gate: The Classic Book of Zen Koans.* Boston, Mass.: Wisdom, 2004.

"Zhuangzi." Translated by Paul Kjellberg. In *Readings in Classical Chinese Philosophy,* edited by Philip J. Ivanhoe and Bryan W. Van Norden, 203–45. New York: Seven Bridges Press, 2001.

Ziff, Israel Rosenfeld. "How the Mind Works: Revelations." *New York Review of Books,* June 26, 2008.

Zulick, Margaret. "The Active Force of Hearing: The Ancient Hebrew Language of Persuasion." *Rhetorica* 10, no. 4 (1992): 367–80.

INDEX

Page numbers followed by f or t refer to figures or tables, respectively. Those followed by n refer to notes, with note number.